Illinois Central College
Learning Resources Center

The Only Good Indian...
The Hollywood Gospel

The Only Good Indian...
The Hollywood Gospel

by
Ralph E. Friar
and
Natasha A. Friar

Drama Book Specialists/Publishers
New York

ISBN: 0-910482-21-7
Library of Congress Catalog Card Number: 72-78907

TABLE OF CONTENTS

To Crazy Horse

Whose image was never captured
on film by the white man

who fought for his people until
the end

this book is respectfully dedicated

"This is a good day to die! Hoka hey!"

In January, 1869, several weeks after Custer annihilated Black Kettle's Southern Cheyenne camp on the Washita River, Gen. Philip H. Sheridan was introduced to a Comanche leader at Ft. Cobb.

COMANCHE:
Me Tochoway. Me good Indian.
SHERIDAN:
The only good Indians I ever saw were dead.

In August, 1941, three homesick Sioux, Raymond Hairy Chin, Robert Elk Voice, and Frank Shooter, quit their jobs as extras in *They Died With Their Boots On* (1941), left Hollywood, and returned home to the Standing Rock Reservation in Ft. Yates, North Dakota.

HAIRY CHIN:
. . . On reservation make $9 a week . . . . Sleep nights. No headaches. Hollywood—phooey.

When asked to work overtime to finish a short scene for *Valley of the Sun* (1942), Juan Concha, leader of the Taos Native Americans spoke to his tribesmen. One replied, "Nope, we tired playing Indian. Go home."

ACKNOWLEGMENTS

Grosset & Dunlap, New York for permission to use excerpts reprinted from *Agee on Film: Vol. I* by James Agee. Copyright © 1958, the James Agee Trust.

The Citadel Press, New York for permission to quote from Milo Milton Quaife's introduction to *My Life on the Plains* by General George A. Custer, edited by Milo Milton Quaife. Copyright © 1962; and *A Pictorial History of the Western Film* by William K. Everson. Copyright © 1969.

The Dial Press, New York for permission to reprint excerpts from *George Catlin and the Old Frontier* by Harold McCracken. Copyright © 1959.

Farrar, Straus and Giroux, Inc, New York for permission to quote from *The Studio* by John Gregory Dunne. Copyright © 1968, 1969.

University of California Press, Berkeley, California for permission to quote from *One Reel A Week* by Fred J. Balshofer and Arthur C. Miller. Copyright © 1967.

Teachers College Press, New York for permission to use an excerpt from p. 12 of *The Rise of the American Film: A Critical History with an Essay, Experimental Cinema in America, 1921-1947*, by Lewish Jacobs. Copyright © 1939, 1947, 1967, 1968.

Yale University Press for permission to quote from *The Last Days of the Sioux Nation* by Robert M. Utley. Copyright © 1963.

Oxford University Press, New York for permission to quote from *Buffalo Bill & the Wild West* by Henry Blackman Sell and Victor Weybright. Copyright © 1955.

University of Nebraska Press for permission to quote from *Black Elk Speaks* by John G. Neihardt. Copyright © 1961.

McGraw-Hill Book Company for permission to quote from *Garbo and the Night Watchman*, edited by Alistair Cooke. Copyright © 1971.

Authors Merle Miller and Evan Rhodes for permission to quote from their book *Only You, Dick Daring!* Copyright © 1961 by Merle Miller and Evan Rhodes. Originally published by William Sloane Associates, New York.

Ladies Home Journal and Mrs. Charles Buddy Rogers for permission to quote from her article "My Own Story" by Mary Pickford which appeared in the August, 1923 issue of the *Ladies Home Journal.*

Cowles Communications, Inc. for permission to quote from "The Indian Style" which appeared in the October 20, 1972 issue of *Look* magazine.

Harper's magazine for permission to quote from "A Man Called Perry Horse" by John Corry which appeared in the October, 1970 issue of *Harper's* magazine.

Edward T. LeBlanc, publisher/editor of the "Dime Novel Round-Up" for permission to quote from the October 15, 1968 issue of "Dime Novel Round-Up."

Smithsonian Institution Press, Washington, D.C. for permission to quote from "The Emergence of the Plains Indian as the Symbol of the North American Indian" by John C. Ewers which appeared in the *Annual Report of the Smithsonian Institution, 1964.*

Directors Guild of America for permission to quote from "Ford and Kennedy on the Western" which appeared in the August-September, 1968 issue of *Action* the official publication of that organization.

Films in Review for permission to quote from "The Indian on the Screen" by Jack Spears which appeared in the January, 1959 issue of *Films in Review* and for permission to quote from "Tim McCoy" by Anthony Thomas which appeared in the April, 1968 issued of *Films in Review.*

Quigley Publishing Company, New York for permission to quote from *The Moving Picture World* and *Moving Picture News.*

Author Art Raymond and Jack Hagerty, editor of the *Grand Forks Herald* for permission to quote Mr. Raymond's review of a *A Man Called Horse.*

Reporter Dan Jorgensen and Anson Yeager, executive editor of the *Sioux Falls Argus-Leader* for permission to quote from Mr. Jorgensen's article on *A Man Called Horse* which appeared in the April 25, 1970 issue of the *Sioux Falls Argus-Leader.*

Associated Press Newsfeatures for permission to quote from Hubbard Keavy's article on *Valley in the Sun.*

W. C. C. Publishing Company, Inc. for permission to quote from articles which appeared in the *New York Herald Tribune.*

The *New York Times* for permission to quote material copyrighted © by the New York Times Company.

Jerry Gambill, editor of "Akwesasne Notes," Mohawk Nation, for permission to quote material from "Akwesasne Notes."

Special thanks is made to the following:

Vietnam Veterans Against the War and their "Winter Soldier Investigation which was broadcast over WBAI-FM, New York.

Film Department, Museum of Modern Art, New York, for film stills.

Film Division, Library of Congress, Washington, D.C. for viewing films and stills.

Eastman House, Rochester, New York.

William K. Everson for viewing films.

New York Public Library Picture Archives.

Theatre Collection, New York Public Library, Astor, Lenox and Tilden Foundation.

A special thanks also to:

Arnold I. Cohen for special photography; Frederick J. Dockstader, Director of the Museum of the American Indian; Heye Foundation for his encouragement; Ms. Buffy Sainte-Marie; Mrs. Robert Pifer; Stephen Feraca; James Bear Ghost; David Humphreys Miller; Mrs. Hilda Gilbert; August Little Soldier; and Herbert Blatchford for allowing us to quote them.

The many people who have generously given of their time and knowledge to help us understand the attitudes and feelings of the Native American.

INTRODUCTION

Jack D. Forbes, in his book *The Indian in America's Past* (1964), wrote: "In answer to the question, 'What is an Indian?' I would state that an Indian is a person whose ancestors lived in India. In my vocabulary, persons whose ancestors were indigenous to America are simply Native Americans; . . ."

The question has been asked, Why did you pick the American Indian for this book, since *all* minorities, cultures, and races have been capriciously invented, stereotyped, and falsified by Hollywood? We found that the very nature of this query made the writing of this book that much more necessary. The assumption implicit in the question is that the Native American is part and parcel of one indigenous ethnic-racial melting pot embracing two continents. Our answer then must be, How is it that the Native American can so thoughtlessly be classified as one more "minority?"

Thanks to the moving pictures, we can, let us say, lump the Apache tribes with the Mohawk Nation, call them "Indians" and assume not only a racial but an *ethnic* relationship as well. We do not, however, arbitrarily lump the people from Hungary with the people from the British Isles to define *Caucasians*, nor do we assume that the two peoples have any ethnic relationship. It might be noted that the geographic distance separating the Mohawks from the Apaches is considerably greater than that which separates Britain from Hungary.

The following will plead our case: Caucasians dubbed these continents "America" to honor the explorer Amerigo Vespucci. Caucasians dubbed the inhabitants of both continents "Indians." Columbus, after all, was on his way to India. The fact that diverse cultures existed on the American continent which

1

were as dissimilar as those on the European continent was considered unimportant.

Spanish, French, English, Dutch, Portugese, Swedish, and Russian voyagers comprised the invading European minority. They came to explore and exploit; they remained to propagate, ravish, and destroy. To insure that we may gullibly accept the historic fallacy that our predecessors came here to create a "free" nation, history books, in conjunction with the makers of filmic history, have conveniently omitted telling us about the many indigenous tribes or nations exterminated on behalf of freedom. Hollywood has continued to perpetuate the myth by creating either (1) a noble red man, or (2) a vicious savage, both of whom deny the white man his proper Christian right to this continent.

No other race or culture depicted on film has been made to assume such a permanent fictional identity. So we cannot understand how the constant extermination of the Native American in films can possibly be analyzed in the same context with other misrepresented ethnic and racial minorities. After all, these other maligned people are trespassers as well. The fact is that the "American Indian" is the only legitimate native of this land. Yet he is *racially*, not ethnically, isolated in our minds as *one minority*. He has been put on reservations apportioned to him on a vague tribal basis. Yet Hollywood has continued to be a co-conspirator in committing cultural genocide by subverting the Native American's various ethnic identities and retaining him as a racial scapegoat. By explicitly justifing the genocide perpetrated by our forefathers, Hollywood utilizes our ignorance to enforce our egoism.

As for genocide: When the white man began to colonize this country, there were about one million Native Americans here. By the late 1800s there were approximately 250,000 left. It was then estimated by historians that it had cost the United States government about one million dollars to kill each Native American. Subsequently, it was decided that it would be cheaper and more convenient to keep the people alive on reservations as paupers.

As for identity: Joan Barthel interviewed Phillip Waxman, the producer of *Tell Them Willie Boy Is Here*, for the *New York Times*, October 6, 1968. He said: "Willie didn't want to be a 'Yassuh, boss' Indian on the reservation; he fights for his identity. Katharine Ross fights for her identity. We're saying that second-class citizens all over the world today are fighting for their identity."

In recent times, many Native Americans have voiced their own anger at being exploited in films, television, by the fashion industry, and in *the* exploitation medium itself—advertising.

Since the number of Indian films made from the inception of the moving picture runs into the thousands, our choice of films must, of necessity, be selective. In this book we have used, out of context, many recent quotes about such films as *A Man Called Horse* (1970), *Tell Them Willie Boy Is Here* (1969), and *Little Big Man* (1971), in order to underscore the hypocrisy of all film-makers who try to justify the making of Indian films on behalf of the Native American.

The term "Native American" will be attributed to "people whose ancestors were indigenous to America." The term Indian" will be used to illustrate the white man's creation which led to the writing of *The Only Good Indian* . . . .

Because we assume that we have been thoroughly Hollywoodized, we will follow the history of the cinematic Indian in documentary scenario form, viewing the jaundiced "white eyes" lens as a mechanical cyclops in a hall of mirrors recording the same reflection endlessly.

WELCOME TO VESPUCCI LAND

SCENE I

Preview of Coming Attractions

FADE INTO

A vast expanse of calm ocean. Threatening clouds hover on the horizon. The wind whips the water with mounting frenzy.

DISSOLVE INTO

A montage of: An ancient map of Europe with drawings of sea monsters and demons of the deep lurking in the West. Various explorers and discoverers—Ericson, Columbus, Vespucci, Champlain, DeSoto—are seen embarking from the Old World or already on the sea of adventure. Upon reaching the New World, each plants a flag claiming the land for his respective sovereign. And always—ever always—in the background, hidden by the forest or the grass or the mist, almost indistinguishable human forms are watching the newcomers.

The very moment the first craft set sail for the New World, the moment the first white man set foot on this continent, the Native American's doom was sealed. That unknown person—misnamed, misunderstood, and mistreated—was cast in a drama not of his making and forced to act out a role not of his choosing.

The strangers came for adventure and so could afford to praise the people they found here. Of the natives in the Carolinas, Arthur Barlow, an Englishman, wrote in 1584: "... very handsome and goodly people, and in their behavior as mannerly and civil as any of Europe."

They came for trade and profit to become desecrators and thieves. Francis Parkman wrote of the traders in 1607:

. . . . the Dutch have found their way to the St. Lawrence,

5

and carried away a rich harvest of furs, while other inter-
loping traders had plied a busy traffic along the coasts,
and, in the excess of their avidity, dug up the bodies of
buried Indians to rob them of their funeral robes.

They came in the name of Christ and religious freedom to
convert the pagans on these shores. A Franciscan missionary,
Father Joseph le Caron, wrote to a friend in 1615:

> It would be hard to tell you how tired I was with paddling
> all day, with all my strength, among the Indians; wading
> the rivers a hundred times and more, through the mud and
> over the sharp rocks that cut my feet; . . . and half starved
> all the while . . . . But I must needs tell you what abundant
> consolation I found under all my troubles; for when one
> sees so many infidels needing nothing but a drop of water
> to make them children of God, one feels an inexpressible
> ardor for their conversion, and sacrifice to it one's repose
> and life.

They came in the name of freedom and enslaved the people.
France's King Louis XIV wrote to Governor de la Barre in 1684
concerning the Iroquois:

> . . . and moreover, as these savages, who are very strong
> and robust will serve usefully in my galleys, I will that you
> do everything in your power to make a great number of
> them prisoners of war, and have them embarked by every
> opportunity that will offer, in order that they be conveyed
> to France.

They came in the name of righteousness and damned the
natives of this continent. In 1702, after living among the
Illinois, Pierre Liette wrote:

> They are proud and vain . . . but in spite of this they are
> given to begging, are cowardly, licentious, and entirely
> given up to their senses . . . . They dress their best when
> they appear in public. They are jealous as Italians, thievish,
> gourmands, vindictive, hypocritical, and perfidious. They
> would prostitute their daughters or sisters a thousand
> times for a pair of stockings or other trifle . . . .

And so they came . . . and they came . . . .

Each succeeding wave of whites wrote a new scene in the
tragedy. Attempts were continually made to subjugate, contain,
reform, assimilate, divide, remove, and exterminate the Native
American.

The Europeans introduced the horse to the New World. A
gift which to the Native Americans came to mean freedom and

mobility. This ironically, might more accurately be seen as embodiment of the prophecy of doom from the white man's Bible: The Four Horsemen of the Apocalypse galloped across the continent, Conquest on a white horse, Slaughter riding a red horse, Famine riding a black horse, and Death, of course, a pale-faced rider on a pale horse.

A fifth Horseman was added by the Europeans—a feather-bonneted brave on a spotted war pony. As the ultimate ignominious triumph and the final humiliating defeat, the white man transformed the Native American into a mythological creature, a symbol, a phantom.

This creature was to wear many masks, changeable, at will, to suit heaven and hell. He was simpleton, wise man, loyal friend, treacherous foe, virtuous or wanton. The Indian became all things to all people. From Samoset and Pocahontas, to Ira Hayes and Billy Mills, the real gave way to fiction, thus to become part of American folklore.

Finally, this schizophrenic image of the Indian became fixed —at once both a bloodthirsty savage and a noble but simple child of the forest. Literature, the only mass medium of the time, pullulated and solidified the concept. Books, poems, journals, plays, essays poured forth from the literary grist mill— some to become classics, others to be deservedly forgotten.

THE MOVING FINGER HAVING WRIT . . .

SCENE II

CUT TO

A clearing in the forest. A white backwoodsman and an Indian emerge from among the trees. They unload their packs, sit on the ground and share their food. Although they do not speak, there is a close bond between them. After eating, they lean against a fallen log and share a peaceful pipe.

James Fenimore Cooper and the concept of the noble savage are synonymous. He was able to idealize the close companionship and camaraderie between red and white soul brothers, making *The Last of the Mohicans* (1826), among others, the springboard for every red-blooded American's fantasies. The reader could be a free spirit by breaking away from civilization, as did Hawkeye, but still know that he was that same civilization's champion simply because he was white. He could "go native," but his primitive alter ego was safely contained within the faithful Indian companion, Chingachgook. The two—white and red—were made one by the tragic death and burial of young Uncas, the last of the Mohicans, as Chingachgook, grieving over the loss of his son, exclaimed:

". . . I am a blazed pine, in a clearing of the palefaces. My race has gone from the shores of the salt lake, and the hills of the Delawares . . . . I am alone—"

"No, no," cried Hawkeye, . . . "no, Sagamore, not alone. The gifts of our colors may be different, but God has so placed us as to journey in the same path. I have no kin, and may also say, like you, no people . . . . The boy has left us for a time; but, Sagamore, you are not alone."

Chingachgook grasped the hand that, in the warmth of feeling, the scout has stretched across the fresh earth, and in that attitude of friendship these two sturdy and intrepid woodsmen bowed their heads together, while scalding tears fell to their feet, watering the grave of Uncas like drops of falling rain.

The durability of *The Last of the Mohicans* is shown by the number of times it has been republished. The result of this production and reproduction in literature, music, drama, and art is that the Indian and his relationship to the white man remains unchanged. In addition, Hollywood has multiplied this reproduction as typified by the many filmed versions of *The Last of the Mohicans*—1911, 1914, 1920, 1932 (serial), and 1936. Most recently (1972), an 8-hour serialized version, filmed and taped in England by the BBC, has appeared on PBS Television in the U.S.

Tradition and myth—Nature's Noblemen—like old soldiers, do not die, but they don't fade away either. Recently, in Ken Kesey's novel *One Flew Over the Cuckoo's Nest* (1962), MacMurphy and Chief Bromden, the modern equivalents of Cooper's Hawkeye and Chingachgook—played on Broadway by Kirk Douglas and Ed Ames—are transplanted from the forest wilderness to the up-to-date wilderness of a mental hospital.

Cooper's works, idealizing the Indian, were avidly read in Europe. In Germany, Karl May (1842-1912), capitalizing on Cooper's success, created his own Teutonic American frontier. He wrote seventy books, which sold over fifteen million copies in Germany and were translated into more than 20 languages. Interestingly enough, none of his books have been translated into English. The first time he saw America was when he was 66 years old.

In the October 15, 1968 issue of *Dime Novel Round-Up*, edited by Edward T. LeBlanc, a letter from Oscar C. Pfaus of Hamburg stated:

> The old time Dime Novel writer Karl May, . . . was the one who had created the imaginary German . . . heroes of Old Shatterhand, Old Surehand, Old Firehand, and others who were also of course all Germans and who were also of course the world's masters of boxing, knifethrowing, rifle and pistol shooting, of the use of the lasso, of the Indian bow and arrow, of tomahawk throwing, . . .

> He also created the imaginary Indian hero, Winnetou, Chief of the Apaches. In May's opinion, the Apaches were the finest, most cultured and most peaceful of all American Indian nations, while the Sioux were described by him

as the most cruel, the most ignorant, and the most cowardly ones!

It has been said in Germany that Hitler himself had read
Karl May's swindle stories about the old American West, and
that he had gained many of his master racial ideas from
May's impossible writings! . . .

An advertisement for a European made Western based on one of Karl
May's novels. Released by Columbia Pictures.

The worst is, that even today German libraries, reading halls, etc., are fully stocked with May's books! They are again read by millions of children, grown-ups, by soldiers and other lovers of adventures, and of stories about the God-Almightiness of the German master-race, of German masterminds, and of always victorious and man-killing German heroes.

And worse still, some of May's stories were made into a series of films. They were shot in Europe in the 1960s, with Lex Barker as Shatterhand or Stewart Granger as Surehand, and Pierre Brice as Winnetou. Deutschland Uber Alles in Apache Land.

Forgotten now, but certainly Cooper's equal in popularity at that time, was Robert Montgomery Bird's *Nick of the Woods, or the Jibbenainosay* (1837). In this story of red versus white on the Kentucky frontier, Bird's Indian is more realistic than Cooper's beau-ideal. Perhaps for the first time in literature the slur "red niggurs" [sic] appeared; a term still commonly used out West today.

Helen Hunt Jackson's *Ramona* (1884), a very popular tragic novel of the California Mission Indians, was truly a stereotypical 19th century woman's book. As described by Albert Keiser *The Indian in American Literature* (1933): "*Ramona* is the story of a pure-hearted half-breed girl who [is loved] by . . . the full-blooded Allessandro, pureminded, open-hearted, and generous-souled, with his passionate heart and repressed nature, . . . whom the influx of ruthless American settlers drives into temporary insanity and a tragic death at the hands of a ruffian." *Ramona* maintained its popularity in several screen adaptations—1910, re-released in 1914 and new versions in 1916, 1928 (which inspired the hit song of the same name), and in 1936.

The Native American in literature remained a favorite subject into the 20th century. In addition to popular appeal, many great books were to be transferred to the screen to reach world-wide audiences. In some cases, lesser books were to achieve fame through their screen treatments.

Edna Ferber's epic *Cimarron* (1929), which had a little red and white romance thrown in as added spice, was originally put on the screen in 1931 and remade 30 years later.

Epic novels were perfect for screen adaption. So there was Kenneth Roberts' *Northwest Passage* (1936), which became a film in 1940; *Across the Wide Missouri* (1947), by Bernard De Voto, came to the screen in 1951; and A. B. Guthrie's *The Big Sky* (1947) appeared as a movie in 1952.

Oliver La Farge, founder of the Association of American Indians Affairs, was awarded the Pulitzer Prize for best novel of the year for *Laughing Boy* (1929), which was transformed into a typical Hollywood romance in 1934.

A supposedly true story of one of the last Apaches to succumb to the white man's rule was Paul I. Wellman's *Broncho Apache* (1936). This was to become *Apache* (1954).

Another story about Apaches, the story of Cochise and Tom Jeffords, was *Blood Brother* (1947), which became *Broken Arrow* (1950).

Biographical stories have always been interesting, especially if they are tragic. *The Hero of Iwo Jima and Other Stories* (1962), by William Bradford Huie, became *The Outsider* (1962), a tragic travesty on Ira Hayes. Harry Lawton's *Willie Boy* (1960) was Hollywoodized as *Tell Them Willie Boy Is Here* (1969).

And, finally, there is Thomas Berger's *Little Big Man* (1964). A spoof on the Old West, it still manages to tell more and have a deeper understanding of Native American ways (in this case, Cheyenne) than many notable scholarly works. It went Hollywood in 1971.

CUT TO

A settler's cabin in flames. Whooping Indians attack the cabin when the door bursts open. A woman, axe in hand, and her three children rush out. The mother protects them behind her skirts as she wields the axe with deadly ferocity. Two Indians are felled by her blows before she is overcome. She and the children are bound and dragged off by the gleeful raiders.

The search for new worlds is legendary. With the discovery of America many felt they had found a new Garden of Eden, and the lure of untold treasures was all too compelling. But the search for El Dorado often led to the discovery of El Diablo. The Native American was blamed for concealing the former and revealing the latter.

The bloodthirsty savage was born with the first letting of blood, followed almost immediately by gory anti-Native American narratives of captivity. One of the earliest was published in 1682, under the improbable title of *The Sovereignty and Goodness of God Together With the Faithfulness of His Promise Displayed: Being a Narrative of the Captivity and Restoration of Mrs. Mary Rowlandson.* She tells of her capture during King Philip's War:

> Of thirty-seven persons who were in this one house, none escaped either present death, or a bitter captivity, save only one, who might say as he, Job 1. 15, *And I only am escaped alone to tell the News.* There were twelve killed, some shot, some stab'd with their Spears, some knock'd down with their Hatchets. When we are in prosperity, Oh the little that we think of such dreadful sights, and to see our dear Friends, and Relations ly bleeding out their heart-blood upon the ground. There was one who was chopt into the head with a Hatchet, and stript naked, and yet was crawling up and down. It is a solemn sight to see so many Christians lying in their blood, some here, and some there, like a company of Sheep torn by Wolves, All of them stript naked by a company of hellhounds, roaring, singing, ranting and insulting, as if they would have torn our very hearts out; yet the Lord by his Almighty power preserved a number of us from death, for there were twenty-four of us taken alive and carried captive.

This bloody, religiously-frenzied best-selling chronicle was reprinted at least 30 times under a much shortened title. The sensationalism of this format was readily exploited to surfeit the public's appetite. This fad got enough mileage to carry it into the middle 1700s.

The most celebrated captive was Hannah Duston. Praised by Cotton Mather and condemned by Nathaniel Hawthorne, she was the first of many recurring hatchet ladies who, with a little help from her friends (another woman and a boy), tomahawked and scalped their captors, including several Native American children. This was done in revenge; for, not only was she forced from bed after giving birth, but her baby was snatched from her arms and its brains dashed out against an apple tree. Throughout, she prevailed to rise up in biblical retribution. Her deed and legend became a monument to motherhood. Many statues of a classic frontier woman clutching both baby and axe were erected.

DISSOLVE INTO
An Indian village. A dead warrior lies near a camp fire. The villagers, honoring their dead, are singing a mournful dirge.

With the various Hatchet Hannahs swinging away, no wonder Indian poetic deathsongs were much the vogue in this country's youth. Philip Freneau, "the Father of American Poetry," wrote such poems, two of which were "The Dying Indian: Tomo-Chequi" and "The Prophecy of King Tammany."

Longfellow, the most popular poet of his time, had been interested in Native Americans for many years. He read their legends hoping to find material for a poem. Using Henry Schoolcraft's *Algic Researches*, a collection of Ojibway folk tales, as a basis, he wrote *The Song of Hiawatha* (1855). Longfellow thought of Hiawatha as "a kind of American Prometheus," and his epic poem was a sensational success, selling 4,000 copies on the first day and 50,000 in its first year and a half. It was translated into several languages, including Latin. Today the poem is either ignored or made fun of, but, in its day, readers sobbed at the death of Hiawatha's Minnehaha:

> And he rushed into the wigwam,
> Saw the old Nokomis slowly
> Rocking to and fro and moaning,

A scene from *Hiawatha* (1909) filmed by the IMP Company. (Motion Picture Section, Library of Congress)

Saw his lovely Minnehaha
Lying dead and cold before him,
And his bursting heart within him
Uttered such a cry of anguish,
That the forest moaned and shuddered,
That the very stars in heaven
Shook and trembled with his anguish.
    Then he sat down, still and speechless,
On the bed of Minnehaha,
At the feet of Laughing Water
At those willing feet, that never
More would lightly run to meet him,
Never more would lightly follow.

But she did follow into three filmed versions of *Hiawatha*—
1909, 1913, and 1952.

"Death and the Noble Savage" has always been a dominant poetic image. How apropos, then, is Fielder and Zeiger's comment in *O Brave New World* (1968), that, for the frontiersman, the only good Indian may have been a dead Indian, but for the popular poet an even better Indian was a dying one.

WHEN I'M CALLING YOU-OU-OU-OU-OU-OU-OU

SCENE III

CUT TO
A close shot of an Indian drum. First, one drumstick starts beating, then another and another. Nothing is heard except DUM-dum-dum-dum; DUM-dum-dum-dum; DUM-dum-dum-dum . . . .

Tammany, said to be the first opera produced in the United States (1794), was mentioned in a 1907 issue of *The New York Dramatic Mirror*: ". . . this piece may be said to have originated that impossible type of stage Indian which claimed allegiance, in Mark Twain's words, to 'an extinct tribe that never existed.'"

Some composers using Indian motifs were: Anton Heinrich (*Indian Fanfares* consisting of *The Comanche revel, The Sioux galliarde,* and *The Manitou air dance*); Charles Skilton (*Indian Dances*); Carl Busch (*Minnehaha's Vision,* based on Long-fellow's poem); Charles Cadman (*Thunderbird Suite*); Antonin Dvorak (*New World* Symphony); Edward McDowell (*Indian Suite*).

Victor Herbert, best known for his operettas, wrote a Grand Indian Opera, *Natoma* (1911). Rudolf Friml had his biggest hit with *Rose-Marie* (1927), which included "Indian Love Call" and "Totem Tom Tom."

Popular songs were something else again. The public's fancy had room for such hits as: "Death Song of an Indian Chief" (1791); "The Indian's Petition" (1835); "The Indian's Lament" (1846); "Navajo" (1903); "Cheyenne" (1906); "From the Land of the Sky-Blue Water" (1909); "By the Waters of Minnetonka" (1921).

Longfellow's poem inspired *The Death of Minnehaha* (1856) and "Minnehaha or Laughing Water Polka" (1856). The Battle

17

Someone must have been singing "Dearest Pocahontas Her Wooing" in 1907.

of the Little Big Horn in 1876 inspired "Custer's Last Charge." And today we have come full circle to the more appropriate and timely "Custer Died for Your Sins."

Much of the early "Indian" music was used for silent screen accompaniment. *The Moving Picture World* had a separate department, "Music for the Picture," by Clarence E. Sinn. One of its main features was a column of suggestions about music to play for certain films. On June 8, 1912, the column contained:

The title page of the hit song "The Death of Minehaha" (1856). Truly a Caucasian fantasy.

"For the Papoose" (Pathe)
1. Indian music ("Os-ka-loo-sa-loo") till man seizes girl, then:
2. Short agitato till "That Same Night."
3. Mysterious till Indian kills sleeping man.
4. Hurry till "Next Morning."
5. Indian sentimental till man throws cloth over Indian girl's head.
6. Agitato till "Be Not Afraid, My Sister."
7. Mysterious agitato till struggle.
8. Hurry till man is seen dead.
9. Indian pathetic till end of picture.

The August 31, 1912 issue offered these suggestions:

"The Arrow Maker's Daughter" (Pathe)
1. "Indian Summer" (by Moret), through first two scenes.
2. "Fawn Eyes" (Or any "Indian" intermezzo), until donkey is led off, then:
3. "Sun Dance" (Witmark), until title: "Paul Starts Across the Desert."
4. "Indian Summer" until title: "Moose Head Finds and Follows the Trail."
5. Mysterious until Paul falls in desert (2nd time), then:
6. Plaintive until end.

When sound came in, this kind of music was not changed, but only elaborated upon on the sound track. "DUM-dum-dum-dum, The Indians are Coming" type of music, or a lyrical flutey passage, became the cue for the appearance of the noble or bloodthirsty phantoms.

ENTER REDSKINS

SCENE IV

DISSOLVE INTO
A medium shot of an elementary school auditorium. The children are presenting their annual Thanksgiving pageant. The camera pulls in as the Indians bring provisions for the feast. The students playing Pilgrims are wearing white collars and cuffs and black hats, all made of drawing paper. The Indians are wearing cuffs, armbands, and headbands with a single feather sticking up or headdresses, all made of colored drawing paper.

The theatre was the perfect mother who nursed and nourished the noble "white" Indian until he awesomely strode upon the silver screen.

One of the first plays was *Ponteach: or the Savages of America* (1766), a tragedy by Major Robert Rogers. It was all poetic and romantic, and concerned nefarious whites who did dirty to noble and innocent Indians. Perhaps Rogers was trying to appease his conscience, since, as a renowed Indian fighter and leader of the famous Rangers, he was responsible, among other notable deeds, for the complete destruction of the Abenaki village at St. Francis, Canada, in 1759.

Although unproduced, the play set the pattern for Indian characters—the proud and stalwart Chief Ponteach:

> Britons may boast, the Gods may have their Will,
> Ponteach I am, and shall be Ponteach still.

And the comely and virtuous Princess Monelia:

> My simple Heart, made soft by so much Heat,
> Half gave Consent, meaning to be his Bride.
> The Moment thus unguarded, he embrac'd,
> And imprudently ask'd to stain my Virtue.

21

Another fiction, that of the pure Indian princess, began to crystallize. Although historically inaccurate, the white man, perhaps intrigued by the idea of homegrown royalty or motivated to raise the Native American to his own supposed high level, gallantly bestowed the misnomer "princess" on the daughters of chiefs and headmen. Virginity was, of course, a woman's ultimate nobility. If there must be miscegenation, let it be with a girl of royal blood and unsoiled to boot. So either one, or preferably both qualities, became prerequisites in story and, eventually, on film. In *A Man Called Horse* (1970), Corinna Tsopei, a Greek starlet playing the Sioux princess, shows Richard Harris her mocassin. It is explained that there is no hole in the sole, which means she is still a virgin. A cliche, no matter how quaintly disguised, is still a cliche.

The legend of Pocahontas blossomed with *The Indian Princess: or La Belle Sauvage* (1808), by James N. Barker. The romantic figure of the virgin princess was further strengthened in Pocahontas by zealously converting her into a "dusky madonna." In Barker's play the relationship between Pocahontas and Smith was immortalized when the princess shrieked, "White man, thou shalt not die; or I will die with thee."

George Washington Parke Custis, step-grandson of Washington, wrote *Pocahontas, or the Settlers of Virginia* (1830). The name of George Washington gave added incentive to include the rescue scene in the repertoire of grade school pageants suitable for appropriate occasions.

Pocahontas saved Smith in this play by confronting her father with these stirring words: "Cruel king, the ties of blood which bound me to thee are dissever'd, as have been long those of thy sanguinary religion; for know that I have abjur'd thy senseless gods, and now worship the Supreme Being, the true Manitou, and the Father of the Universe; 't is his Almighty hand that sustains me, 't is his divine spirit that breathes in my soul, and promptd Pocahontas to a deed which future ages will admire."

Pocahontas: A Historical Drama, by Robert Dale Owen, appeared in 1838. Part of the continuing cycle produced another panoramic spectacle, *The Forest Princess; or, Two Centuries Ago* (1848), by Charlotte M. S. Barnes. As with any story too often repeated, Pocahontas was finally reduced to burlesque and satire with John Broughman's *Po-Ka-Hon-Tas; or, The Gen-*

Pocahontas on stage, 1870
(The Theatre Collection, New
York Public Library)

tle Savage (1855), which contained such characters as O-Po-Dil-Doo and Col-O-Gog.

During this time dramatizations of popular novels, especially those of Cooper, were much produced. Visualization of favorite characters and incidents fondly remembered by faithful readers found a ready-made audience in "Leather Stocking" fans. Louisa H. Medina adapted *Nick of the Woods* in 1838 and Hiawatha was also burlesqued in 1856 with the "Musical Extravaganza" *Hiawatha: or Ardent Spirits and Laughing Water*, by Charles M. Walcot.

The most successful Indian drama was John Augustus Stone's *Metamora, or the Last of the Wampanoags*. Presented in 1829, it was written for and played by Edwin Forrest. As one of America's most popular plays, it made the renowned Forrest rich and famous over the next 40 years, and was seen by hundreds of thousands of people. *Metamora* was a highly melodramatic extravaganza of magnificent proportions with spectacular scenery and stage effects. Much of its success, however, can be attributed to Forrest's performance as described in *The New York Dramatic Mirror* of July 20, 1907: "None but Edwin Forrest, the one and only Metamora, had the capacity to stir the pulse of the Redman in bringing the scent of the prairies over the footlights, . . ." Surely the great Forrest stirred his audience with the impassioned curse of the dying Metamora:

> My curse on ye, white men! May the Great Spirit curse ye when he speaks in his war voice from the clouds! May his words be like the forked lightnings, to blast and desolate! May the loud winds and the fierce red flames be loosed in vengeance upon ye, tigers! May the angry Spirit of the Waters in his wrath sweep over your dwellings! May your graves and the graves of your children be in the path where the red man shall tread, and may the wolf and the panther howl over your fleshless bones! I go. My fathers beckon from the green lakes and the broad hills. The Great Spirit calls me. I go,—but the curses of Metamora stay with the white man!

Broughman, before writing *Po-Ka-Hon-Tas*, burlesqued Forrest's tour-de-force *Metamora* as *Metamora; or, the Last of the Pollywoags* (1847), containing, among others, the characters Wiskeetoddi and Tapiokee.

With the exception of *Metamora* and despite the acting prowess and drawing power of a Forrest, the cycle of Indian

A.S. Lipman as army man and Indian in the 1897 play "The Indian." (Motion Picture Section, Library of Congress)

dramas began to fade in the mid 1800s. If the public rejected the repetitious rantings and ravings of white men's interpretations, how must Native Americans have felt? William Dunlap expressed his feelings in *History of the American Theatre* (1832):

> How these sons of the forest must have despised the sorry imitation of barbarism, who followed in their train, with painted cheeks, rings in their noses, and bladders smeared with red ochre drawn over their powdered locks.

The Indian as a stage subject was revitalized in 1905 with *Squaw Man*, by Edwin Milton Royle. Starring William Faversham, this story of whether a titled Englishman should return home to his son or remain with his Indian wife, was a big hit. A musical version, *White Eagle*, with a score by Rudolf Friml, was produced in 1927. Another hit of 1905 was *Strongheart*, by William C. De Mille, brother of C. B. In this modern story, an Indian football hero at Columbia College in New York was torn between his love for a white girl and returning to his tribe as chief.

The Indian of the stage and the Indian on the screen complemented each other, for the popularity of both continually increased. The July 20, 1910 issue of *The New York Dramatic Mirror* ran a full page ad promoting Miss Della Clarke, who was then in her 47th week as the star in her own play, *The White Squaw*. In 1911 the much praised *The Arrow Maker*, by Mary Austin, told how a medicine woman who wants to be a woman first revolts against her holy status.

By the 1930s the eminent cultural domain of the Indian was film. In all other creative areas he was, as a subject, dormant. And in actual dealings with the Native American the norm was a great silence.

The various civil rights movements and marches of the 1950s reactivated interest in the Native American, with many liberal organizations taking up the challenge. Native Americans themselves voiced their anger and protests against such establishment symbols as the Bureau of Indian Affairs. With the same old cyclical consistency, the white man once more rediscovered the Indian. The constant tub-thumping by the pace-makers produced the desired effect when the 1960s witnessed a renaissance of Things Indian. With fashions, advertising, life styles, with a persistance that pervaded everything, the Indian was in.

The Native American was—and is—fighting to stay alive and reclaim some of his land while everyone else plays Indian with beads, headbands, and fringe. And so the whiteskin puts on his redskin grease paint and walks once more upon the stage.

CUT TO
A street in Broadway's theatrical district. The time is now. A theatre marquee advertizes *Indians*. People begin to congregate preparatory to entering the theatre.

DISSOLVE INTO
A montage of newspater, magazine, and television ads pushing films, plays, and books on Indian subjects, and ads with Indian themes pushing every type of product or service imaginable.

CUT BACK TO
Theatre playing *Indians*. The authors emerge from a cab and join the milling ticket-holders as they go into the theatre.

Straightening the record may have been the aim of Arthur Kopit in *Indians*. This excursion of the liberal establishment opened on Broadway in October, 1969, to generally favorable notices. Although a play, it was as much Hollywood as any "B" horse opera. It will probably end up that way, albeit an expensive "B," since the film rights were sold with the idea of Paul Newman playing Buffalo Bill.

Kopit tells of the tragic plight of the Native American from Buffalo Bill's point of view, using the latter's Wild West Show. And that's exactly what the author does, he tells us and tells us. Despite fancy staging by Gene Frankel with strobe lights, slow motion effects, an impressive set, emotional writing, and even more emotional acting, the play is a didactic, finger-wagging preachment. We are told of the Indians' problems but never experience them. Kopit even tells us who the heroes and villains are; the play ends up exactly like an old-fashioned Western—all too black and white; the good guys versus the bad guys. Only here, the good guys are the Indians and the bad guys the whites. The play is brought up-to-date with a little convenient psychology so essential nowadays for adult Westerns. Granted that the theatre is allowed certain dramatic license, to allow *Indians* this same license does not excuse the play's gross inaccuracies; minor, but notable, is the costuming, which smacks of Hollywood's long unimaginative treatment of the Native American.

Also, in true Hollywood fashion, the Indians are played by non-Indians. A Fiji Islander (perhaps a reverse kind of racist casting) plays Sitting Bull as though he were the King in *The*

King and I. He is anything but a Native American. He is anything but a great medicine man. He is certainly not Sitting Bull.

Kopit tips his hand when a character, mistaken for a Comanche, is shot. He rises up from the dead to explain to the audience that he is actually a Sioux and implies that he was killed because the white man cannot tell one Indian from another. The point, of course, is completely lost and makes no difference, anyway, since the actor is white and costumed in a nondescript, all-purpose Hollywood Indian suit. The author and all those concerned allowed their liberalism on the Indians' behalf and their let's-tell-it-like-it-was attitude to blind them. For, although many Native American tribes are part of the play, there is no difference, whatsoever, in their depiction. For the creators, too, an Indian is an Indian is an Indian.

> CUT TO
>
> The authors and their son, Kenneth, queuing up in a long line of viewers during Christmas, 1970. The attraction is a window display at Lord and Taylor's department store in New York City which depicts a few Southwestern tribes in a village setting. The scene includes a snake dancer, a Kachina, an eagle dancer, and other figures representing very sacred ceremonies. All of them turning, twirling, jumping—mechanical puppets caught in a St. Vitus' dance.
>
> We hear, in Voice Over, the display's creator being interviewed on WBAI-FM, New York City. He says that careful research was done to be authentic, accurate and, above all, in order not to profane any religious ceremonies, so he could not understand why several protests from Indians were voiced.
>
> Segue into author's Voice Over: Why isn't there a window showing priests at Christmas midnight mass raising and lowering The Host? Hey . . . why not a rabbi moving a Torah from side to side for the Chanukah trade?

Off-Broadway had Sam Shepard's *Operation Sidewinder*, which premiered in March, 1970, at the Lincoln Center Repertory Theatre. Some of the characters in this intricately plotted play were: white tourists, a prospector, Air Force personnel, a crippled eccentric German scientist (a la Dr. Strangelove), Hopi Indians, and black and white revolutionaries. The Air Force loses a self-sufficient mobile computer in the shape of a giant serpent; the Hopi find it and believe an ancient legend is coming true. Another plot, among the many, is white boy revolutionary meets white girl tourist; boy loses girl; boy gets girl in Happy Hopi Land.

Shepard's idea is never fulfilled: the clash of two parallel societies, technocracy and traditionalism, as symbolized by the U.S. Army and the Hopi. In the end, the giant serpent brings about the death and destruction of modernism while tribalism lives and triumphs. Much time is spent developing the various themes but the Hopi are given short shrift. A redskin renegade finds salvation when an ancient Hopi guru tells him the legend of the snake. This brief, meaningless, and obscure scene is supposed to prepare a thoroughly, by then, confused audience for the second act which is almost completely devoted to the Hopi Snake Dance.

The most sacred tribal ceremony, the Snake Dance is somewhat authentically presented. Certain concessions had to be made for the sake of theatricality, but, at least, the attempt was made. An experienced and excellent Hopi dancer, Louis Mofsie, trained the non-Indian performers and staged the dance sequence. Because of its sacred significance, complaints by Native Americans were voiced against its use. It was, however, one of the few times New York audiences were exposed to an accurate Native American dance. Although the audience snickered and laughed, this reaction is understandable, for they have been so completely corrupted by the Hollywood Indian.

The critics, the great harbingers and defenders of our tastes and cultural values, were most confused in reviewing *Indians* and *Operation Sidewinder*, especially in the dance department. *Indians* was so influenced by Hollywood that the Indian dancing, at best, is a Broadway choreographer's hallucination of a Hollywood dance director's fantasy and, at worst, a sheer mockery of beautiful, simple ritual. Yet Clive Barnes, drama and dance critic for the *New York Times*, wrote in his review of *Indians*: "... how great, for example, is the Julie Arenal choreographed Indian dance in all it [sic] bloodstained, ethnic tragedy . . . ." There is much doubt as to the greatness of such choreography. There is no doubt, however, that the tragedy lies in how greatly profaned was the most sacred of all Plains tribes rituals, the Sun Dance.

On the other hand, the attempt at accuracy and authenticity in *Operation Sidewinder* was dismissed by *Time's* critic as "... Broadway Indians doing a Broadway Snake Dance." If we are ever going to set the record straight, let's start with the critics and their ignorance of that in which they presume expertise.

THROUGH INDIANLAND WITH BRUSH, CHISEL, AND WET PLATE

SCENE V

CUT TO
Otto Becker's famous lithograph, "Custer's Last Fight." The camera pans and zooms, picking up different bits of action: a feather-bonneted warrior tomahawking a soldier; a mounted brave galloping into the fray; another feather-bonneted warrior knifing a soldier.

CUT TO
A close-up of the Indian-head penny.

CUT TO
A long shot of Cyrus Dallin's statue, "The Appeal to the Great Spirit." The camera comes in to pick up the details.

CUT TO
Edgar S. Paxson's "masterpiece"—"Custer's Last Fight." The camera again singles out the bits of action.

CUT TO
A shot of both sides of the "buffalo nickel," which will include details of the Indian head and the buffalo.

CUT TO
Charles Russell's statue, "Scalp Dance." The camera explores the two dancing figures.

DISSOLVE INTO
Russell's single figure sculpture, "The Scalp Dancer."

CUT TO
Russell's figure of "The Medicine Man" drumming and singing.

CUT BACK TO
Russell's single and double dancing figures.

DISSOLVE INTO
The figure of "The Medicine Man."

31

DISSOLVE INTO
A shot of the U.S. five-dollar bill containing the protrait of the
Sioux Chief Onepapa.

The word *Indian* will usually bring one particular image to
mind—a Plains warrior in a flowing feather bonnet on a
prancing war pony.

The graphic arts were a very important factor in bringing the
Native American to the attention of the world. If one couldn't
see an Indian in the flesh, the next best thing was to look at a
picture of him.

PLATE IV   THE SENECA INDIANS, NEAR BUFFALO
From the manuscript volume Our Travels *(1822)*
in the collection of the New York State Library.

(New York Public Library)

Visual images made a far greater impact than the written
word. Since literacy was limited in the colonies as well as
abroad, the earliest mass exposure of Europeans to Native
Americans came through the graphic arts. Artists here painted
and sketched the Native American in his own setting. Many of
the tribes portrayed on canvas have long since been exterminated. More often than not early painters attributed Caucasian features to their subjects, adding their own embellish-

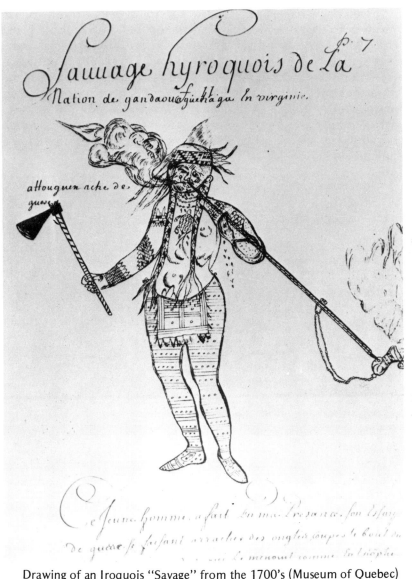

Drawing of an Iroquois "Savage" from the 1700's (Museum of Quebec)

ments as to the latters' mode of dress. As with that of writers, the original works were copied in Europe by artists who had never set foot on this continent, who, in turn, further embellished their own fantasies about the red man, creating for him an aspect mythical.

Driven by that spirit to see for themselves, some artists traveled to remote frontiers to paint the Native American. Three 19th century artists who colored the public's image were George Catlin, Karl Bodmer, and Alfred Jacob Miller. All were noted for their paintings of Plains tribes. These works played an important role in establishing the Plains Indian as the popular image of the Native American. It reached a point where no matter what the tribe was depicted from no matter what part of the country, the subjects always ended up looking like Plains Indians.

"Indians" of South Carolina, 16th Century. (New York Public Library)

John C. Ewers, in his article, "The Emergence of the Plains Indian as the Symbol of the North American Indian," from the *Smithsonian Report for 1964*, makes this evaluation:

> Together the works of Catlin and . . . Bodmer, appearing almost simultaneously, greatly stimulated popular interest in the Plains Indians in this country and abroad, and had a strong influence on the work of many other artists.

> They influenced the pictorial representation of Indians during the mid-19th century in three important ways. First, the Catlin . . . Bodmer example encouraged other artists to go west and to draw and/or paint the Indians of the Plains in the field . . . .

> Secondly, they encouraged some of the most able illustrators of the period, who had not visited the western Indian

Country, to help meet the popular demand for pictures of Plains Indians by using the works of Catlin and Bodmer for reference . . . .

Finally Catlin and Bodmer powerfully influenced those lesser, poorly paid artists who anonymously illustrated a number of popular books on Indians as well as school histories; these began to appear within a very few years after the books of Catlin and Bodmer were published.

Catlin became a one-man bandwagon for promoting the Native American. He assembled his pictures, costumes, and artifacts for a national tour of exhibitions and lectures. His "Indian Gallery" opened in New York City's Clinton Hall on September 25, 1837. Harold McCracken states in *George Catlin and the Old Frontier* (1959):

> . . . George Catlin became the first person to present a *Wild West* exhibition for the entertainment of the American public . . . . [The exhibit] marked the beginning of one of the longest surviving of all the popular interests our country has experienced. Curiosity brought New Yorkers to see what Catlin had brought back and hear what he had to say about the little-known wilderness of the Far West. They crowded into the gallery to gaze at the pictures . . . .

When he opened his show in England in 1840, Catlin got even closer to the Wild West Show concept as explained by McCracken:

> Never content with a goal achieved, Catlin devised a plan for adding greater interest and effectiveness to his exhibitions. This was the introduction of a *tableaux vivans*, in which a group of carefully selected actors were trained to perform Indian dances, ceremonies and scenes of warfare, all properly garbed in costumes from his collection, with their bodies and faces appropriately painted, and instructed in the red man's songs and yells and warhoops . . . .

Still looking for ways of improving his show, he hired 14 Ioway Native Americans stranded in London to do what the white performers had been doing, and now Europeans were treated to the real McCoy.

Catlin's work continues to exert tremendous influence today. The publicity department for the film *A Man Called Horse* proudly proclaimed that this "is perhaps the first motion picture to treat the American Indian in every detail of his life with unparalleled accuracy. Sharpened to a cutting edge with authenticity, 'A Man Called Horse' is definitely a film of the '70's . . . a motion picture that takes its strength by 'telling it like it was.'" To one who has seen the film, this becomes one of the funniest statements ever written. There certainly was "unparalleled accuracy," for many of Catlin's paintings were copied in great detail. The only trouble was that the film had the wrong Indians. The tribe depicted in the film was supposedly Sioux, but the Catlin paintings so faithfully reproduced were of just

The torture ceremony from part of the Mandan O-Kee-Pa, a lithograph by George Catlin.

The "Sioux" Sun Dance from *A Man Called Horse* (1970) after Catlin.

about every other tribe. To give a few examples: the earth-lodge in the Sioux camp is Mandan. The Sun Vow ceremony, which is the focal point of the film's promotion campaign, as well as the high point of the film, is a Mandan O-Kee-Pa ceremony which was done primarily to attract the buffalo. The Mandan was a sedentary tribe and, unlike the Sioux, depended on the buffalo coming to them. Catlin painted and wrote of this.

A drawing of a Sioux Sun Dance by No Heart, Teton-Dakota (Sioux). (Smithsonian Institution National Anthropological Archives, Bureau of American Ethnology Collection)

Richard Harris, during the torture ceremony, faints and has a vision in which the "Sioux chief" is seen in full war regalia astride a rearing charger. This is an exact reproduction of Catlin's Ba-Da-Ah-Chon-Du, He Who Outjumps All or He Who Jumps Over Everyone, a Crow chief. The Sioux and the Crow were hereditary enemies. One of the worst slurs that could be hurled at a tribesman was to refer to him as a member of an enemy tribe. Nothing could be more insulting, but not so far as *A Man Called Horse* is concerned. The producers may have loaded their picture with "authenticity" but certainly not with integrity.

Besides Catlin, other famous artists are associated with the Western Indian: Charles Schreyvogel, Rufus Zogbaum, Frederic Remington, Edgar Paxson, and Charles Russell. Their West is easily identified in TV and film Westerns, since their works are so often used or misused, as was Catlin's, for resource material.

Ba-Da-Ah-Chon-Du, He Who Outjumps All or He Who Jumps Over Everyone, a Crow chief. (American Museum of Natural History)

CUT TO
John Ford and director Burt Kennedy talking as reported in August-September, 1968, issue of *Action*. Ford is speaking: But you try to get a format for each picture. For instance, on *She Wore a Yellow Ribbon* I tried to make it as Remington as possible, though it didn't come out that way. On another picture I might try to make it as if it were seen by Charlie Russell.

The beginnings of commercial art could be seen in the world of advertising, books, dime novels, and Wild West Shows. Mass production of lithographs, with a company such as Currier and Ives leading with quantity and quality, plus mass distribution of calendars, brought art into every home.

"The Scout" by Cyrus E. Dallin. (New York Public Library)

Not to be ignored is the influence sculptors had in molding public opinion. Russell and Remington are also well known for their work in this field. But their works are dwarfed when compared to the monumental statues of Cyrus E. Dallin. Several of them can still be seen in cities throughout the country: "The Appeal to the Great Spirit" in Boston; "The Medicine Man" in Philadelphia; "The Scout" in Kansas City; and "Massasoit" (who looks amazingly like a Plains Indian) in Plymouth. New York City, not to be outdone, has its own kind of sardonic statue. Gigantically, Theodore Roosevelt fronts the Museum of Natural History, sitting high in the saddle. Now, Roosevelt was no lover of Indians; he disliked them more than somewhat. But noblesse oblige: Teddy is flanked by two beneficiaries of the

40

white man's burden—on one side a feather-bonneted Native American and on the other a Native African.

Photography did much to spread and popularize the Native

Sitting Bull and Buffalo Bill in a publicity shot for the Buffalo Bill Wild West Show. (Smithsonian Institution National Anthropological Archives, Bureau of American Ethnology Collection)

American throughout the world. Three men, William S. Soule, L. A. Huffman, and Edward Curtis, were able to take photography—in its early days, a crude and cumbersome process—and, through their portraits of Native Americans, transform it into an art form.

Souvenir photos and postcards became another example of big business know-how. A famous photo of Buffalo Bill and Sitting Bull standing together and captioned, "Foes in '76, Friends in '85" was sold by the thousands at the Wild West Shows. Sitting Bull learned to scrawl his name and sold autographed photos of himself at a dollar a print while he was with the show. Walter Havighurst, in a children's book *Buffalo Bill's Great Wild West Show* (1957), tells:

> Sitting Bull, like all Indians, was fond of children, and he was a hero to them. Clusters of small boys hung around his tent and followed him across the lot. They copied his limping gait and stuck paper in their hair for want of eagle feathers. At the refreshment stand he bought them popcorn and candy.

> Newsboys and shoeshine boys roamed over the grounds, looking for business. Sitting Bull was their best customer. He couldn't read a paper and his moccasins wouldn't take a shine, but he handed out nickels and dimes all day long . . . .

DIME NOVELS AND PENNY DREADFULS

SCENE VI

CUT TO

A close-up of a white man's face looms on the screen. He has a moustache, goatee, long flowing hair and wears a large 10-gallon white hat. The camera pans right to a leering Indian profile wearing a full feathered bonnet. The camera pulls back revealing the white man, in colorful Western garb, staying the hand of the Indian, who, with a knife in one hand and a rifle in the other, is about to stab another white man lying on the ground. Continuing back, the camera shows that this is a cover of *The Buffalo Bill Stories*. The title of this early 1900s dime novel is *Buffalo Bill's Raid of Death or The Border Robin Hood*. A boy is seated under a tree engrossed in the story. He reads aloud: "And when the orator sat down, amid a whirlwind of applause, outside of the lodge the squaws were telling each other how they would torture the white men and the white women and children who should be brought to that village as prisoners. The whole thing made Buffalo Bill's blood boil. But he could do nothing, except sit there and listen to the venomous words, and pretend that he approved them. "Sioux very mad—heap mad!" said Wild Wolf, finding an opportunity to speak thus to him. "Yes, Wild Wolf," the scout answered. And he reflected that if it should become known that he was the army scout Buffalo Bill, those Indians would delight in tearing him limb from limb. Those yelling squaws outside would like nothing better than to poke his eyes out with knives, and torture him to death by inches. For of all fiends in this world, a savage Indian Squaw, with her anger aroused, is, perhaps, the worst."

The boy looks up concerned over the safety of his hero. All he can do is mutter: Wow!

And so ends chapter IV of Buffalo Bill's latest adventure.

From its first appearance in 1860, the dime novel exerted tremendous influence in formulating the detrimental image of the Native American. Although cheap literature had been pub-

43

"NOW, RED—SKINS, YOUR ARROWS HAVE GOT TO BE SHARP TO
GO THROUGH THIS TOUGH BREASTWORK, SO FIRE AWAY." (From
the collection of Edward T. Le Blanc)

lished for many years prior, this publishing and literary phenomenon clicked at this time because of the introduction of mass production, distribution, and advertising. Dime novels were read by the hundreds of thousands by both sides in the Civil War. The habit, once established, flourished. The popularity of these stories also reached across the seas.

The Indian was a predominant figure from the start. It was not by accident that the first novel to be published by Irwin Beadle and Co., soon to become one of the leading publishers of dime novels, was a reprint of *Malaeska: the Indian Wife of the White Hunter*, by Mrs. Ann Stephens. As described in Albert Johannsen's *The House of Beadle and Adams* (1950): "The scene of the story is in and around New York City and the Catskills in early Colonial days. It deals with the tribulations of the wife of a squaw man."

The story that sent dime novel sales skyrocketing was number 8 in the original Beadle series, *Seth Jones; or the Captives of the Frontier* (1860), by Edward S. Ellis. Again the Indian menace appeared, as shown in Johannsen's synopsis: "Life in the early settlements of western New York when Indian horrors were common. The capture of a girl by Mohawks and her rescue by two scouts is the theme of the story." More than 400,000 copies of this novel were sold as a result of a heavy advertising campaign. The fantastic success of *Seth Jones* was the turning point in the dime novel boom.

The two scouts in the Ellis story suggest the influence of Cooper. Writers capitalized on Cooper's earlier successes and elaborated on the Leather-Stocking type characters. The name, Natty Bumppo, rings no romantic bells. But—Hawkeye—there's a name to reckon with. A heroic image to embellish one's dreams. And, in the dime novels, these visions were as varied as the name game. In 1863 Beadle's published Warren S. John's *Single Eye. A Story of King Philip's War.* Again, from Johannsen:

> Metacom, commonly called King Philip, retaliates for wrongs inflicted by the English in Massachusetts. The Pokanokets, Narragansetts, and Wamponoags war against the English and their allies, the Mohigans. A one-eyed hunter, Peter Simpson, called 'Single Eye,' and his Mohigan friend, Assawomset, perform wonders.

Then appeared William J. Hamilton's *Eagle Eye; or, Ralph*

Warren and his Red Friend. A Story of the Fall of Oswego (1865).

In 1869 we had Lewis Jay Swift's *Keen-Eye, the Ranger; or, the Hunter's Daughter*.

In 1873, Beadle and Adams published *Sharp-Eye, the White Chief of the Sioux. A Romance of the Far West*, by Max Martine, the pen name of Henry M. Avery who, in real life and true romantic style, had been a trapper, Indian fighter and, while a captive of the Sioux, was adopted by them and married the chief's daughter.

Glass Eye, the Great Shot of the West, by "Bruin" Adams was published in 1874.

Buffalo Bill Cody, as an author, got into the act with *Deadly-Eye, the Unknown Scout* (1875).

The dime novels advocated the slaying and subduing of the Indian in the name of morality, nationalism, and patriotism. The "pesky redskins" weren't just killed singly or in pairs but by the gross. The bloody flag was not only waved but was rammed down the "red varmits'" throats. Kit Carson, in one story and with one hand, killed seven Indians while supporting a fair, swooning damsel with the other.

Writers, in attempting to outdo one another, included gross exaggerations and misinformation about the Native American. These stories deceived and influenced readers here and abroad.

A classic example that stretched the credibility gap to absurdity was a story by Oliver Gloux, a Frenchman who wrote under the name of Gustav Aimard. He lived among Native Americans for many years as a hunter and trapper and returned to France to write of his adventures, several of which were published here. Using his imagination more than vividly, his accounts of life among the savages were no more exaggerated than those of other authors who were not quite as obvious. This is how Aimard pictured Indian life in *Prairie Flower* (1878):

> In the prairies of the Upper Missouri, at the time of our story, ostriches were still abundant, and their chase one of the numerous amusements of the red-skins and wood-rangers . . . .

> A characteristic trait of the ostriches is their extreme curiosity. In the Indian villages, where they live in a tamed state, it is a frequent occurrence to see them stalking through groups of talkers, and regarding them with fixed attention.

Evidently readers did not question the existence of ostriches in America. Nor did they seem to question *Young Wild Running the Gauntlet; or, The Pawnee Chief's Last Shot* (1903), which contains an excellent example of the influence dime novels exerted on movies—in this case the "ugh" school of dialogue:

"Ugh!" grunted the chief, pausing in front of the captive.
"Ugh!" answered Wild, in the same fashion.
"How?" said the Pawnee, smiling sardonically.
"Pretty fair," retorted the young Prince of the Saddle, who knew the Indian fashion of asking a person how they were, or how they felt, etc.
"Paleface boy heap smart. Blue Horse know him. He come to catch Blue Horse and take him to soldiers at the fort. Young Wild West heap much brave, but he no take Blue Horse to the fort, for tomorrow morning, before the sun gets over the top of the mountains he will die!"

This excerpt illustrates how misinformation was passed along to the public. "How," which is usually spelled *hou*, is a Sioux word, a form of greeting. The word was not part of any other Native American language. It continued to be used in films as a "peace greeting," accompanied by an upraised hand, for all their Indians. In addition, the invention of the word "ugh" became part of the process which reduced the image of the Native American to that of a grunting, mentally retarded, monosyllabic idiot.

The Arthur Westbrook Co. published the short-lived *American Indian Weekly* from 1910 to 1911. The reason for its quick demise might be due to the increasing popularity of the Indian in movies.

Practically every type of cliche used in pictures originally appeared in dime novels. Although the association between films and dime novels is often implied, in some cases it was direct. The dime novel collection of Edward T. LeBlanc, one of the country's leading authorities, contains three original copies of *Wild West Weekly*, August 2, September 13 and 27, 1912, published by Frank Tousey. At the top of each cover page is printed: "NOTICE! This story has been dramatized by the NESTOR FILM COMPANY and can be seen in all the Independent Motion Picture houses in the U. S. A."

Eventually the Dime Novel Indian died, only to be resurrected like some compulsive ghost by the makers of motion pictures.

"WITH LOUD CRIES THEY DRAGGED LALLA TOREDO BEFORE SITTING BULL AND THE GREAT CHIEFS." (From the collection of Edward T. Le Blanc)

LADIES AND GENTLEMEN, INTRODUCING . . .

SCENE VII

CUT TO
A gaudy and garish wagon not unlike a brightly painted circus
wagon. This is a medicine show wagon set up for business in a town
square. A small crowd of "locals" are watching a group of Indians,
bedecked in feathers and buckskins, sing and dance. When they
finish, a white man in a gaudy Western costume puts his arm around
an ancient looking Indian and brings him forward, as he addresses
the crowd: Well, my friends, seeing is believing. You've seen it with
your own eyes—this grand old gentleman, Chief Eagle Claw, dancing
like a young buck. Now you can believe it. And would you believe
this, my friends, that this grand, old gentleman is 110 years old?
Yes, my friends, I repeat, 110 years old and Chief Eagle Claw has
never had a sick day in his life. How is that, you ask? Well, my
friends, I'm about to divulge to you a centuries-old tribal secret.

The heyday of the medicine show lasted from the end of the
Civil War to the turn of the century. There were as many as 150
shows on the road using anything from one wagon to huge
circus tents for pushing their patent medicines. Company names
ranged from the Ginsberg Indian Medicine Co. to the most
famous of all—The Kickapoo Indian Medicine Co., which was
formed in 1881 by Texas Charlie Bigelow and Col. John Healy.
The Kickapoo Company's name for their magical cure-all was
Sagwa. Some "hit and run" shows, capitalizing on Kickapoo's
fame, called their patent medicines Awaga or Saqwah. But most
companies resorted to such appealing names as Wizard Oil or
Herbs of Joy.

In the February, 1967, issue of *The American West*, Arrell M.
Gibson tells, in "Medicine Show," that in order to exploit the

49

COL. T. A. EDWARDS,

AND HIS TROOP OF

WARM SPRING INDIANS.

Now exhibiting   -   -   IN THIS CITY.

(Smithsonian Institution National Anthropological Archives, Bureau of American Ethnology Collection)

country's fascination for Western lore, the Kickapoo Co. organized 30 traveling troupes, each consisting of ten to thirty Native Americans (men, women, and children) plus a "frontier scout." Interestingly enough, none of the Native Americans employed by the Kickapoo Co. was actually from that tribe. Kickapoo contracted with federal Indian agents for the use of, among others: Canadian Mohawks and Crees, New York Iroquois, Pawnees, Sioux, Blackfoot, Cherokees, and Chippewas. They even hired natives from South America.

Although the main purpose was to sell the medicine show "juice," great emphasis was placed on the Wild West Show

An ad from the reverse of the previous photograph. (Smithsonian Institution National Anthropological Archives, Bureau of American Ethnology Collection)

entertainment which was interspersed with the pitch. The pitchman was a "genuine frontier scout" decked out in a colorful Buffalo Bill or Pawnee Bill type costume. The shows usually ended with some kind of rip-snorting show stopper. The audiences must have been rip-snorters, too, since alcohol, the basic ingredient of the tonics, was from 10 to 50 percent of the content. Many tonics also contained morphine. The elixir was a best seller, especially in dry areas. It was easy to keep children sleepily quiet, women discretely tipsy, and men staggeringly happy.

Entertainment values extended beyond the show's visit. The public, while at home, had the opportunity to vary its limited reading with such colorful booklets as *The Indian Illustrated Magazine*, *The Kickapoo Indian Dream Book*, and *Life and*

51

Scenes Among the Kickapoo Indians, and the Discovery of the Wondrous Cures Affected by Them. The writing was wildly exaggerated and flamboyantly grandiose and served to pass the time away during long winter evenings.

The cover of a booklet given away with each purchase of "The Oswego" patent medicine.

As an example of home reading, this is the ending of a story booklet published in Oswego, New York, in 1882, called *The Witch-Woman's Revenge; or, The Golden Secret of the "Oswego,"* by J. Mc.:

> Centuries have passed, and the bones of Wanketo and his noble wife have mouldered into dust, but her secret still lives . . . . At first it was only used in cases of fever, but its potency was rapidly extended even while yet in the hands of the Indians. Gradually its benefits were extended to the whites, and as the Indians faded away before the onward march of civilization the secret passed from their hands into those of the conquering race . . . . It has indeed performed wonderful cures, and deadly diseases, which

have baffled the skill of physicians, are checked by its use and soon permanently cured. Being placed at the low price of twenty-five cents per bottle, it is within the reach of all. It is a sovereign remedy for Biliousness, Dyspepsia, Indigestion, Diseases of the Kidneys, Torpid Liver, Rheumatism, Dizziness, Sick Headache, Loss of Appetite, Jaundice, Apoplexy, Palpitations, Eruptions, and Skin Diseases, all of which these Bitters will cure by removing the cause. Keep the stomach, bowels, and digestive organs in good working order. Ladies and others subject to Sick Headaches will find relief and permanent cure by the use of these Bitters. Being tonic and mildly purgative, they purify the blood by expelling all morbid secretions. For sale by all dealers in medicine.

CUT BACK TO
The boy, previously seen, is lying on his back holding the dime novel, *Buffalo Bill's Raid of Death*, above him. He is still reading aloud: "Give them no time to arm or rally, men! At them with a savage will!" cried Buffalo Bill. "The only way to save the white settlements is to teach these red murderers a lesson they will not forget." And a burst of war cries answered his words, and death held high carnival once more in the home of the red man. In the twinkling of an eye, almost, the village was in ruins, the ground strewn with dead warriors, and hundreds of squaws and papooses were flying for safety to the hills.

By far the most successful hero in dime novels was Buffalo Bill. From 1869, when the first installment of the first Buffalo Bill story by Ned Buntline appeared, until recently, the stories were printed and reprinted hundreds and hundreds of times all over the world. Several issues of *The Buffalo Bill Stories* were reprinted in paperbacks by Gold Star Books in the late 1960s.

One of the blurbs used by Street and Smith in promoting their *Buffalo Bill Stories* was no idle boast: "Buffalo Bill wins his way into the heart of every one who reads the strong stories of stirring adventure on the wide prairies of the West published in this weekly."

CUT TO
A newspaper lying on a kitchen table. The front page has a picture of Buffalo Bill and a headline announcing his death. A young boy sits at the table writing a letter. We hear the contents in Voice Over:
Mr. Buffalo Bill, Denver, Colo.: Dear Sir—My grandpa told me this morning you were ready to start for the happy hunting grounds. He said a long time ago they had perhaps given you the end of a golden string and told you to wind it into a ball and you had it most all

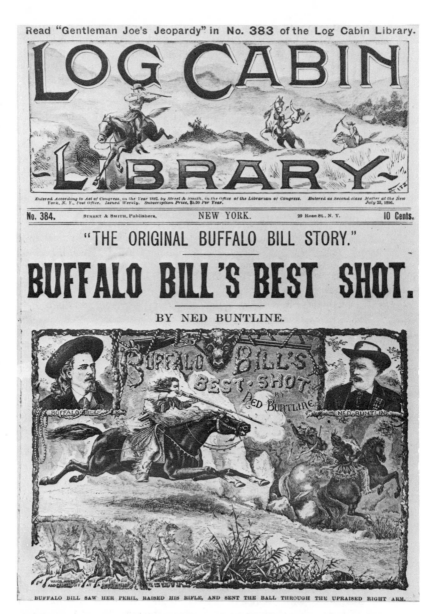

Read "Gentleman Joe's Jeopardy" in No. 383 of the Log Cabin Library.

LOG CABIN LIBRARY

Entered According to Act of Congress, in the Year 1892, by Street & Smith, in the Office of the Librarian of Congress. Entered as Second-class Matter at the New York, N. Y., Post Office. Issued Weekly. Subscription Price, $5.00 Per Year. July 25, 1896.

No. 384. STREET & SMITH, Publishers. NEW YORK. 29 Rose St., N. Y. 10 Cents.

"THE ORIGINAL BUFFALO BILL STORY."

BUFFALO BILL'S BEST SHOT.

BY NED BUNTLINE.

BUFFALO BILL SAW HER PERIL, RAISED HIS RIFLE, AND SENT THE BALL THROUGH THE UPRAISED RIGHT ARM.

"BUFFALO BILL SAW HER PERIL, RAISED HIS RIFLE, AND SENT THE BALL THROUGH THE UPRAISED RIGHT ARM." (From the collection of Edward T. Le Blanc) winded up and it had led you to the happy hunting ground, and after you got there they would lock the gate and throw the key away, as you were the last one they had been waiting for. Mr. Buffalo Bill, I want to go to the happy hunting ground too. It looks to me like a nicer place than just heaven where they have only gold streets and harps and angels and things. Mr. Buffalo Bill, will you please take the key and hold the gate and make room for just me? I am a little fellow and don't take much room nohow, and I will come as soon as I get through here. Then they can lock the gate and throw the key away forever and ever.

—ROBERT CURTISS TALBOTT

The success of the dime novels encouraged "the Knight of the Plains," the Honorable William F. Cody, to embark on two other endeavors, stage shows and Wild West Shows.

The launching of Buffalo Bill's stage career established the standard operating procedure for show business Indians. In 1872 Buffalo Bill starred in the first of his many successful tours: *The Scouts of the Prairie*, by Ned Buntline. The redskins were played by whiteskins and the Indian maiden, Dove Eye, was played by Mlle. Morlacchi, "the Italian danseuse." This successful play was followed by *The Scouts of the Plains*, by Fred G. Maeder, in 1873. The title was only slightly different and so were the parts; that season Mlle. Morlacchi played Pale Dove.

In 1875 and 1876 the standby or alternate play was *Life on the Border*. Don Russell in *The Lives and Legends of Buffalo Bill* (1960) describes this cliche ridden epic: "If *Life on the Border* were to replace a television western without warning, it is doubtful that one in a million listeners would know the difference—except in missing a few slightly less antiquated cliches that haunt that medium."

The 1876 season had them touring *The Red Right Hand; or Buffalo Bill's First Scalp for Custer*, the story of his famous duel with Yellow Hand. Cody modestly described the play in one of his autobiographies: "It afforded us . . . ample opportunity to give a noisy, rattling, gunpowder entertainment, and to present a succession of scenes in the late Indian War, all of which seemed to give general satisfaction." Yellow Hand's scalp and headdress, Cody's blood-stained trophies, were used extensively for advertising purposes. Thus the play afforded ample opportunity to exploit Buffalo Bill's reputation as an Indian Killer and advocate of the white man supreme.

55

CUT TO
A man seated at a desk. Col. William Lightfoot Visscher is writing the final chapter, "The End of the Trail," for *Life and Adventures of Buffalo Bill*. We hear part of what he is writing in Voice Over: For Buffalo Bill was a man's man and yet a boy's man. He was all that was desired, in the form of romantic manhood. His stories were the stories that thrilled—the yarn of his duel with Yellowhand, when the renegade challenged him before thousands of Indians and soldiers, only to meet death at Col. Cody's hand. Then, too, there were the stories of the Battle of Warbonnet and of Summit Springs. There were the stories of trails and of plains—and many a time I have seen the colonel, an island in an ocean of small boys, telling them the stories of the past, the stories of days when the warhoop echoed and the tomahawk was something more than a tradition.

For the new play in 1877, *May Cody; or, Lost and Won*, Native Americans were used to play Indians; Cody hired some Sioux from the Red Cloud Agency, a reservation in South Dakota.

The Knight of the Plains; or, Buffalo Bill's Best Trail, by Col. Prentiss Ingraham, was introduced in 1878. Cody hired some Pawnees and ran into trouble with the Indian Bureau for taking "wards" off the reservation without permission. Under the law, Native Americans were considered wards of the government, supervised by federally appointed agents. One of the neatest rationalizations for the gross exploitation of the Native American was given by Cody, in his life story: "I thought I was benefiting the Indians as well as the government, by taking them all over the United States, and giving them a correct idea of the customs, life, etc., of the pale faces, so that when they returned to their people they could make known all they had seen."

CUT BACK TO
Col. Visscher at his desk. He is writing a section entitled "Pahaska friend of the Indian" which we hear in Voice Over: "He never fought us except when we needed it," old Short Bull, the man who is supposed to have caused the Ghost Dance war, told me one day, "and he was our friend even when he fought us. He killed us because we were bad and because we fought against what he knew was best for us. And when there was peace, he was our best friend. Did he not talk to the Great White Spirit in Washington and help us? Did he not get food for us when we were starving? Did he not give us money from his own hands that we might live? No, Pahaska has not been our enemy. He has been our friend."

CUT TO

A small town street—sunlit, quiet, peaceful, dreamlike. This is Main St., U.S.A. at the turn of the century. Two men, one carrying a bucket of paste and a long-handled brush and the other long rolls of paper, stop at a high, white-washed wooden fence and paste up a large colorful poster. Blazoned across the top of the entire sheet in bold letters is "Buffalo Bill's Wild West and Congress of Rough Riders of the World." As if by some magical magnet, children are drawn to the two men. Shouts of "Buffalo Bill's coming to town," can be heard.

DISSOLVE INTO

A street near the outskirts of town jammed with wagons and people. Indians, cowgirls, American and Mexican cowboys, all on horseback, mill about getting into position.

CUT TO

Buffalo Bill, mounted on a handsome white prancer, waves his great, white sombrero. The cowboy band strikes up a fast and happy march. The big parade is led by Buffalo Bill himself, doffing his hat and bowing to his cheering admirers. Following the great scout is the band wagon; then comes a mounted band of redskins in war paint and feathers brandishing their weapons; Annie Oakley and Johnny Baker ride royally in a carriage; a band of war-painted Indians, on foot, sing and dance up the street; cowboys ride herd on longhorns; and finally comes the famous Deadwood Stage. The parade heads for the show grounds followed by the cheering crowd. Another great day for Buffalo Bill's Wild West is about to begin.

The concept of the Wild West Show was not new. George Catlin had tried one type of exhibition in 1837 with some degree of success. Another kind of Wild West, also on a small scale, was attempted in the summer of 1876 by the former agent of the San Carlos Apaches, John P. Clum. He took some of them along with other Apaches on a not too successful tour. Among the few Apache chiefs who toured with Clum was Tahzay, the son of Cochise, chief of the Chiricahua Apaches.

The tour was initiated, as Clum said, "to permit the effete East to see for itself that Apaches were human, . . ." Their first appearance was in St. Louis and the program did nothing but reinforce all the classic cliches about the Native American. And these lines from a review speak for themselves:

A hand-to-hand combat ensues, resulting in the triumph of the pale faces. There was considerable fighting done, however, and when the knife of the white man gleamed in the face of the Indian, who was held in his strong embrace, the applause, especially from the galleries, was deafening.

Olympic Theatre!

A NOVEL ATTRACTION.

Friday and Saturday Evenings, September 8th & 9th,

And Saturday Matinee,

Only appearances of members of the Famous Indian Tribes of

WILD APACHES

OF ARIZONA,

Under the direction of Mr. J. P. Clum, Ex-Indian Agent, numbering

Sixteen Stalwart Braves and Four Squaws

Without doubt the Finest Specimen of the Aborgine ever seen in this city.

The entertainment will consist of a series of

Stirring Tableaux,

Intensely and accurately illustrative of

Indian Modes & Customs

Never before so faithfully set forth.

FIRST TABLEAU.

THE INDIANS IN FULL COSTUMES.

Introductory remarks by Mr. J. P. Clum.

SECOND TABLEAUX.

AN INDIAN ENCAMPMENT.

The Surprise!   The Fight!   Thrilling Hand-to-Hand Combat!   Taking of the Scalp!   Triumph of the Whites!

THIRD TABLEAU.

AN INDIAN COUNCIL OF WAR.

Speeches in the Indian Language by the noted Braves & Chiefs.

FOURTH TABLEAU.

Indian Woman Mourning the Death of her Husband.

FIFTH TABLEAUX.

Grand War Dance.   Preparing for the War-Path.

OVERTURE,   -   -   -   -   -   ORCHESTRA

PART SECOND—FIRST TABLEAU.

INDIAN TELEGRAPHIC SYSTEM.

SECOND TABLEAUX.

Whites Encamped.   The Indian Attack.
Capture of the Hunter.   Taking of the Scalp.
Securing the Prisoner to the Stake.
His Torture.   Indian Scalp Dance.

THIRD TABLEAUX.

Indian Police Regulations.   Arresting a Renegade.

FINAL TABLEAUX.

The Indian at Home, and at Peace.

Squaws engaged in Domestic Labor.   Social Games.   The whole concluding with A SOCIAL DANCE.

INDIAN MATINEE, SATURDAY

At Reduced Prices, 50 and 25 Cents to all parts of the house.

Monday, Sept. 11, 1876, opening of the Regular Fall and Winter Season,

Mr. C. W. BARRY

In his New Drama, ECHOES.

Chas. E. Ware & Co. Printers, N. E. cor. Fifth and Chestnut Sts

If the applause was deafening for a makeshift show such as Clum's, imagine the tumultuous reception given Buffalo Bill's spectaculars. With such stalwart figures as Buffalo Bill to identify with, the fantastic became real.

> CUT TO
> An empty stage. A young boy walks out and bows to the audience. He begins to recite in his best elocutionary fashion:
> "A Knight of the West." To Col. William F. Cody, Buffalo Bill. A poem by Col. William Lightfoot Visscher.
>
> Who is this gallant cavalier that rides in from the West?
> His horse, and gun, and trappings are the truest and the best;
> He strides his noble thorobred with manly, easy grace,
> And sits the saddle like a sheik, and rides a rattling pace;
> His hair falls white and long adown his shoulders strong and wide,
> And all his bearing has the poise of manliness and pride."
>
> CUT TO
> A large outdoor arena. The stands are completely jammed, with young faces in the majority. A white man wearing buckskins gallops to the center and announces in a booming voice: Ladies and gentlemen, Buffalo Bill and Nate Salsbury proudly present America's national entertainment, the one and only, genuine and authentic, unique and original Wild West Show.

Cody's Wild West started in Omaha in 1883. It was popular; it was entertaining; it was exciting. Audiences thrilled to the Indian attack on a settler's cabin and the rescue by Buffalo Bill and his troupe as the cabin went up in flames. The public was witness to the conquest of the West in all its glory.

> CUT TO
> The flower-filled auditorium of an Elks Club. The casket of Buffalo Bill lies in state as though homage were being paid to a royal prince. An Episcopal minister is reading messages of condolence: "The Rocky Mountain Club sends this message to the mourning world and the bereaved family: 'The News of the passing away of our fellow member, Col. William F. Cody, brings sorrow to all of us. Col. Cody was the one remaining hero of all time whose name is indelibly entwined in the redemption of our great West from barbarism and savagery, making it the hand-maiden of civilization and progress. His fame will shine in history in lines of living light with those other pioneer American crusaders, Daniel Boone, Davy Crockett, and Kit Carson. He was gentle, sincere, brave, loyal, and manly, and the world is the poorer for his passing. His fellow members of the Rocky Mountain Club ask you to present to his widow and family their respectful homage and sympathy.'"

Spectators gasped as redskins ambushed a wagon train and Buffalo Bill and his cronies arrived in the nick of time.

CUT BACK TO
The young boy reading the poem "A Knight of the West." He is now on the third stanza:
"'Mong the willows by the river, on mesa, hill and plain,
They fell beneath his horse's hoofs and 'fore his leaden rain;
Full well he wreaked his vengeance, and he blazed a western path,
With the weapons of his prowess and the scoring of his wrath.
From Missouri's murky waters to the white Sierra's crest,
This knightly man led dauntless men and empire to the West."

Buffalo Bill described a grand finale in his own words: "As a finish there was a Wild Western cyclone, and a whole Indian village was blown out of existence for the delectation of the English audience."

CUT TO
Buffalo Bill seated at a desk. He is writing one of his several autobiographies. We hear it in Voice Over: In concluding, I want to express the hope that the dealings of this government of ours with the Indian will always be just and fair. They were the inheritors of the land we live in. They were not capable of developing it, or of really appreciating its possibilities, but they owned it when the white man came, and the white man took it away from them. It was natural that they should resist. It was natural that they employed the only means of warfare known to them against those whom they regarded as usurpers. It was our business, as scouts, to be continually on the warpath against them when they committed depredations. But no scout ever hated the Indians in general.

Youngsters cheered as Buffalo Bill led the Cavalry in rescuing a scout captured by galloping red devils.

One of the great crowd pleasers was the depiction of Custer's Last Fight, which for some reason still haunts the media. After the battle, with the arena covered with dead Indians and soldiers, Buffalo Bill arrives. He finds Custer's body and, removing his hat, bows his head in silent tribute. Light bulbs flash the obvious in large letters: "TOO LATE."

Another rouser was described in a review in the May 4, 1907, issue of *The New York Dramatic Mirror*. Buffalo Bill had just returned after five years in Europe and his show was playing to capacity houses at Madison Square Garden:

Perhaps the most imposing feature of the performance is a reproduction of the Battle of Summit Springs, in which

Colonel Cody took part as a scout in 1869. The Indians are seen coming into a plain from behind a mountain with their tents, papooses, squaws and the various trappings necessary for the making of a village. They erect the tents, light the fires and proceed to settle down for the night . . . . As the mountain top is tinged with the rays of the morning sun Buffalo Bill is discovered peering over a rock in the distance. He gives the signal to the soldiers, and a vigorous attack is made on the savages, who put up a desperate resistance. They were finally conquered, of course, after a very realistic battle scene.

Soldier and Brave (1963), a book published by the National Park Service, described the real battle: "The Battle of Summit Springs was one of the most shattering defeats suffered by the Plains Indians. It occurred on July 11, 1869, when Major E. A. Carr surprised Tall Bull and his Cheyenne 'Dog Soldiers,' killed fifty and captured more than a hundred with the loss of only one cavalryman . . . ." The fight was quick and deadly, lasting about ten minutes, after which Buffalo Bill claimed credit for killing Tall Bull.

CUT BACK TO
The boy reading. He has finished the first poem and has started reading the second "The Great Scout" by F. P. Livingston. He is on the second stanza:

"What were the thoughts that filled his brain
While waiting for the final call?
Methinks he saw the blood-stained trail,
The rifles flash, the red man's fall.
The war-whoop and the massacre.
Ah, God! His life was one great fight
To master man and elements,
To force the erring mortal right.
　　They called him Bill—
　　Just Buffalo Bill."

A most publicized gimmick was to take famous people on as passengers in the Deadwood Stage while the Indians attacked it. On one of its European tours the passengers were the kings of Belgium, Greece, Denmark, and Saxony, plus the prince of Wales, with Buffalo Bill driving.

The show's first trip overseas was a triumphant year's tour of England in 1887. In 1889 the Wild West was the hit of Paris' *Exposition Universelle.* The most sophisticated Parisian shops

The caption for a European promotional piece reads: "La Troupe Du
Colonel Cody (Buffalo Bill) 1. Le reloi de poste.—2. La chasse aux buffles
dans le Far West.—3. Capture de cheveaux sauvages au lasso.—4. Danses
Guerrieres des Peaux-Rouges.—5. Red-Shirt (La Chemise-Rouge), chef des
Peaux-Rouges.—6. Domptage d'un cheval sauvage par un cow-boy.—7. Le
Colonel Cody (Buffalo-Bill)." (New York Public Library)

were selling Indian and Wild West tourist items. The show toured Europe for 18 successful months.

Although the Indians were a major attraction, Cody knew a kicker was needed. He also knew that the most famous red man of the most famous tribe was Sitting Bull of the Sioux. After the Battle of Little Big Horn, Sitting Bull and his band lived in exile in Canada. With his people near starvation, he was forced to surrender to U.S. authorities in 1881 and became a virtual prisoner of war—finally ending up at the Standing Rock Reservation. He agreed to appear with the Wild West for four months at $50 a week. He and eight other Sioux joined the show at Buffalo, New York in June, 1885. Sitting Bull was given a tipi of his own with his name over its entrance.

At first Sitting Bull and the audiences were not on the best of terms. The public did not forget Custer that easily. Newspapers found that the great medicine man was good copy and sympathetic treatment built sympathetic audiences. The fickle public, always looking for new heroes, found Sitting Bull. They came to jeer and, as if by magic, the bloodthirsty savage turned into a noble one before their very eyes. The red devil had become a matinee idol.

When the show went to Europe in 1887, the Native Americans were headed by Red Shirt and included such famous warriors as Rocky Bear, Flat Iron, Cut Meat, Red Dog, American Bear, Kills Plenty, Poor Dog, and Tall Horse.

The great Sioux medicine man, Black Elk, in John G. Neihardt's *Black Elk Speaks* (1961), had this to say about the show while they were in New York:

> We stayed there and made shows for many, many Wasichus [white men] all that winter. I liked the part of the show we made, but not the part the Wasichus made. After a while I got used to being there, but I was like a man who had never had a vision. I felt dead and my people seemed lost and I thought I might never find them again. I did not see anything to help my people. I could see that the Wasichus did not care for each other the way our people did before the nation's hoop was broken. They would take everything from each other if they could, and so there were some who had more of everything than they could use, while crowds of people had nothing at all and maybe were starving. They had forgotten that the earth was their mother. This could not be better than the old ways of my people. There was a prisoner's house on an

island where the big water came up to the town, and we saw that one day. Men pointed guns at the prisoners and made them move around like animals in a cage. This made me feel very sad, because my people too were penned up in islands, and maybe that was the way the Wasichus were going to treat them.

In the spring it got warmer, but the Wasichus had even the grass penned up. We heard then that we were going to cross the big water to strange lands. Some of our people went home and wanted me to go with them, but I had not seen anything good for my people yet; maybe across the big water there was something to see, so I did not go home, although I was sick and in despair.

This is Black Elk's description of their performing before Queen Victoria:

Sometimes we had to shoot in the show, but this time we did not shoot at all. We danced and sang, and I was one of the dancers chosen to do this for the Grandmother, because I was young and limber and could dance many ways. We stood right in front of Grandmother England. She was little but fat and we liked her because she was good to us. After we had danced, she spoke to us. She said something like this: "I am sixty-seven years old. All over the world I have seen all kinds of people; but to-day I have seen the best-looking people I know. If you belonged to me, I would not let them take you around in a show like this . . . ."

There had been some talk about the mistreatment of the Native Americans in the show. Stories appeared in American papers and Buffalo Bill was in trouble again. The Commissioner of Indian Affairs felt that they should be home on their reservations rather than barnstorming in Europe with a circus. When the show went into winter quarters in 1890, Cody brought the homesick Native Americans back and took them to Washington. Rocky Bear and Red Dog acted as spokesmen at the Indian Bureau. If they praised the Wild West Show, Buffalo Bill, and the dubious benefits derived, it was with the knowledge that the only alternative was slow death on the dreaded reservation.

This was 1890. They told of how well they were treated and cared for. It was the year of the Ghost Dance, the murder of Sitting Bull, and the Wounded Knee Massacre. This was 1890 and the last chance for the Native American.

The Ghost Dance religion was their last hope. The white government wanted them to be farmers but didn't teach them how to farm and the crops failed. The white government wanted them to be ranchers but the cattle given to them died of disease. The food given or sold by the white traders and agents was rotten and uneatable. Everywhere, on the reservations, from the very old to the very young, there was death and starvation. By denying all that was white, believing in a Savior, and praying and dancing for peace and a vision, they believed that the white man would disappear and all would return to as it was in the days of old. This is what the Ghost Dance taught.

Sitting Bull encouraged the Ghost Dance, which made him an even greater threat to the white man. When his arrest was ordered, Buffalo Bill's offer to help was, in the end, of no help at all. Sitting Bull, while resisting arrest, was shot and killed by Reservation Police who were themselves Sioux.

The Ghost Dance, a dance of peace, was the Native American's last hope. The white man's government, convinced it was a dance of war, ordered it stopped at all cost. That cost was 300 men, women, and children of Big Foot's Sioux band who were massacred at Wounded Knee by Custer's famed 7th Cavalry on December 29, 1890. It has been said that this massacre was in retaliation for what had happened to Custer at the Little Big Horn. This unprovoked and senseless slaughter broke the back of Native American resistance. The Ghost Dance died at Wounded Knee.

Robert M. Utley, in *The Last Days of the Sioux Nation* (1963), writes of one tragic aftermath of Wounded Knee:

> General Miles left Pine Ridge for Chicago on the evening of January 26. He took with him twenty-five Ghost Dance leaders, including Kicking Bear and Short Bull, whom he intended to confine at Fort Sheridan, Illinois, until passions had subsided enough for them to return to their people. Buffalo Bill Cody, who had turned up at Pine Ridge in the last days of the campaign as a colonel on the staff of the governor of Nebraska, asked to employ the prisoners as part of the troupe of his Wild West Show, which was about to embark on a European tour. The chance to get these troublemakers out of the country for a year, and at the same time to relieve the Army of their support, appealed to Miles, and he heartily endorsed Cody's application. But Commissioner of Indian Affairs Morgan regarded circus life as demoralizing and had publicly announced that no more Indians would be permitted to leave the reservation for exhibition purposes. Cody went to the Nebraska congressional delegation and

had sufficient pressure applied to Secretary Noble to get the ban lifted, and the prisoners, together with other Sioux recruited at Pine Ridge, joined the show for a profitable trip across the great waters.

The Wounded Knee Massacre became another entertainment

An old poster for a Wild West Show recently used as a cover for *Bandwagon Magazine.*

66

spectacle in the show several years later when the Buffalo Bill and Pawnee Bill shows joined forces.

The phenomenal success of Buffalo Bill's Wild West resulted, naturally, in all sorts of competition. The better known were Pawnee Bill and the Miller Bros. 101 Ranch Real Wild West. When stranded in Europe, Black Elk worked for a show called Mexican Joe's. Every show and exhibition had to have its famous Indian. As a result, Red Cloud, Chief Joseph, Geronimo, Rain-in-the-Face—all played the circuit.

The reduction of a once great people to the status of show pieces caused many Native Americans to speak out in anger. Most notable was Dr. Carlos Montezuma, an Apache, who was a highly successful physician, an untiring fighter for Native American rights and a strong advocate for the abolishment of the Bureau of Indian Affairs. Not only did he speak out against and fight such shows as Buffalo Bill's, which exploited his people, but he also strongly criticized those Native Americans who participated in them for the white man's amusement. Despite his criticism, he did not abandon his fellow Native Americans. When some Native Americans with the Buffalo Bill show were injured in a train wreck, Dr. Montezuma took up their cause in a court of law.

Other voices were heard. At the 1913 conference of the Society of the American Indians, a Sioux, Chauncey Yellow Robe, was one who spoke out:

> Is there anyone here that will tell me that the Wild West Show is a good thing for the Indian? If this Society is in favorable accord with such a practice, I am willing to form a new Wild West Show right here among the members of this Society to take the place of the celebrated Buffalo Bill, . . .
> The Indian is not to be censured for the Wild West Show, for his condition and the present life which the Indian is forced to lead has drawn him into such shows. What benefit has the Indian derived from these Wild West Shows? None, but what are degrading, demoralizing, and degenerating, and all their influences fall far short of accomplishing the ideals of citizenship and civilized state of affairs which we most need to know. Tribal habits and customs are apt to be degraded for show purposes, because the Indian Bureau under our government is constantly encouraging the Indian to degenerate by permitting hundreds of them to leave their homes for fraudulent savage demonstrations before the world. All these Wild West

67

Shows are exhibiting the Indian worse than he ever was
and deprive him of his high manhood and individuality.

We see the Indian. He is pictured in the lowest degree of
humanity. He is exhibited as a savage in every motion
picture theatre in the country.

As the Wild West began to fade, it ended up as a circus tag-on
presented after the main performance. This continued in many
circuses through the 1930s and finally disappeared.

But it is no shock to learn that Buffalo Bill and the Wild West
Show are alive and well. The magic, glamor, and glory of the
Wild West were made even more so in the 1940s with Broadway's *Annie Get Your Gun*. When the MGM gloss was added to
the movie version in 1950, directed by George Sidney, the
magic, glamor, and glory positively glowed.

New generations were exposed to the white man's forked
"There's No Business Like Show Business" tongue. Bosley
Crowther in the *New York Times*, March 11, 1954, commented
about *Saskatchewan* (1954, Raoul Walsh*): "So many cowboys
and Indians—or, let us say, so much Wild West Show—have not
been seen in the movies since the last time Custer made his last
stand."

CUT BACK TO
Buffalo Bill Reading a letter from William Tecumseh Sherman, Gen.,
U.S. Army: "Fifth Avenue Hotel, New York. Col. William F.
Cody: Dear Sir— . . .So far as I can make out, you have been modest,
graceful, and dignified in all you have done to illustrate the history
of civilization on this continent during the past century . . . . As
nearly as I can estimate, there were in 1865 about nine and one-half
million of buffaloes on the Plains between the Missouri River and
the Rocky Mountains; all now gone, killed for their meat, their
skins, and their bones. This seems like desecration, cruelty, and
murder, yet they have been replaced by twice as many cattle. At
that date there were about 165,000 Pawnees, Sioux, Cheyennes, and
Arapahoes, who depended upon these buffaloes for their yearly
food. They, too, have gone, but they have been replaced by twice or
thrice as many white men and women, who have made the earth to
blossom as the rose, and who can be counted, taxed, and governed
by the laws of Nature and civilization. This change has been salutary,
and will go on to the end . . . ."

*When a film is first mentioned, the director, when known, appears
after date of film release.

WELCOME TO MOVIELAND

THE IMAGE MAKERS BEGIN: THE SILENT ERA

SCENE VIII

CUT TO
Herbert Blatchford typing a letter to the authors. Mr. Blatchford, a Navajo, is director of the Gallup, New Mexico, Indian Community Center. We hear excerpts of what he is writing in Voice Over: The crux of Indian opinion toward witnessing Indians on movie or television screen can be summed up in the following analogy: A number of children who were viewing a western movie were asked: "Are you an Indian?" They all answered that "I am a Navajo" (or other tribal names). "Are you a Navajo Indian?" "No, I am a Navajo . . . . Indians are bad people." This serves to lead me to believe that the identification of the contemporary Indian with the movie Indian is somewhat removed, one from the other. They can see, many times, that the dress, styles of activity, and settings are not what they are accustomed to; so . . . they are different.

SLOW DISSOLVE INTO
Broadway and 27th Street, New York City. It is Spring, 1894. A long line of people stand in front of Holland Bros.' Kinetoscope Parlor at 1155 Broadway. The camera comes in and pans the crowd into the "theatre." The people are waiting to see the newest craze, Edison's peephole box, the Kinetoscope. Inside, there are ten machines and the management makes sure there is only one person at each machine. For 25 cents each viewer is given five different but short examples of the magic of moving pictures.

Since the Indian had always been popular, it was only natural that some of the first film vignettes made by Edison for the penny arcade peep shows should have titles such as *Sioux Ghost Dance* (1894), *Parade of Buffalo Bill's Wild West* (1898), *Procession of Mounted Indians and Cowboys* (1898), *Buck Dance*

(1898), *Eagle Dance* (1898). They went from one ignominy, *Indian War Council* (1894), to another, *Serving Rations to the Indians* (1898).

Although considered a novelty, the Kinetoscope and its competitor, the Mutoscope, became popular. Screen projection was introduced two years later. The process called Vitascope had its premiere in New York City on April 23, 1896, at Koster and Bial's Music Hall where Macy's Department Store now stands.

The filmic cultural genocide of the Native American begins with such commercializations as *Sioux Ghost Dance*. There is no evidence that the dance filmed in 1894 was actually the Ghost Dance. But since Wounded Knee had occurred only four years before and the late Indian Wars were still very much news, we see the beginnings of motion picture ballyhoo. *Webster's Dictionary of Synonyms* (1942) defines ballyhoo: ". . . applied to any kind of advertising, publicity, or promotion which the speaker or writer regards as sensational, insincere, misleading, unduly obtrusive, and the like; . . ."

We also see the beginnings of motion picture exploitation. *Webster's Seventh New Collegiate Dictionary* (1963) defines exploitation: ". . . an unjust or improper use of another person for one's own profit or advantage . . ."

> CUT TO
> Segments of *Sergeants Three* (1962, John Sturges) containing references to the Ghost Dance: our heroes find out that the renegade Indians are "ghost dancers" which is a "dance of death"; Dean Martin and Sammy Davis go to the ghost dancers' cave which has an altar covered with skulls; the dancers wear large African-like masks and hop around shaking rattles; they listen to Indian leader Henry Silva paraphrasing Eduardo Ciannelli's famous "kill" speech from Gunga Din.

Film makers have been notorious for miscreating Native American rituals. That which is synonymous with Hollywood has managed to destroy that which is true, denigrate that which is real, and desecrate that which is holy.

> CUT TO
> The Pine Ridge Sioux Reservation in 1913. There is much activity filming the "adventures" of Buffalo Bill. A hand-cranked camera is being adjusted by a cameraman in britches and puttees and a cap turned backwards. The director, wearing riding clothes, is mounted on a cow pony, and gives instructions through a large megaphone he

is holding. Several well-known people can be seen: Buffalo Bill, Johnny Baker, Gen. Miles, Short Bull, Jack Red Cloud, and Dewey Beard.

There had been some success with filmed versions of the Buffalo and Pawnee Bills' show and other Wild Wests. Mr.

(Theatre Collection, New York Public Library)

McQuinn, manager of "The Two Bills" pictures in Ontario, Canada, in a letter to *The New York Clipper*, August 5, 1911, reported: ". . . business was big all along the line."

To keep pace with growing competition in the film industry and still capitalize on his name, an old and financially troubled Buffalo Bill wanted to do a film depicting the Indian Wars and the conquest of the West using events in his own life. Toward this end "The Col. Wm. F. Cody (Buffalo Bill) Historical Picture Co." was formed. The Secretary of War approved the use of troops and equipment. The Secretary of the Interior approved the use of Pine Ridge and its Sioux. Gen. Miles agreed to appear in the film. The Essanay Company agreed to handle the production.

Charles J. ver Halen in a story in *The Motion Picture News* of November 22, 1913, gave a contemporary view of the shooting of the picture:

> With the return of the producers, cameramen and others . . . , a permanent record has been made of a bit of history which very nearly eradicated a mighty nation, the Sioux Indian . . . .
>
> Chiefs, bucks, and squaws, generals, officers and soldiers who held arms against each other in the battles of '90 and '91 again opposed each other on the very field they did some twenty odd years ago. Memories stirred in them of the real affray and they lived over again a period of their life which was at once painful in its recalling.
>
> . . . For several days previous to the taking of the first battle scene the air seemed to be charged with danger; both Indians and soldiers were loath to commence operations. It was during this battle many years ago that so many on both sides were lost, not only soldiers, but women and children.
>
> During the entire taking of the picture the squaws chanted their death song as they did years ago when they saw the brave warriors fall under the rain of bullets. Many of them broke into tears as the vividness of the battle recalled that other time when lives were really lost and everything was actual.
>
> Even the chieftains, now grown gray, and used to the sight of bloodshed from the innumerable battles, told of those days with a tremor in their voice. That battle was not only the start of a warfare that deprived them of power, but of brothers, relations, wives and children.
>
> Such battles [as that] of Wounded Knee and the Battle of the Messiah form part of this production . . . . Dewey

72

Beard, still considered a hero among his tribe, appears in his ghost shirt, which still bears the marks of five bullet holes. Dewey Beard was the last to surrender at the time of the battle, and held off soldiers for fourteen hours from his place of vantage.

Brave men's names as these appear little in history, however their heroism deserves the praise of all. Its [sic] memory should live forever. Besides General Miles and Colonel Cody, Colonel H. S. Sickel, who is now in command of the Twelfth Cavalry, was then a lieutenant in the Seventh; General Muas, General King and General Lee were there to replay their parts . . . .

It was publicized in *The Moving Picture World* of November 15, 1913, that, "the films are to be a record in the War Department at Washington, and will be used to enlist recruits for the army." *The Indian Wars*, directed by Theodore Wharton, was first shown to an audience of cabinet members, Congressmen and other "dignitaries" in Washington. From *The Moving Picture World*, March 4, 1914:

. . . Another difficulty presented itself, for the Indians refused to remain "dead" after being "killed" unless they were absolutely without ammunition, and then they would roll over that they might get a better view of the antics of their brothers. Thus, often comedy is injected into an otherwise very serious affair. No five-cent novel of our boyhood days is nearly as exciting as are these pictures . . . . The effect of the pictures on an audience was evidenced by the alternate handclapping, cheers and hisses which greeted individual action . . . .

Following the "action," one is carried into more peaceful scenes where Indian boys and girls in the uniforms of the schools which they attend are seen saluting the American flag, Indian-farmers bringing in the results of a season's work, the schools, agencies, and other modern buildings, and we may also see the last word in civilization, a seven-passenger touring car.

All was not so grand and glorious as the various reports would have us believe. There had been trouble while shooting the picture which Henry Blackman Sell and Victor Weybright tell about in *Buffalo Bill and the Wild West* (1955):

. . . a number of Indian villages had been constructed along the creek at Wounded Knee. The technicians and their movie cameras moved in. The plan called for the battle to take place right over the Indian graves, which seemed to the Sioux a horrible desecration. General Miles could see nothing wrong with the idea, however, for that would

73

make everything historically accurate. Johnny Baker came to see the Colonel. He understood how the Indians felt, and talked to them.

Nevertheless the Indians were resentful, remembering how the white soldiers had massacred their tribesmen and the women and children. Iron Tail came to Buffalo Bill's tent and warned him there would be trouble. Colonel Cody told him to call together the old men of the tribe. Short Bull and No Neck came to the council. Buffalo Bill told them how hopeless it would be to turn this movie battle into a real one, to shoot real bullets at the white men, for the Indians would be pursued and caught, and probably tried for murder. The Sioux warriors finally saw his point, and the following day the sham battle went before the cameras. No one was hurt.

The report of the Washington premiere also expressed the uneasiness so strongly felt by the Sioux participants:

> Of the Indians, "Short Bull," still a moving spirit in a more moderate religious sense among his people, led in person hundreds of warriors, many veterans of the warpath of the powerful Red Cloud, Ogllalla and Spotted Tail Brule, Sioux, through the familiar scenes. The greatest difficulty encountered in getting these men together was to convince them that the purpose of this mobilization was merely to reproduce the wars and not to annihilate them, for when they saw the Hotchkiss guns, the rifles, revolvers and cases of ammunition, there was a feeling of unrest, as though the time had come when they were to be gathered in by the Great Spirit through the agency of the white men . . . .

Survivors of Wounded Knee gave statements about the massacre. These later appeared in James H. McGregor's *The Wounded Knee Massacre* (1940). The statement of one of the survivors puts Cody's and ver Halen's ideas and racist views of frontier history in proper perspective. Edward Owl King, with Henry Standing Bear as interpreter, said, in part:

> These people are first time giving the straight story of it. Some years ago they had a moving picture taken of this Massacre. The Indians without thinking went ahead and performed in the ways that were directed by some white people, not truthfully but just the way they wanted it presented in pictures. That tells the wrong story. There may be a book written on that but that would be an error if it was based on that picture. They all agree that the presentation of the Massacre by the picture was all wrong.

74

These old men say that they are giving you the right truth now.

Cody died on January 10, 1917. To capitalize on his death or as a memorial to his life, Essanay released the *Adventures of Buffalo Bill* just 19 days later. This was accomplished by using most of the footage from the 1913 film, *The Indian Wars.*

In 1894 a film was made called *Sioux Ghost Dance.* In 1913 *The Indian Wars* reenacted the Ghost Dance and Wounded Knee. In 1914 an Indian potboiler, *The Last Ghost Dance*, was shown. In 1917 the *Adventures of Buffalo Bill*, remake of *The Indian Wars*, was released. In 1970 there were rumors that the Sioux of South Dakota had resurrected the Ghost Dance.

HISTORY IN THE REMAKING—1898-1908

SCENE IX

CUT TO
A typical, busy, neighborhood city street at the turn of the century. Among the many stores is a redone storefront covered with posters and signs announcing that this is the Orpheum Nickelodeon with its latest moving picture attraction. The camera follows some people as they pay their nickels at the cage box office cubicle, go through the door, around a large black curtain and into a dimly lit room. It is filled with every type of kitchen chair imaginable, most of which are occupied by noisy patrons, eating and commenting on the flickering screen image over the sound of the accompanying piano.

For a few years, the peephole machine parlors and the screen theatres flourished. People were content to watch parades, street scenes, waterfalls, and trains charging at them from the screen. There was enough excitement in *Indian Day School* (1898) and *Circle Dance* (1898) to make audiences think they got their nickel's worth. But soon, just watching something move was not enough. Patrons grew tired of *Buffalo Bill's Wild West Parade* (1901), *Moki Snake Dance by Wolpi Indians* (1901), *Sham Battle at the Pan-American Exposition* (1901), and *Club Swinging, Carlisle Indian School* (1902). Edwin S. Porter's *The Great Train Robbery* (1903) was the first one-reel film with story continuity. It was in the best Wild West Show tradition. It had everything except Indians, and those redskins were just over the next cinematic hill.

The success of Porter's film revolutionized and revitalized the movies. One-reel story films were the sensation and nickelodeons and movie making companies were fruitful and multiplied. Audience demand was so great that theatres changed their bills once or even twice a day. If a movie clicked, everybody jumped in and, within a few days, several versions of the same story would be playing, and pirated dupes would also be making the rounds. This was the first application of the industry's first commandment: "If it makes money, make it again."

> CUT TO
> An Indian chief in a full-feathered headdress staring directly into the camera. The camera pulls back to show the chief wrapped in an Indian blanket with his arms folded across his chest. In the background are some tipis and a group of Indians doing Indian things—tanning hides, repairing canoes, cooking. The chief puts his hand above his eyes and stares off into the distance as he surveys the 1900s "western" wilderness of Ft. Lee, New Jersey.

Buffalo Bill clearly proved that the West just wasn't the West without redskins. The movie makers knew this too. The obvious step was to use the savage in the "plot" film. Following *The Great Train Robbery*, the fabled frontiersman, Kit Carson, began taking on those redskins in *Kit Carson* (1903). We also had the beginning of happy Western endings with *Rescue of Child from Indians*.

Movie makers formulated their second commandment: "If it works once, use it again." Consider: *Indian Revenge* (1905), *The Indian's Revenge* (1906), *The Indian's Revenge or Osceola, the Last of the Seminoles* (1906), *Attack on Fort Boonesboro* (1906), *Daniel Boone or Pioneer Days in America* (1907).

In 1904 audiences saw *Brush Between Cowboys and Indians*, which begat *Cowboy Justice* and *Cowboy's Narrow Escape*. Certainly cowboys and Indians influenced those first movie makers as they still do. It appears that common usage of that phrase started in the late 1800s along with Buffalo Bill's Wild West's exaggerated emphasis on cowboys and Indians. Its common acceptance and continual usage can be attributed to the repeated emphasis in films.

> CUT TO
> A stretch of field on the Pine Ridge Reservation, South Dakota. It is summer, 1966. Ralph Friar looks on as some Sioux boys armed with "made in Japan" cap pistols and "made in Hong Kong" toy bows and arrows are playing cowboys and Indians. Or, rather, they are making a futile attempt at playing since none of the boys wants to be an Indian. One boy, in particular, almost driven to tears, is yelling that he does not want to be an Indian because the others keep beating him up and he is always losing the game.

On August 16, 1967, the *New York Times* carried the following story:

MAN BURNS TO DEATH IN A COWBOY GAME

San Antonio, Tex., Aug. 15—A game of cowboys and Indians was blamed here today for the fiery death of a 20-year-old man.

Lieut. David Keene of the Homicide Bureau said Arturo Garcia was fatally injured during an accidental flash fire last Friday that occurred after he was tied to a post by two fellow employees.

One of the employees, also 20, was booked for negligent homicide.

Lieutenant Keene said the man booked admitted in a statement as did the other 18-year-old companion, that they had been playing the cowboys and Indians game.

"They were just horsing around the warehouse where they all work," Lieutenant Keene said. "It seems ridiculous men that age play such a game, but that's what they said they were doing . . . ."

By inference and example, for three quarters of a century moving pictures have had an unparalleled influence on our lives.

Lewis Jacobs, in *The Rise of the American Film* (1939), looked at the first audience:

The content of American motion pictures since their inception has been, in fact, not only an important historical source but a stimulant and educator to American life itself. Besides offering a social occasion and an emotional experience, they supplied audiences with information and ideas. Immigration was at its peak in 1902-1903, and the movies gave the newcomers, particularly, a respect for American law and order, an understanding of civic organizations, pride in citizenship and in the American commonwealth. Movies acquainted them with current happenings at home and abroad. Because the uncritical movie-goers were deeply impressed by what they saw in the photographs and accepted it as the real thing, the movies were powerful and persuasive. More vividly than any other single agency, they revealed the social topography of America to the immigrant, to the poor, and to the country folk. Thus from the outset movies were, besides a commodity and developing art, a social agency.

The moving picture became the working man's chief source of entertainment and, to paraphrase Jacobs, his textbook. It was also a narcotic that offered a few moments of pleasure and relief. It was gloriously successful. On October 13, 1906, *The*

Billboard commented: "Store shows and five-cent picture theatres might properly be called the jack rabbits of the business of public entertaining—they multiply so rapidly."

Everyone accepted what they saw. Even people who had lived through the taming of the frontier began to prefer what they saw on the screen to the reality they had experienced. Thus they tacitly approved the history chronicled by the filmmakers—a history scripted by the rewrite men.

The lure of the Western was just as great in Europe. Attempts made by Europeans to reproduce the Wild West were wild indeed. French producers had cowboys greet one another in typical French manner: they kissed each other on both cheeks.

In 1907 Pathe of France produced *Cowboys and Indians*, which was weird as well as wild. The cowboys were costumed like gypsies, the Indians like phantasmagorical spectres. Pathe's *Justice of a Redskin* (1908) and Gaumont's *Red Man's Revenge* (1908), both filmed in France, were almost identical in plot: A miner and his faithful Indian companion are robbed; as the title indicates, the Indian seeks revenge. This story line was lifted almost intact from the American *The Indian's Revenge* (1906, Vitagraph).

The New York Dramatic Mirror on August 1, 1908, published this review of *Texas Tex*, A Great Northern filmed in Copenhagen:

> The Indian, desiring the girl for himself, kills the bad cowboy, and is dancing a lonesome war dance around the fair prisoner, when Texas Tex arrives and puts an end to the redskin and the captivity of the girl at the same time. It is true that the scenery in which the pictures are made is not strictly Texan in appearance, nor is the Indian's toy bow and arrows suggestive of a present day Indian—but let that pass . . . . The Indian is genuine and so are the cowboys and their horses, being recruited no doubt from a wild west show touring in Europe.

America had its fictional Indian football heroes, as in Broadway's *Strongheart* (1905). But the nation had its own real live hero in Jim Thorpe, who helped Carlisle Indian Industrial School beat such formidable foes as Penn, Minnesota, and Harvard in 1907. The next year a minor cycle was started with *A Football Warrior* and *The Call of the Wild*, the latter directed by Griffith. In *Warrior* a white girl loves the Indian football hero who, in turn, is hated by his white rival. In *Wild* the situation is reversed: Indian hero loves white girl.

Both films are good examples of an early plot which concerned the Indian who was educated at Carlisle, some other school in the East, or at a mission school, and who returns home to the tribe. Most of the stories concerned an Indian man but, occasionally, there was a nod to an Indian "maiden." Various conflicts were provided for the Indian: should the white loved one be given up; should the good life of the East be given up for the harsh life of the West; once returned, do his people accept or reject him; and if rejected, does he turn to drink; and if he turns to drink, . . . and so on with other sundry problems.

A scene from *Pocahontas* (1908) filmed by the Edison Company. (Motion Picture Section, Library of Congress)

As blatant as the stealing of stories was the "borrowing" of cliches. *The Cattle Rustlers* used that classic character of the dime novel: the dirty, no-good, half-breed; in this film he was the leader of the gang. In *The Cowboy's Baby* there was the equally classic Wild West Show wagon train attack. *The Kentuckian* concerned a squaw man, an overworked dime-novel character. In fact and in fiction, a squaw man was a non-Indian who married or lived with or otherwise enjoyed conjugal rights with his "squaw."

1908 begat *The Discoverers, Forced into Marriage, In the Days of the Pilgrims, An Indian's Honor, The Red Girl, Pocahontas, Pioneer Crossing the Plains in '49, Red Cloud, The Redman and the Child, A Round-Up in Oklahoma, 'Twixt Love and Duty, The White Chief.*

1908—Enter Broncho Billy

CUT TO
A settler's cabin in a valley. Two Indians drag a struggling young white girl out the door. A burly cowboy rides up, jumps off his horse, and clouts the Indians; they sneak off as he bravely clasps the fainting but grateful girl in his arms.

The new Western produced its first cowboy star in Gilbert M. "Broncho Billy" Anderson. Born Max Aronson, he first appeared as an extra in *The Great Train Robbery* (1903). Eventually he formed the Essanay "The Film With the Indian Head" Co. with George K. Spoor.

In 1908 Anderson was working in Niles, California, where he shot his first Western. In it he played a character named Broncho Billy. It was successful; he made a few more and fan mail started coming in. The character stuck, the name stuck and the enormously popular Broncho Billy series was launched.

Anderson was interviewed by Ezra Goodman, parts of which appeared in *The Fifty Year Decline and Fall of Hollywood* (1962):

> "I directed, wrote and acted in 175 of those dang things in seven years," he recalled. "There was *Broncho Billy's Love Affair, Oath, Bible, Mexican Wife, Leap, Christian Spirit and Redemption*, to name a few. I did one every seven days, shooting from a brief outline."

In 1911 Essanay's publicity department was claiming that Anderson was being seen throughout the world every day by hundreds of thousands of people. When Goodman first interviewed him in 1948, Anderson appeared somewhat cynical about Westerns:

"They're just like I used to make, . . . except they talk a little. Most of them are mediocre. They all have the same formula . . . . It's one big stew out of the same stew-pot . . . . They [Western producers] cater to the low mentality that wants nothing but excitement and doesn't care why the stagecoach goes over the cliff as long as it goes over . . . . You can kill six Indians with one bullet, as long as you shoot them dead. The more impossible and incongruous westerns are, the more audiences like them . . . . I was never anything more than a competent rider, . . . and I used doubles for the sensational stunts. And as for marksmanship—heck, in those movies a blank used to turn a corner and kill a man . . . . The movies? . . . They're still what they were—the maximum amount of entertainment for the mimimum amount of price. Today's westerns are not improvements on the early ones. They got the recipes from those pictures and they juggle the in-gredients upwards, backwards, forwards and sideways."

Broncho Billy Anderson (left) in *Broncho Billy and the Red Man* (1914) filmed by Essanay Company. (The Museum of Modern Art/Film Stills Archive)

Anderson's cavalier approach to making films in no way changed the image of the red man, since he used dime novels for inspiration. He was the noble white man helping the noble red man in *An Indian's Friendship* (1912). He was a noble clergyman teaching the commandment "Thou Shalt Not Kill" to Indian maidens in *Broncho Billy's Teachings* (1915). Broncho Billy was forever rescuing girls, white or red, who were forever falling in love with him, or, at the very least, admired him rather strongly: *Broncho Billy and the Indian Maid* (1912), *Broncho Billy and the Navajo Maid* (1913), *Broncho Billy and the Settler's Daughter* (1914). An advertising blurb for *Broncho Billy's Indian Romance* (1914) read: "Tender love story of the Indian maiden who loves and loses. Broncho Billy is the idealized object of her affections, but his girl comes back to him when she learns that he is sick, and then there is no place for the little Indian."

His famous Broncho Billy series was wearing thin by 1915, and so the other characters Anderson played were being pushed. The *Essanay News* of Novermber 20, 1915, had a publicity blurb from which the following is taken:

> G. M. Anderson, in "The Indian's Narrow Escape," appears in one of the most thrilling and dramatic of all the western plays, which abound with quick action and intense climaxes. Mr. Anderson takes the part of an Indian, and makes the most of dramatic situations offered in the play.
>
> There also is an intense human interest touch in the photoplay that reaches the hearts of all. The plea of the two little children for the life of the Indian, whom a posse is planning to lynch, is full of pathos and grips every spectator.

The times were quickly passing Anderson by. In 1915 William S. Hart, playing a new type of Western hero, began to replace the Broncho Billy image. Anderson tried to revive Broncho Billy briefly in 1919 but his dime-novel character was already obsolete. Anderson, Hart, and other Western heroes came and went, leaving a long, long trail of cinematic chiefs, bucks, maidens, squaws, braves, and half-breeds awinding into the land of our dreams.

MOVIES AND THE "INDIAN" FIND A HOME

SCENE X

CUT TO

A New York street in the 1900s. (All action should be at a jerky, speeded-up pace.) Several people emerge from a building. One man carries a long object wrapped in a blanket; the others carry suitcases. They get into an open touring car and drive off as the camera follows. Weaving in and out of traffic, they head for Central Park. They stop at a secluded section of the park; the actors, opening their suitcases, change into their costumes. One man gives directions. The object is unwrapped and set up; it is a camera. The heroine, in Western garb, and the villain, in Indian garb, go through a series of antics around a rock. The hero leaps from the top of the rock and clouts the Indian who runs off. The director stops the action; the cameraman wraps up the camera and they disappear over a knoll as they go to their next location.

The Motion Picture Patents Co., commonly referred to as the "Trust," had been formed by seven U.S. companies including Edison, Biograph, and Broncho Billy's Essanay. They wanted total control of the film industry and sought to obtain it by licensing patented cameras and projectors and charging fees for their use.

The lure of big fast money was too much for the independents, who cashed and crashed in by using bootleg equipment rather than pay what they considered blackmail to the "Trust." Spies, counterspies, goons, guards, hidden cameras and, occasionally, fighting became part of a day's work. The long and often bloody battle was one of the influencing factors for the move to Hollywood. It offered a convenient back door escape to Mexico to avoid any action by the "Trust," legal or otherwise.

85

But the first film center was Ft. Lee, New Jersey. It was rugged enough for Westerns, and was close to New York but remote enough to keep away the Patents people. One outfit which shot its Westerns in Ft. Lee was Bison. Fred J. Balshofer, the company's co-founder, wrote about making a film in 1909 in *One Reel a Week* (1967):

> We had acquired a story with the unlikely name of *The True Heart of An Indian* and had hired an actor who also had done some work with the Biograph, to play the Indian character lead. The actor . . . was Charles Inslee, who wore a black wig parted in the center with two braids that reached below his shoulders. He was costumed in a breech-cloth, giving him an excellent opportunity to display his fine physique. Again we used Evelyn Graham as the leading lady, *and for realism and color, we added two authentic Indians to the cast, Young Deer and his wife Red Wing* [italics ours].

The plots, action, and acting in all these films were elemental and crude. The Indians were solemnly, stoically, and stereotypically portrayed by whites in bad make-up, bad costumes, and ghastly wigs and skull caps. They were forever shading their eyes to illustrate their acute vision. In some films, paradoxically, some characters used this same gesture while staring at objects just a few feet away. They were forever folding their arms, a gesture which film makers must have thought represented a particular brand of stoicism; it was not always a male gesture—women resorted to this type of posturing as well. The costuming for the white red man can be dismissed as a hodge-podge of authentic items added to the film maker's own fantasy. The movie maker can always work on the premise that anything goes since the audience probably knows as little about the subject as he does.

To keep costs down and mobility up, producers used small stock companies with actors playing several parts in each film. It was not unusual for an actor to play an Indian one minute and find himself as the cavalryman chasing that same Indian the next minute. The sun dictated the shooting schedule and the day wasn't long enough to bother with quality.

In 1909, movie companies had to contend with the ever increasing pressure of the Patents Co., compelling them to shoot in places further away from New York. Balshofer tells how Bison reacted:

... in the summer of 1909 we sneaked out of New York City up to the small town of Neversink in the Catskill Mountains . . . . Inslee again was cast as an Indian. Often just Inslee, Arthur [Miller], and I would pack off some distance to remote locations to get scenes of the lone Indian as he dodged around boulders and swam across streams busily tracking down the enemy for the white man, or as he arrived just in time to save a child or a fair maiden in distress. On these occasions, Arthur cranked the camera . . . . Inslee made a striking appearance on the screen, and the ladies simply went gaga over him. Oh's and ah's came from them whenever he appeared on the screen in one of his naked Indian hero roles, so naturally most of his pictures were on that order. The names of the players did not appear on the film but Inslee had a flock of fans anyway, with letters coming to him through our New York office addressed to "The Indian," "The Lone Indian," and so on. Since he was human, these letters caused him to throw his chest out even further than he did in his moving picture roles.

CUT TO
A small town stucco, Spanish-style station; a train is coming in. People get off, gather in groups and collect their luggage as the camera pulls. Some people point to a large banner hung across the building. They clap their hands and cheer with "play-acting" enthusiasm. The sign reads: "Welcome to Los Angeles! The Moving Picture Paradise! 350 Good Shooting Days out of 365!"

Once the move began, there was no stopping it. In 1907, Selig was one of the first outfits on the coast, using an abandoned Chinese laundry as a studio. Bison set up in a barn and feed store in 1909. In 1910, Biograph, with D. W. Griffith in charge and Mary Pickford in tow, set up shop for the winter in an old carbarn. Nestor was there in 1910, too.

Soon there were over a dozen companies located in Hollywood and the majority of them were shooting Westerns. In 1911, *The Moving Picture World* commented: "Los Angeles and vicinity have acquired their reputation in the production of Western and Indian pictures. Here, of all places, is the ideal location for the production of such films." That same paper in 1913 pointed out that they were "simple, inexpensive to produce and capable of giving large returns . . . . They cost little to make, required comparatively little story and yet sold tremendously well."

Goodman reported that, according to Broncho Billy Anderson, each "Billy" picture was budgeted at $800 and grossed up to $50,000.

THE DELUGE—1909-1914

SCENE XI

Many producers used Indian movies to launch their companies. While fighting the "Patents Trust," Carl Laemmle, head of Imp, later to become Universal, released *Hiawatha* (1909), with the following promotional: "Length 988 feet. Taken at the Falls of Minnehaha in the Land of the Dacotahs. And you can bet it is classy or I wouldn't make it my first release."

Kalem was organized in 1907; in 1909 director Sidney Olcott and a company went on winter location to Florida where they made *The Seminole's Revenge* (1909), *The Seminole's Vengeance* (1909), *The Seminole Halfbreeds* (1910), and *The Seminole's Trust* (1910).

The number of Indian films almost doubled in 1909. About 50 of them were produced. More films necessitated repeating old or finding new formulas.

Indians and animals were an unbeatable combination. In 1909 Balshofer boasted: "Snowball [a pure white stallion] became well known to movie audiences throughout the country . . . . With our famous horse and Inslee in his naked Indian hero roles, our Bison pictures were outselling most of the pictures made by members of the trust."

The Priest of the Wilderness tells of a Catholic missionary among the Iroquois, while *Yiddisher Cowboy* speaks for itself. Meanwhile, *A Squaw's Revenge* begat *The Squaw's Sacrifice*.

Col. Richard Dodge wrote in *33 Years Among Our Wild Indians* (1882 and 1959):

> When the white trader invaded the solitudes of the
> Indian, he took with him, or soon picked up, a small stock

89

of words, which, by his constant use among the tribes, have become, as it were, common property; thus "squaw," the Narragansett name for woman; the Algonquin "papoose" for child; "chuck," food; and many other words, have become universal among all the North American Indians east of the Rocky Mountains, when speaking to a white man, or Indian not of their own tribe.

Although the word squaw actually meant wife in some tribes, as used by the white man it took on the meaning of slut or prostitute and was applied generally to all Native American females. The term became so degrading that Native Americans stopped using it except when referring to a particular woman of that particular persuasion. However, the word has remained in common use, especially among white people associated with the movie industry.

CUT TO
The following series of quotes are flashed on the screen: From *Variety's* review of *A Man Called Horse*, April 29, 1970, signed Murf.: "... Corinna Tsopei (who eventually becomes Harris' squaw) ...." From Vincent Canby's review of *Horse*, the *New York Times*, April 30, 1970: "The ancient squaw, who looks like Mammy Yokum in a fright wig, is actually Dame Judith Anderson .... An old squaw acknowledges the death of her son by slicing off several fingers ...." From the pressbook on *Horse*: "Buffalo Cow Head is the name of the Sioux squaw played by Dame Judith Anderson ..."

Film reviewers began to pay more attention to the Western and to question credibility. In *The New York Dramatic Mirror*, October 10, 1908, a review of *Pocahontas* mentioned that the Indians of Virginia were using Navajo blankets. In the May 22, 1909, issue of the same paper, the reviewer of *In The Bad Lands* wondered why in the fight between soldiers and Indians "... only two of them [whites] fall, while the Indians are almost wiped out."

The next week, May 29, in a review of Broncho Billy Anderson's *The Indian Trailer* the same paper wondered: "The Indian is on foot, but he has no difficulty in keeping ahead of the party of cowboys, although in every scene they are shown to be riding like mad .... All parties keep up an incessant firing of revolvers without apparent object or aim and surely without results."

Eccentric shooting in most Westerns was obvious. Rifles and pistols were fired every which way with more deadly results than the *Dramatic Mirror* observed. The guns were fired up, down, and around while piles of redskins bit the dust.

A scene from *Buying Manhattan* (1909) Edison Company. (Motion Picture Section, Library of Congress)

In the July 10, 1909, issue of *The Moving Picture World* there appeared a short article entitled "Accuracy in Indian Subjects." Its author, "Wild West," was concerned about the accuracy of such things as costuming and certain Indian attitudes. He maintained that "squaws" always wore belts and were always sedate. Many more critics, correctly or otherwise, pointed to inaccuracies, or what they thought to be inaccuracies, in Indian dress and customs. But not once did any of those self-annointed scholars question the total cultural distortion Hollywood was perpetrating.

CUT TO
Montage of 1909 movies including: *Across the Divide, Boots and Saddles, The Bride of Tabaiva, Buying Manhattan, A Child in the Forest, Children of the Plains, A Close Call, A Colonial Romance, Comata, the Sioux, Custer's Last Stand, Dan Blake's Rival, Dove Eye's Gratitude, The Falling Arrow, The Famine in the Forest, A Friend in the Enemies' Camp, The Gold Prospectors, Half Breed's Treachery, Hiawatha, In Old Arizona, In the Bad Lands, The Indian, The Indian Runner's Romance, The Indian Trailer, An Indian Wife's Devotion, Iona, the White Slave or Iona, the White Squaw, Leather Stocking, The Mended Lute, On the Warpath, Onawanda, Outcast or Heroine Pale Face's Wooing, The Pony Express, The Priest of the Wilderness, The Red Man, The Redman's View, Red Wing's Gratitude, The Seminole's Revenge, The Seminole's Vengeance, A Squaw's Revenge, The Squaw's Sacrifice, The Trail of the White Man, The True Heart of an Indian, The Warrior's Sacrifice, A Western Hero, Yiddisher Cowboy.*

CUT TO
The Kalem Co. in a 1910 ad from *The New York Dramatic Mirror.* When the ad hits the screen, we hear a fanfare of trumpets: An epoch in the Motion Picture Industry. Beginning March 2nd, we will release on Wednesday of each week a magnificent and thrilling INDIAN PICTURE—These pictures are all historically true, being founded on incidents in the lives of celebrated INDIAN FIGHTERS and SCOUTS who blazed the way for the settlement of the great Middle West. NOTHING SO GREAT BEFORE ATTEMPTED.

In 1910 at least 100 Indian films were released. Here are some of them, followed by the names of the producing companies and excerpts from ads or reviews of the day. Since advertising dollars bought glowing reviews, there wasn't much difference between a press release and a review.

The Indian Scout's Revenge—Kalem: "Dime-action . . . scout cleans out an entire tribe of Indians, single-handed . . ."

The White Captive of the Sioux—Kalem: "An Indian picture of the better sort. A study of human nature under strange conditions."

White-Doe's Lovers—Melies: "A drama of elemental passions. Cowboy valor against Indian strategy."

The Maid of Niagara—Pathe: "A stupendous Indian depiction of the old legend of the falls. Not a pale face in the film."

An Indian's Gratitude—Pathe: "An exciting and thrilling Indian drama. Only two palefaces appear in the picture, the rest of the characters are natives."

The Girl From Arizona—Pathe: "A sensational and thrilling western drama made in this country with genuine cowboys and Indians."

A Cheyenne Brave—Pathe: "An Indian drama that is a classic. The best example of native life and customs ever depicted."

The Heart of a Sioux—Lubin: "Written by a former Indian agent who knows whereof he writes . . ."

White Fawn's Devotion—Pathe: "A thrilling story of the plains, produced under the direction of a native Indian chief."

Attack by Arapahoes—Kalem: "Real Indian fighting by real soldiers and redskins."

The Indian Raiders—Selig: "A Regular Smash, Bing, Bang, Full-of-Ginger Kind—the Selig way of doing the Redskin pictures."

No aspect of things Indian was left unexploited. Like a roll call at a convention, there were all kinds of tribal representations: *Apache Gold, Attack by Arapahoes, The Cheyenne Raiders, A Daughter of the Sioux, Fighting the Iroquois, The Navajo's Bride, The Sacred Turquoise of the Zuni, The Seminole Halfbreeds, The Uprising of the Utes.*

In addition, an absurd variety of emotional states became the motivation for Indian characters: *Chief Blackfoot's Vindication, Starlight's Devotion, The Indian Girl's Romance, Young Deer's Gratitude, Indian Pete's Gratitude, Iron Arm's Remorse, Red Wing's Constancy, Red Wing's Loyalty, The Seminole's Trust, The Woman Hater.*

Critics' remarks were getting more to the point. From an unsigned article titled "The Indian and the Cowboy (By One Who Does Not Like Them)," in a 1910 issue of *The Moving Picture World*: "Whether the field is worked out, or whether producers have grown somewhat careless, the Western pictures have a certain degree of sameness and monotony which is fatal to sustained interest."

Kalem's *Lo! The Poor Indian* was a portent of things to come. All-Indian films—those with just Indian characters—were the trend with more Native American "Indians" being used. Many films had used them exclusively but the casting of non-Native Americans in Indian roles has never been reversed.

CUT TO

A press party being held by the producers of *A Man Called Horse*. Various members of the cast and crew are talking to newspeople.

CUT TO

Producer Sandy Howard: We assembled a gallery of talented, creative individuals to insure that *A Man Called Horse* would not be just another Western or Indian picture. Members of the Rosebud Sioux Reservation appear in featured roles, and 200 members of the tribe worked behind the scenes to make the tipis, costumes, and the weapons, all created with precision to detail and authenticity. *A Man Called Horse*, therefore, is not just another Hollywood version of the Indian legend but the Indians' own statement of their trails.

CUT TO

Montage of 1910 movies including: *Across the Plains, Apache Gold, Attack by Arapahoes, The Attack on Fort Ridgely, Big Medicine, Brave Hearts United, or Saved from the Indians by a Woman's Wits, The Buffalo Bill's Wild West Show and the Pawnee Bill's Far East, The Call of the Blood, A Cheyenne Brave, The Cheyenne Raiders, Chief Blackfoot's Vindication, The Cliff Dwellers, The Colonel's Errand, Company D to the Rescue, The Cowboy and the Squaw, The Cowboy's Devotion, Cowpuncher's Sweetheart, A Daughter of the Sioux, Days of the Early West, The Debt Repaid, The Dumb Half-Breed's Defense, Early Settlers, Elder Alden's Indian Ward, The Exiled Chief, Fighting the Iroquois, The Flag of Company H, A Frontier Hero, The Girl from Arizona, The Girl from Triple X, Glimpses of an Indian Village, The Golden Secret, Government Rations, Hannah Dusten, The Heart of a Cowboy, The Heart of a Sioux, Her Indian Mother, His Indian Bride, In the Dark Valley, In the Wilderness, The Indian and the Cowgirl, The Indian and the Maid, Indian Blood, The Indian Girl's Awakening, The Indian Girl's Romance, The Indian Land Grab, An Indian Maiden's Choice, Indian Pete's Gratitude, The Indian Raiders, The Indian Scout's Revenge, An Indian's Gratitude, Iron Arm's Remorse, Justice in the Far North, Kit Carson, The Law of the West, The Legend of Scar Face, Lo! The Poor Indian, The Maid of Niagara, A Mohawk's Way, The Navajo's Bride, Nevada, Onoko's Vow, The Paleface Princess, Perils of the Plains, Raiders of the Plains, Ramona, Red Eagle's Love Affair, Red Fern and the Kid, The Red Girl and the Child, Red Hawk's Last Raid, Red Wing's Constancy, Red Wing's Loyalty, The Rescue of the Pioneer's Daughter, The Return of Ta-Wa-Wa, Riders of the Plains, A Romance of the Western Hills, Romantic Redskins, The Sacred Turquoise of the Zuni, Saved from the Redmen, The Seminole Halfbreeds, The Seminole's Trust, The Sheriff, A Shot in Time, Song of the Wildwood Flute, Spotted Snake's Schooling, Starlight's Devotion, Stolen by Indians, The Trapper and the Redskin, The Uprising of the Utes, The Voice of Blood, The Way of the Red Man, Wenonah, Western Justice, The White Captive of the Sioux, White-Doe's Lovers, White Fawn's Devotion, White Man's*

Money—The Indian's Curse, The White Princess, The Woman Hater,
Young Deer's Gratitude.

In 1911 close to 200 Indian pictures were released. Tom Mix began his career at Selig. And *Ramona* (1910) gave birth to *Ramona's Father* in 1911.

The Moving Picture World, January 21, 1911: "Six million people go to the picture plays every day in the year in the United States. There are more than 10,000 5-and 10-cent picture play houses in this country, giving an average of three exhibitions a day, with an average attendance of 200 persons for each exhibition."

DISSOLVE INTO
A series of stills from some 1911 films. Each is captioned with an excerpt from an ad or review: *What the Indian Did—*It was wonderful; they stole a lot of U.S. uniforms and went on the warpath. *An Up-To-Date Squaw—*A new idea in Indian pictures—an Indian comedy. *Grey Wolf's Grief—*An Indian Tale—'Nough Sed. *Silver Tail and His Squaw—*A thrilling tale of a rejected redman's revenge. *The Battle of Redwood—*A villainous agent sells the Indians' food. Indians starving set out on warpath and are smitten hip and thigh by the soldiers. *The White Medicine Man—*997 feet of peculiarly exciting and charming Western Film—rapid and virile—delights the eye and stirs the heart. GET IT! *Owanee's Great Love—*An Indian romance between a Sioux warrior and a Blackfoot maid. The Sioux is killed in battle and the girl, mourning over his body, is taunted by a rejected suitor. In frantic rage she attacks her tormentor, kills him, and then destroys herself. *A Warrior's Faith—*Showing the dangers of early missionaries among the savages. A captive priest converts an Indian maid, and through her intervention the lives of the white prisoners are saved. Many thrilling incidents and stirring battles.

In the *World's* "Letters to the Editors" column on March 18, 1911, a letter was printed from I. Lee, a Native American from Rochester, New York, in which he complained: "... Do you believe that five pioneers could drive away ten or twelve Indians with guns without the latter offering any resistance .... Well! I don't—I think it quite improbable. I know the way of my people and am sure they would resist. The picture I have in mind is 'Robby and the Redskins.'" What Robbie's redskins were like can be imagined from the critic's comments in the *World* of February 18: "... they are the most extraordinary Indians I ever saw .... In my limited wanderings amongst the Redskins I never met any of this brand—or heard of them."

One of the better critics of the day was W. Stephen Bush, who wrote in *The Moving Picture World* in 1911:

MOVING PICTURES ABSURDITIES

The greatest of them all is the Indian. We have him in every variety but one. We have Indians á la Francais, "red" men, recruited from the Bowery and upper West End Avenue . . . . General Sherman said that there were no good Indians except the dead ones. He had never seen the moving picture Indians . . . . You cannot escape the moving picture Indian . . . . I studied the audiences . . . while the Indians were doing their worst on the screen, and noticed no feverish enthusiasm denoting approval. I sincerely believe they were tired of them, especially as the music with these pictures is always the same . . . . The surest path to success is the one where "no track of steps has worn a way." Originality is the life of the moving picture.

Ridiculous plots kept rolling merrily along. *For the Sake of the Tribe* tells about three white men who steal supplies from an army post. Indians have trouble with the army, attack the fort and also steal supplies. Three Indians surrender and dig their graves before facing a firing squad. Meanwhile, the original three thieves get drunk, fight, one is wounded and confesses all. The three Indians are saved and now their tribe is given supplies by the army. The final fadeout shows the army commander and the Indian Chief smoking a peace pipe while standing in front of Old Glory.

In *Incendiary Indians* (1911), the usual bunch of red pyromaniacs raid a fort and set fire to a cabin. Amidst the arson, the few redskin extras find time to crowd together to make sure they all get into the shot. It looks much like the old Ritz Brothers routine of picking the handsome one in the middle.

Sacrifice of Silver Cloud tells of a renegade Indian who helps the whites beat his fellow tribesmen. This was a popular theme, with all sorts of rationalizations given for the Indian's traitorous acts, as in *The Broken Trap* and *The Silent Signal*.

In Bison's *The Pioneer's Mistake*, he makes a terrible one by shooting a feathered-headdressed Indian, mistaking him for a bird. As a result, the Indians go on the warpath.

CUT TO
A large meeting room at the Fourth National Conference on Indian Health, New York, 1966. Robert Moran, President of the Lakota

Tuberculosis and Health Association, White River, South Dakota, representing the Rosebud Reservation, is speaking:

> One day I was out in the field and a couple of elderly ladies from the East came along and were looking through field glasses. It came to my attention they were looking for something. I said, "What are you looking for?" They said, "For Indians." So I said, "What would you do if you saw an Indian?" One of the ladies said, "Maybe it would just scare me plumb to death." "Well," I said, "I hate to be the cause of your death but I want to introduce my father here and my nephew and myself. We are all Indians." She said, "Where are your feathers?" I said, "We usually shed them this time of the year. It is a little hot . . . ."

CUT TO
The Capitol Building in Washington, D. C., 1911. There is a demonstration on the steps. We see several Native Americans, in full tribal regalia, angrily talking to government officials and newsmen.

For the first time Native Americans voiced their strong objection to their portrayal in films. To emphasize their case, the Shoshoni, Cheyenne, Arapahoe, and Chippewa took their case to Congress and threatened to go directly to President Taft if no action was taken. They were supported by Indian Commissioner Robert G. Valentine.

A part of the story was reported in *The Moving Picture World*, March 18, 1911. It said: "One of the protesting Indians said to-day that he had gone into one of the motion picture theaters here, where a picture was shown in which a young Indian graduate of one of the non-reservation schools was the chief figure. He was shunned by the members of his tribe upon his return to them, took to drink, killed a man and fled, but was killed after a long chase. This was denounced as an untrue portrayal of the Indians."

The Moving Picture News handled the Washington protest from another angle:

> Let the moving picture man beware! Chief Big Bear and Chief Big Buck are in full war paint. Their Cheyennes and Arapahoes have taken to the scalp dance. At any moment the noble redman may be hard on his trail.
>
> Why? Because Poor Lo has seen a moving picture show.
>
> Of course, we do not mean to say that Chief Big Bear and Chief Big Buck will necessarily take the warpath just because they have seen a moving picture show. They are not that sensitive. Neither are they preachers nor uplifters nor protectors of the legitimate drama. But Chief Big Bear and Chief Big Buck were in Washington last week to have a

little talk with their White Father, President Taft, and in seeing the sights they took in a "photo-play"—a "heap bad" photo-play that hurt their feelings, insulted their dignity and roused their fighting blood.

Chief Big Bear threw savage stoicism to the winds and freed his mind right there in Washington. Translated from English into the well-known jargon that stamps all Indian utterances as authentic, his utterance runs thus:

Ugh! Me heap big Injun. Me Arapahoe chief. Me Big Bear. This show heap bad. Heap big lie. Pictures show Injun men bad and do heap bad things all time. Injun men in pictures heap lie. No Injun man; pale face dressed up like Injun man; poor Injun get blame for bad pale face. Me got to go home to-day or me go to Great White Father and ask him to stop heap bad show—show heap big lie. You wait. Big Bear and Big Buck go home. Then Big Bear and Big Buck raise heap fuss. Picture man look out. Ugh! . . .

CUT TO

A Montage of 1911 movies including: *The American Insurrecto, Arizona Bill, As Things Used to Be, At the White Man's Door, Back to His Old Home Town, Back to the Prairie, The Bad Man's First Prayer, The Battle of Redwood, Bear Hunt Romance, The Black Chasm, Black Cloud's Debt, The Blackfoot Halfbreed, A Branded Indian, Brave Swift Eagle's Peril, The Broken Trail, The Broken Trap, By the Aid of a Lariat, The Call of the Wilderness, Captain Brand's Wife, A Chance Shot, Charlie's Buttie, The Cheyenne Medicine Man, The Cheyenne's Bride, Cheyenne Frontier Days, The Chief's Daughter, Chief Fire Eye's Game, The Chief's Talisman, The Conspiracy of Pontiac, Crow Chief's Defeat, The Curse of the Red Man, Daniel Boone's Bravery, A Daughter of the Navajos, The Deerslayer, The Desert Well, Driven from the Tribe, The Empty Tepee, The Faithful Indian, Fighting Blood, The Flaming Arrows, Flight of Redwing, The Flower of the Tribe, For the Tribe, For the Squaw, A Frontier Girl's Courage, Gathering of the Council of the Six Nations, George Warrington's Escape, Grey Wolf's Grief, Grey Wolf's Squaw, The Gunfighter, The Half-Breed's Atonement, A Halfbreed's Courage, The Half-Breed's Daughter, The Half-Breed's Plans, The Hair Restorer and the Indians, Heart of an Indian Girl, The Heart of an Indian Mother, The Heart of a Savage, The Horse Thief, How Tony Became a Hero, In the Day's of Gold, In the Day's of the Six Nations, In the Early Days, In Frontier Days, Incendiary Indians, An Indian Brave's Conversion, The Indian Brothers, The Indian Flute, The Indian Fortune Teller, An Indian Hero, An Indian Legend, An Indian Love Story, The Indian Maid's Sacrifice, An Indian Martyr, The Indian Rustlers, An Indian Trapper's Prize, An Indian Vestal, An Indian's Elopement, An Indian's Love, The Indian's Sacrifice, Kit Carson's Wooing, The Last Drop of Water, The Last of the Mohicans, Lean Wolf's End, The Legend of Lake Desola-*

tion, Lieut. Scott's Narrow Escape, Life on the Border, Little Dove's Gratitude, Little Dove's Romance, Little Ingin, Lone Eagle's Trust, Lone Star's Return, The Long Trail, Love in a Tepee, Maiden of the Pieface Indians, The Mascot of Troop "C", The Medicine Woman, The Message of the Arrow, The Mission Waif, The Missionary's Gratitude, A Noble Red Man, Ogallalah, Old Indian Days, Old Wyoming Days, On the Warpath, Only a Squaw, Owanee's Great Love, The Passing of Dapple Fawn, The Pathfinder, Percy and His Squaw, The Peril of the Plains, A Perilous Ride, The Perversity of Fate, The Pioneer's Mistake, The Plains Across, Poisoned Arrows, Priscilla and the Pequot, Prisoner of the Mohicans, Puritans and Indians, Ramona's Father, The Ranger's Stratagem, The Rebuked Indian, Red Cloud's Secret, Red Deer's Devotion, The Red Devils, Red Eagle, Red Feather's Friendship, A Red Girl's Heart, The Redman's Dog, The Red Man's Penalty, Red Man's Wrath, The Redskin's Secret, Red Star's Honor, Rescued in Time, Return of Company D, The Rival Stage Lines, Robbie and the Redskins, Romance of the Desert, A Romance of the Rio Grande, Running Fawn's Chief, Sacrifice of Silver Cloud, A Sacrifice to Civilization, The Saving Sign, The Seminole's Sacrifice, Sergeant Dillon's Bravery, The Silent Signal, Silver Leaf's Heart, Silver Tail and His Squaw, A Sioux Lover's Strategy, A Sioux Spy, The Spirit of the Gorge, The Squaw and the Man, A Squaw's Bravery, The Squaw's Devotion, The Squaw's Love, The Squaw's Mistaken Love, Starlight the Squaw, Starlight's Necklace, The Story of the Indian Ledge, Tangled Lives, The Totem Mark, Three Men, Too Much Injun, The Trail of the Pomos Charm, Trailed by an Indian, The Trapper's Fatal Shot, The Tribe's Penalty, The Twin Squaws, An Up-to-Date Squaw, A Warrior's Faith, The Warrior's Squaw, A Warrior's Treachery, The Way of the Red Man, Wenona's Broken Promise, A Western Postmistress, The Westerner and the Girl, What the Indians Did, When the West Was Wild, White Brave's Heritage, The White Chief, White Fawn's Escape, White Fawn's Peril, The White Medicine Man (Nestor), The White Medicine Man (Selig), The White Red Man, The Will of a Western Girl, The Winning of Wonega, A Young Squaw's Bravery.

In 1912 production of Indian films was down to approximately 150.

Native American actor-director James Young Deer and his actress wife, Red Wing, had become well-known personalities since their 1909 Bison days, when they were first used "for realism and color." James Young Deer was hired by Pathé Western as a director to bring the stamp of authenticity to their Indian films. Young Deer wrote the screenplays he was to direct. For reasons difficult to imagine, George Gebhart, a well-known white actor, was to play the Indian romantic leads in Young Deer's films, with Red Wing as Gebhart's leading lady.

Typical of the pictures Pathe was turning out in those days were:

The Squawman's Sweetheart. A white hunter's wife joins him in the West and so his Indian maiden lover must return to her people. The Indians are upset at this rejection. They capture the hunter's wife, and send her hat to him as proof of her captivity. The hunter, in turn, captures an Indian, ties him to a tree, puts on his clothing, and in this disguise goes to the Indian village. Inevitably there is a hand-to-hand struggle between the Indians and the white man who finally rescues his wife from a tipi. They escape in a canoe. In the meantime, back at the tree, the Indian unties himself and gets his fellow tribesmen to go after the fleeing couple, how else but in canoes. Unaccountably the final scene shows the hunter and his wife escaping in wagons while the Indians burn their cabin.

Red Man's Honor. A red man and a red woman are lovers but she is already married to another red man by whom she has had two children. The affair is discovered and the red chief calls a council in the tipi village where it is decided to punish the lovers by tying them in a blanket and setting them adrift in a canoe which all too quickly begins to sink in the next scene. They are rescued by the woman's children who have been following them in their own canoe. (Follow that canoe.) They meet their father who wants to kill the mother, but the children cling to him and he relents, then forgives, and they all go back to the village together.

Swift Wind's Heroism. A white woman rebukes the advances of a Mexican man. She is saved by an Indian man. The Mexican man shoots himself because of his love for the white woman. An Indian maiden finds the suicide note. A white man is accused of killing the Mexican man and is sentenced to hang. The Indian man, who saved our heroine, gives himself up to take the place of the white man who wants to see his white girl-friend before he dies. The agreement is that if the white man does not return in time, they will hang the Indian. He does not come back in time, and the Indian is to be hanged. The Indian maiden brings the suicide note written by the Mexican man to the white man and they ride to the rescue of the Indian.

Stories were still based on Wild West dime novels. In *Young Wild West Cornered by Apaches,* based on the dime novel of the same title, "Starlight, a beautiful Indian girl, is betrothed to

Young Bull, the chief's son, whose love she does not reciprocate. Young Wild West comes in the nick of time and saves Starlight from the clutches of her savage adorer."

In *A White Indian*, the message conveyed is that an Indian who does a good deed is a "white" Indian.

In *The Penalty Paid*, Black Hawk and Red Fox fight and Red Fox is killed. The other is "condemned to wander the plains with the body of Red Fox tied to his back."

And there was *The Heart of the Red Man*: "The stubborn warlike Sitting Bear disapproves of his daughter Fire-Fly's match with a young brave, by name Ardent Heart, with whom she is in love."

The White Brother's Text "depicts a new type of an Indian in a beautiful story." The Indian is a converted Evangelist.

There were other items of note for 1912. Mack Sennett made one of his crazy comedies, *The Tourists*, with Indians and sightseers involved in the climactic chase. A pre-serial Pearl White played in *The Arrowmaker's Daughter*. And critics were getting somewhat wiser. Gaumont's *The Prairie on Fire*, made in France, provoked this comment: "Some of it may make American audiences laugh . . ."

CUT TO
Montage of 1912 movies including: *Across the Plains or War on the Plains, Anona's Baptism, An Apache Father's Vengeance, An Apache Renegade, The Army Surgeon, The Arrowmaker's Daughter, At Cripple Creek, At Old Fort Dearborn, The Battle of the Long Sault, Battle of the Red Men, Before the White Man Came, Blazing the Trail, A Brave Little Indian, Broncho Billy and the Indian Maid, The Buffalo Hunt, The Bugle Call, The Cactus County Lawyer, Captain King's Rescue, Chief White Eagle, The Chief's Blanket, A Child of the Wilderness, Cholera on the Plains, The Colonel's Peril, The Colonel's Ward, The Cowboy's Mother, The Crisis, The Curse of the Lake, Custer's Last Fight, Darkfeather's Strategy, A Daughter of the Redskins, A Daughter of the West or The Old Chief's Dream, The Deer Slayer's Retribution, The Disputed Claim, The Fall of Black Hawk, The Famous Scout to the Rescue, The Fight at the Mill, The Flower of the Forest, For the Honor of the 7th, For the Honor of the Tribe, For the Papoose, The Forest Rose, The Frenzy of Fire-water, A Frontier Child, A Frontier Soldier of Fortune, General Bunko's Victory, Geronimo's Last Raid, The Half-Breed's Sacrifice, The Half-Breed's Treachery, The Half-Breed's Way, The Heart of the Red Man, Her Indian Guardian, Her Indian Hero, A Heroine of Pioneer Days, His Little Indian Model, His Punishment, An Hour of Terror, How the Boys Fought the Indians, In God's Care, In the*

Nick of Time, The Indian and the Child, An Indian Idyl, Indian Jealousy, The Indian Massacre, Indian Romeo and Juliet, An Indian Sunbeam, The Indian Uprising at Santa Fe, New Mexico, An Indian's Gratitude, An Indian's Loyalty, The Invaders, Iola's Promise, Isleta, N. M. Indian City, Justice of Manitou, The Lieutenant's Last Fight, Life and Customs of the Winnebago Indians, The Life of Buffalo Bill, The Little Indian Martyr, The Loneliness of the Hills, The Lonesome Trail Pioneers, Lucky Jim, Man's Lust for Gold, The Massacre, The Massacre of the Fourth Cavalry, The Massacre of the Santa Fe Trail, Memories of a Pioneer, A Messenger to Kearney, The Mortgage, On the Brink of the Chasm, On the Warpath, Orphans of the Plains, The Outcast, The Parson and the Medicine Man, The Penalty, The Penalty Paid, Peril of the Plains, A Picnic in Dakota, A Plucky Ranch Girl, The Post Telegrapher, The Prairie on Fire, The Price He Paid, The Price of Gratitude, Pueblo Indians, Albuquerque, N. M., A Pueblo Legend, The Redemption of Red Rube, The Redemption of White Hawk, The Redman's Burden, A Redman's Friendship, Red Man's Honor, A Redman's Love, A Redman's Loyalty, The Redskin Raiders, A Redskin's Appeal, The Renegades, The Rights of a Savage, The Seal of Time, The Sergeant's Boy, Silver Moon's Rescue, Silver Wing's Two Suitors, A Soldier's Furlough, A Soldier's Honor, A Squaw Man, The Squawman's Sweetheart, The Story of the Savage Modock Mine, The Swastika, The Tale of the Wilderness, A Temporary Truce, The Tourists, The Trade Gun Bullet, The Trail Thru the Hills, Trapped by Fire, The Tribal Law, The Unwilling Bride, The Vanishing Race, The Vengeance of Fate, Waneta's Sacrifice, A Wasted Sacrifice, A Western Child's Heroism, When the Heart Calls, The White Brother's Text, White Cloud's Secret, White Dove's Sacrifice, White Fawn, A White Indian, The White Lie, The White Savior, White Treachery, Winona, The Witch's Necklace, The Wooing of Wathena, The Wooing of White Fawn, Yellow Bird, Young Wild West Cornered by Apaches.

In 1913 studios released over 100 Indian films.

DISSOLVE INTO
The Tournament of Roses parade, Pasadena, California, 1913. The camera pulls in, picking out several Indian floats, as we hear quotes in Voice Over from *The Moving Picture World*, January 18: James Young Deer, of the Pathé West Coast studio at Edendale, entered a representative float called "Indian Life—Past and Present." One end of the float showed a smartly dressed college-graduated Indian. On the other end was a tipi with an aged squaw sitting before it. In front of her stood an Indian hunter in full costume, who had just laid before her the body of a dead deer. At his side was a live wolf which he had trained to hunt. The three Indians who rode on the float are members of the Pathe company. Behind the float rode a cavalcade of Indians and cowboys in costume, also from the Pathe studio . . . .
The Universal company contributed Indians, soldiers, and cowboys

to the parade . . . . The Kay-Bee company sent more than 100 Sioux Indians, men, women, and children, from its Santa Monica ranch. They gave demonstrations of Indian life, such as making camp, breaking camp, going on the march, a number of tribal dances, and various games. Miller Bros., 101 Ranch company contributed rough riders, lariat tossers, and broncho busters who gave exhibitions of many kinds . . . .

CUT TO

A segment from a Gaumont 1913 Western starring Onesime, a well-known French baggy-pants, slapstick comedian. The French Indians look, dress, and act quite Hollywood-like. They slap him around in what is supposed to be a tipi as he shamelessly mugs for the camera.

CUT TO

A series of stills from various 1913 films with appropriate quotes in Voice Over: *The Barrier of Blood*—A Young half-breed loves a girl, but cannot marry her because of his doubtful blood. *The Friendless Indian*—His only reward is a nod of thanks, for, of course, he is a redskin and as such is doomed to walk the world alone. *The Squawman's Awakening*—Paleface Magee, who has married a squaw and almost forgotten civilization, meets one day a white woman being made captive by two Indians. *Commencement at Indian School, Carlyle, Pa.*—Not as good a picture as one would be led to expect with such a title. The students drilling, a group of parents in costume, and Congressman Carter, an Indian, and Chief Three Bears shaking hands are shown. Surely there is more of interest than that.

As if these were not comic enough, the "comedies" continued with *Grease Paint Indians* and *The Indian Servant*, as well as the all-Indian picture, *An Indian Maid's Strategy*. The popular animal of that particular year was a horse named Peggy, who was featured in *Peggy and the Old Scout*:

> Bill Cody, an express messenger, is entrusted with a bag of gold which he is to carry over the Broken Trail. He is mounted on his pet horse, Peggy, which he has taught to perform some clever tricks. The length of the journey necessitates a night's encampment. While sleeping, a band of Indians make him prisoner. He refuses to tell where the gold is hidden and is tied to the stake but Peggy with her teeth unties the knots that bind him. Cody is pursued by the men—while fighting them off Peggy races back to town and summons some cowboys who soon rout the Indians, thus allowing Peggy and the Old Scout to continue their journey.

Good old Peg repeated her bit in *Saved by His Horse*. This

time she untied herself after being bound by an Indian, proving that even a horse can outwit a red man.

Henry Wadsworth Longfellow's noble Hiawatha, and James Fenimore Cooper's noble Chingachgook appeared once more. *Hiawatha*, made by Kinemacolor, had an all-Indian cast. It was praised by the critics and applauded by the public. Of the white producer, *The Moving Picture News*, March 29, 1913, commented:

> Mr. Moore . . . who, through his work with the Indians, has become an authority on them, says, "The Indian is all right as long as he works out of doors and keeps away from fire water . . . ."

The March 1 issue of the same paper had this to say about the film itself:

"HIAWATHA," THE INDIAN PASSION PLAY IN PICTURES

> An event most interesting to critics and other thinking individuals occurred . . . when Frank E. Moore exhibited . . . a four-reel motion production of Longfellow's poem, "Hiawatha."
> "Hiawatha" as an outdoor play has been presented most successfully by Mr. Moore during the past few years with a cast of Indian players at various parks and private estates. These same Indians, some 150 strong, have participated in the most remarkable manner in the production of the picture play . . . . It is intensely interesting to note the work of these full-blooded Pagan Indians. There is a dignity, a strong dramatic instinct and a natural grace about the American Indian that cannot be denied . . . . Natural and free from affectation as children, they participate in the action of the play in a manner that is most delightful.

Vitagraph filmed a version of *Deerslayer* in 1911, and remade it in 1913, which featured Wallace Reid playing Chingachgook very badly. This was one of Reid's first appearances prior to becoming a superstar of the silent screen.

Louis Reeves Harrison wrote of *Deerslayer*, in *The Moving Picture World*: "In this Cowboy-and-Indian period of motion-picture evolution, this era of revolver and scalping knife, of fringed trousers, war paint and feather bonnets, the supreme delight of five-year-old boys, a revival of James Fenimore Cooper's stories seems highly appropriate . . ."

Whereas the noble red man attracted many, it was the savage Indian who made money for the studios. *The Big Horn Massa-*

cre, made by the Kalem Co., evoked this critical judgement: ". . . Indian pictures failed because they were tame; not because they were Indian pictures, and . . . 'The Big Horn Massacre,' is a savage Indian picture, and is likely to excite comment where it is seen, because it is so savage, so vigorous in the quality of its action; because the camera shows 'stomach' in taking it."

"Vigorous quality" was again displayed in *The Last Blockhouse*. A wicked half-breed, played like a wicked witch, lusts after a white woman. He incites the Indians to attack the fort, forcing the settlers to the last blockhouse, which, of course, is promptly set afire. Before the blockhouse is blown to smithereens—because of the gun powder therein—the half-breed captures the girl. Then the blockhouse is blown up. Miraculously, there is one survivor. He hurriedly warns the hero, who is busily chopping wood in the forest. The hero, in turn, gets the soldiers to attack the Indian village. Meanwhile, the half-breed escapes with the girl, the hero gives chase, and there is a fight. The half-breed is killed and the hero and heroine are reunited and all's well that ends well.

Cinema history reached another milestone in 1913. One and two reelers grew into feature length films. Buffalo Bill's *The Indian Wars* was advertised in a 1914 issue of *The Moving Picture World*: "As a Money-Maker this film is without an equal . . . . The advertising possibilities of the picture are unlimited . . . . It is a FIVE REEL THRILLER THAT WILL LIVE FOREVER—1000 INDIANS, many of whom were leaders in the original battles . . . HISTORICALLY CORRECT and all scenes TAKEN ON THE EXACT LOCATION of the original battles . . . THE POSTERS will STOP THE CROWDS . . ."

CUT TO
Montage of 1913 movies including: *Across the Chasm, After the Massacre, The Apache Kind, An Apache's Gratitude, At the Half-Breed's Mercy, The Attack at Rocky Pass, The Barrier of Blood, The Battle at Elderbush Gulch, The Battle of Fort Laramie, The Bear Hunter, The Big Horn Massacre, The Blindness of Courage, The Branded Six-Shooter, Bred in the Bone, Breed of the North, Broncho Billy Gets Square, Broncho Billy and the Navajo Maid, The Buckskin Coat, The Call of the Blood, Campaigning with Custer, Camping with the Blackfeet, Camping with Custer, The Cheyenne Massacre, Children of the Forest, The Counterfeiter, Commencement at Indian School, Carlyle, Pa., A Dangerous Wager, Darkfeather's Sacrifice, The Death Trail, Deerslayer, Dorothea and Chief*

Razamataz, A Dream of the Wild, Early Oklahoma, The Eleventh Hour, The Faithless Friend, A False Accusation, The Fight at Grizzly Gulch, The Flaming Arrow, For the Peace of Bear Valley, The Friendless Indian, General Scott's Protege, The Good Indian, Grease Paint Indians, The Green Shadow, A Hair Raising Affair, The Half-Breed Parson, The Half-Breed Sheriff, Harvest of Sin, The Heart of an Indian, Her Indian Brother, Hiawanda's Cross, Hiawatha, In the Long Ago, An Indian Maid's Strategy, The Indian Maid's Warning, The Indian Servant, The Indian's Secret, The Iron Trail, The Land of Dead Things, The Last Blockhouse, A Matter of Honor, Maya—Just an Indian, Mona, The Mystery of Yellow Aster Mine, The Oath of Conchita, On the Frontier, Over the Cliffs, The Pale-Face Squaw, Partners, Past Redemption, The Peace Council, Pecos Pete in Search of a Wife, Peggy and the Old Scout, Piegan Indians, The Pride of Angry Bear, A Prisoner of the Apaches, The Quakeress, A Redskin's Mercy, The Romance of the Utah Pioneers, Saved by His Horse, The Secret Treasure, The Sheriff's Baby, The Skeleton in the Closet, The Snake, The Song of the Telegraph, The Squaw Man, The Squaw Man's Reward, The Squawman's Awakening, The Stolen Mocassins, The Trail of the Silver Fox, The Transgressor, The Trapper's Mistake, Trooper Billy, The Waif, The Water War, When the Blood Calls, When the West Was Young, The White Squaw, The White Vaquero, Wynona's Vengeance, The Yaqui Cur.

CUT TO
A busy New York City street in 1914. A movie theatre with a new front and marquee stands out. It reads: Opening Today—The All New Odeon—First Features—Latest News From Europe—Continuous performances. Although the box office is still closed, people are beginning to queue up.

In 1914 the Great War started in Europe. Cecil B. De Mille's career was launched with the release of *The Squaw Man*. William S. Hart also started on his way to becoming the greatest Western star of them all, and Tom Mix began to make himself apparent. Besides World War I, 1914 begat the serial *Perils of Pauline*. In the second episode, "Goddess of the Far West," there is a cherished moment. Pauline has been captured by Indians who think she is a goddess and there is much bowing and dancing. But there must be proof that she really is. Even Indians know that gods do not die; that deities have the strength to overcome anything. They decide to put her to the test. The Indians dance her to a high rock for the ordeal while the following subtitle is flashed on the screen: "This test should reveal her immoral [sic] strength."

Criticism of Westerns had been building and, by now, everyone said they were out of style. Yet close to 150 Indian films were made during this year.

One outfit, calling itself Albuquerque-Warner's, was credited

Kalem ballyhooing its accomplishments in 1914. (Theatre Collection, New York Public Library)

with *The Toll of the Warpath* and *The Lust of the Red Man*, both written by Dot Farley and directed by Gilbert P. Hamilton. The critical comments are most revealing. *Toll*: "It will delight all those who like Western drama, painting the Indian in black colors, and causing the spectator to feel no sympathy for him or his misfortunes." *Lust*: "One idea seems to have been uppermost in the minds of both [director and writer], and that was to paint the Indian as a true villain of the worst possible sort. They have succeeded in their idea, and due to this the picture is unpleasant at times. No sympathy goes out to the redskins . . ."

The following comments from reviews seem more typical of the day:

The Arrow's Tongue—"Another absolutely unique story of the old West. Picture this: A dying half-breed boy with an arrow in his breast dashing across the plains on a white horse . . . . Everywhere the . . . boy and the white horse and the bloody arrow spread the message of the coming redskin hordes. And in the scenes that ensue you can almost hear the warwhoops."

Lo, the Poor Indian—"A thoroughly delightful comedy. Charlton King as the Indian is splendid. The picture is taken in the South. A professor brings an Indian into civilization. His antics at seeing water flow from a tap, and on finding 'fire water,' make excellent comedy."

CUT TO
A sequence from the 1914 Fatty Arbuckle comedy, *Fatty and Minnie He-Haw*, showing how "he gets into a world of trouble with an Indian squaw who desires his hand in marriage."

While W. C. Fields and Groucho Marx were able to carry humorous names to the sublime, the rest of Hollywood got only as far as the ridiculous. *Reggie, the Squaw Man*, "a petted and pampered scion of aristocracy, falls in love with Annie Wagon-tree, daughter of Chief Pump Handle." In *The Indian Suffragettes*, "an Indian Farce Comedy," the heroine is Dishwater of the Oompah tribe. And with *Colonel Custard's Last Stand*: "It seems almost a shame to burlesque such a subject. Some very humorous names, such as Chief Standing Cowski, instead of the original Sitting Bull are introduced. Good comedy of that class." Then there was the snappy boast of the Appollo Company for *Some Bull's Daughter*:

"Did Big Chief Love His Daughter
Every Appollo is a Comedy Reel—
Any Appollo is a Real Comedy!"

The Moving Picture World, January 17, 1914, ran a story about Tom Mix and the making of *In the Days of the Thundering Herd*. Mix, who claimed to be part Cherokee, had been making pictures for only three years and had not yet reached the heights of stardom:

> . . . Mr. Campbell and Mr. Mix, with a host of Indians and white men, were engaged in making an old-time, historical buffalo hunt production . . .
>
> "Pawnee Bill's" . . . ranch of 6000 acres was used for the hunt. The animals were hunted and killed by Indians and white men just as they were in the days long ago on the plains, and eight bulls altogether were killed in the chase.
>
> There will be quite a difference between the methods of the Indian and the white man in bringing down this big game, as shown in the films. The Indians will be seen stalking the herd in their own way and then killing their quarry with bows and arrows. Then the Indian methods of drying, curing, and jerking the meat will be shown, affording quite an interesting lesson to the spectator . . . .

CUT TO

A montage from *The Way of the Redman,* as we hear in Voice Over: A very good Indian story with Tom Mix as the Indian. He befriends a gambler who in turn steals his wife from him and mistreats her. The redman returns to his forefather's idea of punishment and ties the gambler to a stake and places food just out of reach. When, through the little girl, the gambler attempts to escape, there is a death struggle between Indian and white man.

CUT TO

A montage from *The Ranger's Romance,* which is described in Voice Over: A western drama by Tom Mix, featuring an exciting running fight between a prairie schooner and a band of drink-maddened Indians.

The Princess myth was a perfect device for Hollywood to use both on and off the screen. One of the best known of the early Native American stars was Mona Darkfeather. The people at Kalem, the studio which made her films, had trouble deciding on her status. In 1914 she made at least 34 pictures. In 20 of them she was publicized as a "Princess"; in the other 14 she was just the plain ordinary Indian girl in the next tipi. Appearing with her were many well-known and popular Native American players of the day: Little Thunder, Art Ortega, Big Moon, Chief Phillippi, Lone Bear, Two Feathers, Eagle Eye, Eagle Feather, Eagle Wing. Her 1914 films include: *At the End of the Rope, Brought to Justice, The Call of the Tribe, The Cave of Death, The Coming of Lone Wolf, Defying the Chief, The Fate of a Squaw, The Fight on Deadwood Trail, The Fuse of Death, The Gambler's Reformation, Grey Eagle's Last Stand, Grey Eagle's Revenge, His Indian Nemesis, The Hopi Raiders, The Indian Ambuscade, Indian Blood, Indian Fate, The Indian Suffragettes, An Indian's Honor, Kidnapped by Indians, Lame Dog's Treachery, The Legend of the Amulet, The Medicine Man's Vengeance, The Navajo Blanket, The New Medicine Man, The Paleface Brave, Red Hawk's Sacrifice, The Redskins and the Renegades, The Squaw's Revenge, The Tigers of the Hills, The Vanishing Tribe, The Vengeance of Winona, The War Bonnet.*

Indian football heroes were back giving it the old college try in *Strongheart*, who was at Columbia University taking the blame for selling football plays. And screen adaptations of stage plays were continuing with *Pierre of the Plains* and *Eagle's Nest*.

The Indian was as incredulous as anything yet made. At the beginning of the film, we see Chief War Eagle with his twin sons, Blue Feather and Red Feather, wearing matching little Indian outfits as they coyly pose for the camera. The rest of the film tells the story of the twins. One is raised as a white and becomes an army officer while the other stays with his tribe and becomes a warrior. Predictably, they meet; predictably, there is a white woman.

CUT TO

Montage of 1914 movies including: *Andy and the Redskins, The Angel of Contention, The Arm of Vengeance, Around the World in 80 Days, The Arrowmaker's Daughter, The Arrow's Tongue, At the End of the Rope, The Blood Test, The Bottled Spider, The Brand of His Tribe, Breed o' the North, Broncho Billy and the Redskin, Broncho Billy and the Settler's Daughter, Broncho Billy's Indian Romance, Brought to Justice, The Call of the North, The Call of the Tribe, Cameo of Yellowstone, Captain Junior, The Cave of Death, Colonel Custard's Last Stand [sic], The Colonel's Orderly, The Coming of Lone Wolf, The Cross on the Cacti, Dan Morgan's Way, A Daughter of the Plains, A Daughter of the Redskins, The Daughter of the Tribe, The Death Mask, The Death Sign at High Noon, Defying the Chief, The Desert's Sting, The Devil Fox of the North, Eagle's Nest, The Fate of a Squaw, Fatty and Minnie He-Haw, The*

Fight on Deadwood Trail, The Final Reckoning, The Final Verdict, The Fires of Ambition, The First Nugget, The Forest Flame, A Frontier Mother, The Fugitive, The Fuse of Death, The Gambler of the West, The Gambler's Reformation, The Ghost of the Mine, Grey Eagle's Last Stand, Grey Eagle's Revenge, The Half-Breed, Hearts United, The Hills of Silence, His Indian Nemesis, Hopi Raiders, The Hour of Reckoning, In the Days of the Thundering Herd, In the Wolves' Fangs, The Indian, The Indian Agent, The Indian Ambuscade, Indian Blood, An Indian Eclipse, Indian Fate, The Indian Suffragettes, The Indian Wars, An Indian's Honor, Kidnapped by Indians, Lame Dog's Treachery, The Last Ghost Dance, The Last of the Mohicans, The Legend of the Amulet, The Line Rider, Lo, the Poor Indian, The Lost Arrow (also billed as The Last Arrow), Love's Sacrifice, The Lure of the Windigo, The Lust of the Red Man, The Mad Hermit, The Medicine Bag, The Medicine Man's Vengeance, Meg of the Mines, The Navajo Blanket, The New Medicine Man, Northern Lights, Orphans of the Wild, Out of the Valley, The Paleface Brave, The Panther, The Perils of Pauline, Pierre of the Plains, The Raid of the Red Marauders, The Ranger's Romance, Red Hawk's Sacrifice, The Red Man's Heart, The Redskins and the Renegades, Reggie, the Squaw Man, The Renegade's Sister, The Renunciation, A Romance of the Pueblo, The Sea-Gull, The Severed Thong, Shorty and the Fortune Teller, The Silent Way, Sitting Bull, the Hostile Sioux Indian Chief, Slim and the Indians, Some Bull's Daughter, The Squatter, The Squaw's Revenge, Star of the North, The Story of the Olive, Strongheart, A Tale of the Desert, A Tale of the Northwest Mounted, A Test of Western Love, The Tigers of the Hills, The Toll of the Warpath, The Unlawful Trade, Under Arizona Skies, The Vanishing Tribe, The Vengeance of Winona, The Village 'Neath the Sea, A Waif of the Plains, The War Bonnet, The Way of the Redman, When America Was Young, Where the Trail Divides, The Whiskey Runners, White Wolf, Wolfe, or the Conquest of Quebec, The Word of His People, Yellow Flame.

RAIN MAKERS

SCENE XII

Enter D. W. Griffith

Griffith made well over 400 pictures, some 30 of which were about Indians. Most of these were made for Biograph. His second film, *The Redman and the Child*, told of a Sioux Chief, played by Charles Inslee, who clandestinely works a claim on a Colorado river and hides his gold in a tree. The following quotes are from a review in *The Moving Picture World*, August 1, 1908:

"There camped a Sioux Indian, who besides being a magnificent type of the aboriginal American, is a most noble creature, as kindhearted as a woman and as brave as a lion . . . . It is needless to say that he was beloved by those few who knew him, among whom was a little boy, who was his almost constant companion."

The noblest savage of them all was Griffith's.

Two white meanies steal the gold, kill the boy's grandfather and kidnap the boy. The noble Indian chases after the villains.

"Clutching him by the throat, the Indian forces his [the villain's] head beneath the surface of the water and holds it there until life is extinct, after which he dashes in pursuit of the other . . . . A ferocious conflict takes place on the sands terminating in the Indian forcing his adversary to slay himself with his own dagger."

The bloodthirstiest savage of them all was Griffith's.

White man's lust for gold was always a good device for getting Indians to oppose prospectors, gold seekers, or treasure hunters. According to Hollywood, many Indians were as preoccupied with the thought of gold as the white man. But, in actuality, unlike the cultures to the South—Aztec and Mayan—most Native American tribes couldn't have cared less for gold. They had no need, desire or use for it. And the thought of cutting or scarring their Mother Earth to get it was totally repellent to them. Sadly enough, contact with the white man was to alter many concepts. The lunacy of gold fever was all too contagious.

Mary Pickford, in "My Own Story" for the August, 1923, issue of *The Ladies Home Journal*, told of those early Biographs: "The stories were sudden, abrupt and somewhat disconcerting. They attempted to cover too much and the treatment was always sacrificed to the happenings, which were often not too closely related."

A lot always happened in Griffith's films even if you couldn't figure out a reason for its happening. The Indian football hero, educated at Carlisle, is in love with the white heroine in *The Call of the Wild* (1908). His rejection by the girl's father causes him to go berserk and he tears off his white man's clothing. He returns to his savage ways by donning his war bonnet and buckskins and gets drunk. The only possible reason we can come up with for this extreme, bizarre behavior is that the Indian is mentally unbalanced.

Griffith seemed to enjoy depicting Indians going berserk. In *Leather Stocking* (1909), several of them do so as they pounce upon a group of whites, killing, scalping, and dashing babies' brains out.

Plains Indians, some wearing Sioux bonnets, attack a wagon train in a desert in *The Last Drop of Water* (1911). The Indian attack was a convenient device for the inevitable Griffith "galloping last minute rescue." This is also true of *The Battle At Elderbush Gulch* (1913). Not only are we puzzled to find Plains Indians in the desert but we are equally puzzled by an attack motivated by no apparent reason.

In *A Pueblo Legend* (1912), the Indian hero, after what seems like months of searching for a sacred stone, and, after much fighting, returns home empty-handed only to find that the Indian heroine, Mary Pickford, had found the stone buried under her very doorstep. Nothing could be more disconcerting.

In 1908 the *New York Dramatic Mirror* began publishing film reviews by Frank Woods, who devoted much space to Griffith's work. Woods later sold story ideas to Griffith on the side. According to the former Mrs. Griffith in *When Movies Were Young* (1969), Woods took his reviewing seriously:

> Frank Woods now set about to criticise the pictures with the same seriousness with which he would have criticised the theater. He bought books about the Indian and let the producers know there was a difference between the Hopi and the Apache and the Navajo. With a critical eye, he picked out errors and wrote them frankly, and his influence in the betterment of the movies has been a bigger one than is generally known outside the movie world. Mr. Woods is really responsible for research . . . .

Eventually Woods became head of Biograph's scenario department, working closely with Griffith for many years. "Daddy" Woods, as he was affectionately called by the Biograph family, apparently did father the concept of Hollywood experts, who are just as "responsible for research" as Mrs. Griffith states.

CUT TO
A pressbook: "'A MAN CALLED HORSE' is an extraordinary story about a most extraordinary man. It . . . is perhaps the first motion picture to treat the American Indian in every detail of this life with unparalleled accuracy. Sharpened to a cutting edge with authenticity, 'A MAN CALLED HORSE' is definitely a film of the '70s . . . a motion picture that takes its strength by 'telling it like it was . . . .' 'A MAN CALLED HORSE' is a totally authentic motion picture, a statement of the courage, discipline and savagery of the Indians as they were prior to the white man's plundering of their birth rights."

CUT TO
A protest outside a theatre in Minneapolis, Minnesota at the premiere of *A Man Called Horse*. A long line of pickets from the American Indian Movement—AIM—is circling outside the theatre. The pickets are shouting as they try to dissuade people from entering. Placards read: "How To Make an Indian Movie"; "Buy 40 Indians"; "Totally humiliate and degrade an entire Indian nation"; "Make sure all Indians are savage, cruel and ignorant"; "Satisfy Indian groups by seeking authenticity"; "Import a Greek to be an Indian Princess"; "Introduce a white man to become an 'Indian' hero"; "Make the white man compassionate, brave and understanding"; "Make the white man an 'Indian' leader to save the souls of the weak"; "Desecrate the Indian religion"; "Pocket the profits in Hollywood." On the back of each sign is printed: "Every dollar going into the theatre boxoffice is a vote for bigotry."
While the above sequence is shown, we hear in Voice Over: This

article was written by an Oglala Sioux, Art Raymond, and published in the *Sioux Falls Argus-Leader* on April 25, 1970:

"'Lila Sicha.' In Lakota, that means 'really bad.'"
If *A Man Called Horse* ... is authentic, my name is George Armstrong Custer. *A Man Called Horse*, under the "historical expertise" of former North Dakota employee Clyde Dollar, has been billed from coast to coast as authentic. Its premier in the land of the Sioux has been blazoned across the country on radio, television and by newspaper. "The film presents the American Indian and his customs with fascinating realism," says one review published in advance. The same review goes on to say that much of this film's authenticity is owed to its technical advisor—"Clyde Dollar, Sioux historian and veteran student of Indian custom." Movie makers cannot be expected to know. Dollar certainly ought to. The stupidity and ignorance of Sioux ways (and the film is about the Sioux), is gross. Dollar didn't even know the Sioux mounted their horses on the right side—not on the left as do the Wasicu (white men).
One of the key romantic and emotional parts of the film is Hollywood's alleged desertion of the old people by the Sioux. This simply is not true. In the Siouan culture, the elderly held one special place of honor and never, never, never were deserted. On the contrary, they received very special care.
The Sioux, in *A Man Called Horse*, were depicted as cruel with no finer instincts for understanding human nature. In truth, the Sioux were implacable enemies once their animosity was aroused. However, their entire culture was one in which altruism and love for fellow man held the highest of places. The film is preceded by propaganda which says it shows the way of life and custom. To extract one segment of that life and let it represent the entire way of life and culture is a gross injustice to the Sioux of today.
The scenery is beautiful; the photography the best, and the fictionalized story line dramatic; the language is real and most (but not all) of the songs authentic.
Who could complain if this were simply billed as another portrayal of white man's version of Indian wars in which the white man wears the white hat and the Sioux the black hat; That is wrong, of course, but the Sioux have come to expect that. To bill this as an authentic film which accurately portrays the life and custom of the Sioux is not only wrong and injust. It is a lie.

In his review of *The Mended Lute*, August 14, 1909, Woods wrote:

... Without exaggeration it may be said that this film bears almost the same relation to many past Indian pictures as Longfellow's Hiawatha bears to a redskin dime novel .... The story is of the Dakotas when that Indian race occupied the Central West. An Indian maiden is given by her father to a favorite warrior, although she is in love with a young brave. She escapes . . . and joins the . . . brave. Together they flee from the warrior and his followers, who pursue in canoes, furnishing the most thrilling realistic canoe chase the writer has ever seen.

This type of film, more than all prior media, was to establish the white man's distortions and inventions as fact. The Sioux or Dakota and other Plains "races" did not use canoes—as surely as canoe users did not use tipis. Most Plains tribes followed the buffalo. It is most difficult to paddle after a buffalo. About *A Mohawk's Way*, Woods wrote on September 21, 1910: "It is the noble red man of James Fenimore Cooper that we see in this film—the Indian of romance who, as some people claim, never existed, but who is nevertheless the ideal type for story telling."

Sioux-Bonnetted Navajo rug salesman? A scene from Griffth's *Fighting Blood* (1911) Biograph. (The Museum of Modern Art/Film Stills Archive)

117

DISSOLVE INTO

A montage of scenes from some of Griffith's films: *The Red Girl* (1908), *The Indian Runner's Romance* (1909), *The Redman's View* (1909), *The Indian Brothers* (1911), *Fighting Blood* (1911), *Iola's Promise* (1912), *The Massacre* (1912). Each scene blends into the next with either chase or rescue. The contents of the segments follow in this order: Indians molesting white women; scalping; chase; white men mauling Indian women; clubbing; rescue; Indians manhandling babies; tomahawking; chase; Indians fighting white men; stabbing; rescue; Indians fighting each other; shooting; chase; burning of cabin; rescue; burning wagon train; chase; burning whites at stake; chase; rescue. Each segment is finally superimposed one upon the other until a totally black Fade Out. During the above sequence, we hear in Voice Over: James Agee once wrote: My veneration for Griffith's achievements is all the deeper when I realize what handicaps he worked against, how limited a man he was. He had no remarkable power of intellect, or delicacy of soul; no subtlety; little restraint; little if any "taste," whether to help his work or harm it; Lord knows (and be thanked) no cleverness; no fundamental capacity, once he had achieved his first astonishing development, for change or growth. He wasn't particularly observant of people; nor do his movies suggest that he understood them at all deeply. He had noble powers of imagination, but little of the intricacy of imagination that most good poets also have. His sense of comedy was pathetically crude and numb. He had an exorbitant appetite for violence, for cruelty, and for the Siamese twin of cruelty, a kind of obsessive tenderness which at its worst was all but nauseating. [*Agee on Film* (1964)]

Of all Biograph personalities, Mary Pickford was a favorite Griffith "Indian." Mary herself tells of her reaction to playing Indians in "My Own Story:"

> . . . as I had dark eyes, I had to play Indian maidens, and Indian dramas were very frequent in the early picture days. I had my head in a bowl of bolarmenia—the skin stain for Indian make-up—all the time. With heavy black wig, alligator teeth round my neck, leather clothes and beaded leggings, I'd have to tramp day after day over the hills . . . . We made a film version of Helen Hunt Jackson's story, *Ramona*. This was a departure in several ways, for we bought the story, and also, so far as I know, it was the first time that a film company actually went to the exact locations of the story.

Griffith paid the publishers $100 for the film rights to *Ramona* (1910), a high price then, and, with "our Mary" playing the title role, it was touted as being the most expensive picture ever made. Biograph considered it Griffith's most artistic film.

In 1912 Griffith and his company made a picture, *A Pueblo Legend*, which included battle scenes between Pueblos and Apaches in which arrows shot from bows with weak-wristed will just plopped to the ground. Yet many a man staggered about pierced with arrow. But let Mary Pickford who played the Indian Maiden tell the story:

> . . . On our way from California to New York we stopped off at Albuquerque, New Mexico, to make this supposedly historical picture. *In those days motion-picture companies did not have research departments, and no work of this sort was done by anyone. Today a great deal of thought is given to this matter alone* . . . . [italics ours]
>
> Undoubtedly this Indian picture was filled with mistakes. The dress of the Pueblos is very modest, and they wear a sort of tunic or nightgown effect under the dresses. We obtained dresses like theirs, but did not use the under dress and our arms were bare. So, too, were our legs, for we did not trouble to bind them with rawhide, which is worn as a protection against snake bites. We were told that this and the under garment had not been used formerly, and as ours was a historical picture we dispensed with these things.
>
> We proceeded to the Indian village of Isleta, sixteen miles from Albuquerque, where the inhabitants were shocked when they saw us in our incomplete dress. None of them knew what motion pictures were except a few who were Carlisle graduates. Among these was the chief's daughter.
>
> A Frenchman who was cast for the part of a medicine man had been given permission to select a costume for himself from the museum in connection with the Harvey Hotel at Albuquerque. He had the ill luck to choose a very weird one with a short skirt trimmed with bells. When he came dancing into the scene with bathing trunks underneath his short skirt the Indians were furious, because they thought we were trying to make fun of them. It seems that this was a sacred skirt, and they insisted that he take it off or that we all leave the village . . . .
>
> The Indian chief . . . demanded that our chief, Mr. Griffith, come to their kiva, or councilroom, which was in the middle of the village . . . .
>
> Mr. Griffith was detained there all afternoon, and the rest of us did not know what to do. He told us

afterwards that through the long session his hair stood on end several times. There was only one Indian who spoke English, and Mr. Griffith had no idea whether he was translating his speeches fairly or not. He could not tell from the Indian's faces, as they were quite expressionless. He offered them two thousand dollars if they would allow us to stay the rest of the afternoon; but the council decided that no matter how much money we had, we must leave the village. We had insulted them and had made fun of them. Finding that there was nothing that would tempt them, Mr. Griffith sent me word that the camera was to be secreted and that I was to walk down their village street and steal the scene. If we did not get this particular bit, all that we had done before they stopped us would be wasted.

I have never been so terrified as I was when I walked trembling down that street. I did not like the job; but in those days the director was king—Mr. Griffith's word was law, and none of us would have thought of disobeying him. As I walked down that road I could feel eyes watching me from every corner and crevice. Finally there was a split in the tribe, and about one-fourth of them came with us when we went back to Albuquerque to finish the picture there. The chief's daughter acted as interpreter, and I heard afterwards that she had to leave the village, that her father was furious with her for going with us. Incidentally, the picture was not much of a success when released.

We hear Miss Pickford repeating in echo effect and Voice Over: In those days motion picture companies did not have research departments . . . . Today a great deal of thought is given to this matter alone.

CUT TO

Clyde Dollar, historian, for *A Man Called Horse*, and John Hartl, a reporter for the *Seattle Times*. Dollar is talking about the film: I don't say that it's perfect. There are still mistakes in it, but I'd defy anyone but an expert to detect the factual errors. Some schools have already made the film required viewing in their anthropology classes. We have tried to communicate the dignity and mysticism of Indian religious ceremonies—and this is something few white men have experienced. When the movie was shown in Minneapolis last week, members of the American Indian Movement protested, charging that it portrays Indians as savage, cruel and ignorant. It's less a protest against the film than a tribal complaint. The AIM is made of Winnebagos, Chippewas, and urban Indians—all traditional enemies of the Sioux. When they complain that the film shows the Sioux as savage, it's their way of finding a gimmick to let their feelings about the Sioux be published.

This kind of tribal feuding is fairly common. For years, the Eastern Sioux considered the Western Sioux crude, ignorant, stupid, savage —and the Western Sioux considered the Eastern Sioux to be panty waists. As a white man AND an accepted member of the Sioux, I can move freely from one tribe to another, from Sioux to Crow, and communicate as Indian members of the tribes usually cannot.

CUT TO

A newspaper ad for the film as we hear in Voice Over this from the *Minneapolis Tribune*, April 28, 1970: The Minnesota Department of Human Rights announced Monday it is urging all citizens to boycott the film, *A man Called Horse* [sic], on the grounds that it is an affront to the dignity of Indians. "The department has viewed the picture and feels that the story line perpetuates a Caucasian superiority and neglects to consider the sensitivities of the American Indian nation . . . ."

CUT TO

The Washington Monument and the surrounding area. As the camera comes in, we see red, white, and blue bunting everywhere. American

There goes the neighborhood. A scene from Griffith's *America* (1924). (The Museum of Modern Art/Film Stills Archive)

121

flags of all sizes are flying. Workmen are building a large stage and the setting is an outdoor theatre. The authors are watching this on television. It is "Honor America Day," July 4, 1970. Throughout the day, WTOP-TV, Washington, D.C., keeps plugging that the day's televised activities will end with the premiere TV presentation of Griffith's "immortal" 1924 "classic epic," *America.*

But Griffith's *America* proved very mortal. It was a long, dull film and, when first released, not very successful. Nevertheless, it did have its admirers.

Using some actual factual material, the film creates its own version of America's history. The Indians in this movie are ignorant, easily beguiled, arm-folding stoics, or crazy, drunken, torturing fiends. The costuming is as atrocious as the acting. The famous Griffith panoramic scenes are in evidence at this time, showing Indians slaughtering settlers and laying waste the Mohawk Valley.

Considering Griffith's grotesque distortions of the Native American, using this film to help celebrate "Honor America Day" is in perfect keeping with the best American tradition.

ENTER THOMAS INCE

CUT TO
Mr. Ince being interviewed by a reporter. Mr. Ince is speaking: They never put on a real Wild West Show until I found it could be done. Oh, of course, they had horses and cowboys and fake Indians, but they never had any real Indians. They said, "You can't teach Indians to act. They're savages." That didn't sound reasonable to me. The Hundred and One Wild West Show was playing not so very far away from us, and I went over and hired the whole crew for the winter. I found the Indians were the best actors ever. They have a great sense of humor and a sense of the dramatic, and even if they don't understand more than a quarter of what you're saying to them, they're the greatest mimics in the world. All you have to do is show them once and they have the idea for good.

In 1911 Thomas Ince came to Hollywood to work for Bison Films. Ince's influence in making Indian films was immediately felt. A review of *An Indian Martyr,* in *The Moving Picture World*, December 30, 1911, notes:

The opening scene of this film shows one of the most convincingly set Indian villages that this reviewer remembers. The photographs throughout give clear detail portraits in both foreground and middle distance. An Indian maid of the village is loved by a Sioux who is not acceptable to her father, the chief. The Sioux is captured, brought in and condemned to death. She persuades another chief to set her lover free and this man is the martyr; he suffers in place of the Sioux. The tone of the photographs is soft brown and in some of them there is a myopic, Corot mistiness that is extremely lovely. The story is well designed and made very effective by sincere and restrained acting.

As a director and later producer, using the Miller Bros. 101 Ranch Real Wild West Show and their company of Sioux plus 18,000 acres of mountainous range, Ince standardized the mass-production method of making movies.

The Sioux employed by Ince came from the Pine Ridge Reservation in South Dakota. They were often asked to recreate battles from a history still vividly remembered. As a result, they would, at times, resent participating in battle scenes in which they were defeated. Very often these Native Americans found themselves carried away by the spirit of the battle and departed from the scripted action. Because of this, Ince had their tomahawks and war clubs padded to protect the white actors. Nonetheless, their women still urged the warriors on by singing traditional songs of victory.

George Mitchell, in "Thomas H. Ince," *Films in Review*, October, 1960, wrote of Ince's use of the Sioux: ". . . Since they were wards of the U.S. government, he had to arrange with the local Indian agent not only for their care, but also for their schooling. Though docile, the Indians were averse to work, and they 'appropriated' such brightly colored props as rugs, blankets, etc. They also got drunk, and local saloon keepers would call Ince in the middle of the night and complain that some of his 'wards' were disturbing the peace."

Reaction to the Ince and 101 combination can be seen in these excerpts from an article on their first film, *War on the Plains*, or *Across the Plains*, in *The Moving Picture World*, January 27, 1912:

> The history—the true history—of early life in the Wildest West is being written on the film. The famous Bison 101 Ranch aggregation is now at work on a stupendous series of films that will be a revelation to the outside world of the actual life and experiences of the early settlers in the Far West, the Indian tribes, the gold prospectors, the cattle herdsmen, etc. We have been surfeited ad infinitum ad

nauseam by the Diamond Dick novel kind of Western film.
[And, by the way, the Bison trademark of old proclaimed
the source of too many of these travesties on Western life
and human intelligence, many of which were so ridiculous
that exhibitors in Western states dared not show them.]
We have had plenty even of the Fenimore Cooper style of
Western drama, based on fact, no doubt, but lurid, highly
colored and imaginative to a degree. It marks a distinct
step in advance when a manufacturer sees his mistakes and
now sets forth to present to the public the great West as it
really was and is . . . . It should also be mentioned that
Bison 101 pictures will all be two-reel subjects. One double
reel each week on Fridays. Eminent moving picture
authorities have long pointed out that the two and three
reel subject was the logical development of the business if
it was to advance . . . .

The film was well received by all, as were most of Ince's
productions.

Battle of the Redmen, released in March of that year, concerned Cheyennes and Sioux battling each other. Those participating in the film were, of course, Sioux. We wonder how they
must have felt when called upon in the story, not only to
portray, but to fight their friends and allies, the Cheyennes.
Only 36 years had passed since both tribes had fought Custer at
the Greasy Grass.

CUT TO

The interview with Ince as he continues: Then, too, I was the first
man who paid $50 for a scenario. I realized that you had to have
good scenarios or you wouldn't make good no matter how much
effort and expenses you put into the film. It's like having a good
cover to a book and nothing inside. They said I'd ruin the picture
business, paying prices like that but pretty soon they all met my
prices, and now of course, since the competition has grown to be
what it is, $50 isn't considered exactly what you'd call ruinous.

CUT TO

Buffy Sainte-Marie and the authors talking before her New York
Central Park concert on August 14, 1970. Miss Sainte-Marie is
speaking: It's the writers' fault. That's what I object to. Hollywood
keeps using the same old white writers over and over again. They
don't say anything important and they don't know what they're
writing about. There's no empathy. Even the so-called authentic
movies like *A Man Called Horse*—that's the whitest of movies I've
ever seen. Everything they do; everything they write has to go
through layers and layers of white cheesecloth and it's all bound up
in rolls and rolls of white tape. And it's the audience that ends up
getting gypped because they don't know what they're getting.

124

This, in reality, is what an Ince film was like: in *Blazing the Trail* (1912) Indians attack a settler's wagon. The parents are killed, their son wounded, their daughter captured. Her boyfriend, having escaped capture, follows her. The son is found by people in a wagon train who, upon hearing his story, decide to help. Meanwhile, the boyfriend has sneaked into the Indian village and reaches the girl by slitting the back of the tipi, which is guarded only at its entrance. Their escape is foiled, he is tied to the stake, tortured, and finally is made to run the gauntlet. They are rescued at the last minute by her brother et al.

William K. Everson commented in *A Pictorial History of the Western Film* (1969):

> Films like Ince's *The Indian Massacre* were meticulous not only in documenting the Indian's way of life, but in establishing him as a human being of nobility and recognizable emotions. *The Indian Massacre* was one of the best of these films, presenting both sides of the picture, stressing the problems and courage of the white settlers, but emphasizing most of all the tragedy of the relentless extermination of the Indian. Its closing scene—a silhouette of an Indian woman praying beneath the woodframe burial pyre of her dead child—was as beautifully composed and photographed as anything in later John Ford films.

Having read Mr. Everson's remarks about *The Indian Massacre*, one might conclude that this is a sensitive and accurate appraisal. However, having viewed the film, we have serious doubts about Mr. Everson's judgements. A cliched, stereotyped creature can hardly be called a human being. The Native Americans depicted in *The Indian Massacre* were, in fact, portrayed no differently than they had been in the worst of the Indian films.

The Indian Massacre (1912) was re-released in 1913 under the title of *The Heart of an Indian*. Louis Reeves Harrison wrote a prose version of the film which appeared in the *World*, March 9, 1912. When it comes to "the relentless extermination of the Indian," there are no two "sides of the picture:"

> ... the entire war party joined in stampeding the food supply of the whites on the hoof while skirmishers undertook the enlivening duties of braining settlers, burning their cabins and carrying off their wives for outrages unspeakable before slavery, or death by torture .... She knew of her fate in advance. A woman so comely was usually taken by one of the younger bucks as his wife—the

penalty of any attempt at escape being torture more hideous than crucifixion—then traded to another when the first brave was tired of her and so on down to abject slavery beneath the Indian squaws and children who would lose no opportunity to inflict humiliation, to an end in horrible death with her mutilated body rolled in mud to express red hatred for the white race . . . . The worst that would occur for an attractive white woman in the hands of redmen arose when the captors holding Mrs. Brown began to dispute for her possession. This meant instant death for the captive, or outrageous torture upon the return of the war party . . . . The horrible torture inflicted upon white women by Indians of the plains was a matter of common knowledge among frontiersmen, but it was not needed to stir up the Brownsville terrors . . . . Many of the tribes were still in the wigwams, though a few braves had been occupied since the break of day in preparing for an orgie [sic] of torture almost as refined as that enjoyed by the citizens of Rome during a period of ancient civilization. Twigs and boughs were already smouldering near the contrivance of pegs and thongs used to fasten a naked prisoner to the ground during torture, as one of the few pleasures of the noble red man was to build a small fire on the stomach of his captive and sit around enjoying the agonized writhing and screams of his victim . . . .

Is this Everson's human being of nobility with recognizable emotions?

Mr. Harrison reviewed several Ince pictures. In an article, "The 'Bison-101' Headliners," he continued his blatantly racist ramblings in *The Moving Picture World*, April 27, 1912:

There were probably less than a million Indians scattered over that part of the continent now known as the United States, subject to the ravages of relentless killing and torture—[among themselves]—cruel, crafty and predatory—with no universal language, no marks of gradual enlightenment and incapable of contributing anything of value to human evolution when European races began to fight their way from ocean to ocean under all sorts of difficulties, including methods of warfare disastrous to the invaders. The natives were so well protected by natural advantages and their methods of fighting that it was a difficult matter to kill a redskin, whereas the whites were constantly exposed by their peaceful occupations to indiscriminate slaughter.

There is no discovery of rights and wrongs involved in this Bison production. Conditions alone are presented, especially those which existed after the government attempted to regulate and control the various tribes, according them privileges still unenjoyed by white citizens, and punishing with severity acts of outrageous cruelty by the natives, and less severely acts of oppression by responsible whites. Race hatred was unavoidable and it is only modified to-day. The average descendent of colonial families has little use for the red man, regards him with distrust and, with poetic exceptions, considers him hopelessly beyond the pale of social contact.

The Indian, however, remains one of the most interesting and picturesque elements in our national history. He is almost typical of the fighting male, a restless, dominating, ever-struggling human creature, principally engaged in works of destruction, but representative of the ancestral strain that conquered all the other creatures delivered from the fertile womb of Mother Earth. He was essentially a man of physical action, using only that part of his brain which enabled him to be crafty in the hunt for food, though he had vague poetic ideals and nebulous dreams of barbaric splendor. Mentally he was far below the Egyptian of 6,000 years ago, but he was the physical superior of any man on earth except the strong-armed European who cultivated brain along with brawn.

The United States Government first tried to lead the tribes into civilized pursuits, but Mr. Redman was not strong of arm nor strong of purpose. He took to drink on small provocation and had a drunkard's lack of ambition, was satisfied with enough to keep him going and oppressed by an ingrowing distaste for work of any kind. Many Americans of high intelligence exhibited a genuine friendship for the Indians; the establishment of schools and colleges for them shows that. On the other hand, a lot of heartless scoundrels like those now preying on white people robbed the redman by much the same methods, and constant "uprisings" ensued as a consequence.

These uprisings became a habit with the tribes, as they are also with the New York motion picture company directors. If the plain truth be told, we know in advance that the Indians are going to have a war dance and attack the settlers, that some hero or heroine will go through all sorts of perils to reach the military post, and that the troops will arrive in the nick of time. This pounding on the tom-tom of one idea indicates that the plays are made on the spot, and the sameness is only relieved by one strong outreach for sympathy. That occurs in "The Crisis"—it might better have been called "The Weakling" . . . .

The New York Motion Picture Company has not gone to extremes one way or the other in revealing the characteristics of the American Indian. There has been a lot of slush written and voiced on this subject, but here is a middle course that is nicely balanced. One of the Indians of the company—he enacts the part of a chief—is a star actor. His gestures and movements are a source of perpetual study. The directors have apparently let Lo play his own role and he does it to perfection. The chief is quite as good in comedy as tragedy—a delight in one and impressive in the other.

I must take off my hat to the directors for showing the pioneer as he was, one of the hardest fighters in the world, pitted against a barbarian who would have swept the barbarians of Europe from the face of the earth. The early settler was a man, every inch of him, and the iron in his blood has descended to those who freed the country from British rule and fought every way for liberty since then, who took under their protection the unhappy children of all nations, and at last tried to give them opportunity to enjoy life, liberty and the pursuit of happiness.

A scene from Ince's *Custer's Last Fight* (1912) Bison. (Theatre Collection, New York Public Library)

CUT TO

The last scene in *Custer's Last Fight* (1912), showing the Custer Monument being dedicated and the little white girl placing a wreath of flowers on Custer's tomb. As the scene unfolds, we hear the following about the Sioux from *The Moving Picture World*, August 24, 1912: . . . They are selected for their physical development, and are splendid types of the fast vanishing race. They plunge into the picture-making with a seriousness that is at times uncomfortable, and they have to be under careful watch at all times.

The climax in *Custer's Last Fight.* (Theatre Collection, New York Public Library)

Sessue Hayakawa and Tsuru Aoki, early Japanese stars, were frequent players in Ince's Indian films. In 1914 they appeared as Indians in the following films: *The Death Mask, Desert Thieves, Last of the Line, Star of the North, Village 'Neath the Sea.*

In *Last of the Line*, Hayakawa played the educated Indian turned drunkard and renegade. His father, a chief and friend of the white man, kills his son during an attempted army payroll robbery. To salvage his son's honor, the chief makes it look as if his son died saving the money. The son, now a hero, is buried with full military honors.

CUT TO

Buffy Sainte-Marie on stage at her Central Park concert in August,

129

1970. She begins to sing "My Country 'Tis of Thy People You're Dying."

She continues singing as we

DISSOLVE INTO

A series of stills from some Ince films: *A Frontier Child* (1912), *The Invaders* (1912), *His Sense of Duty* (1912), *The Land of Dead Things* (1913), *The Colonel's Orderly* (1914), *The Death Mask* (1914), *The Secret of Lost River* (1915), *Satan McAllister's Heir* (1915).

ENTER C. B. DE MILLE

CUT TO

A vast valley. Dust clouds swirl about everywhere. As they clear, we see a lone figure and a movie camera on top of a cliff way off in the distance. The man waves his hat and his voice re-echoes throughout the valley: Anytime you're ready, C. B.

Claims have been made that *The Squaw Man* (1913) was the first feature made in Hollywood and there are claims that deny this. Anyway, it was C. B. De Mille's first film. The Jesse L. Lasky Feature Play Co.—later to become Paramount—had been

De Mille's 1918 version of *The Squaw Man.*

formed by Lasky, Goldwyn, and De Mille. They hired a cameraman and a director, Oscar Apfel, to work on *The Squaw Man.*

The movie was a big financial success; it made a screen star out of stage matinee idol, Dustin Farnum, and brought even greater fame to Red Wing. The film was to be an important factor in De Mille's professional life—since he remade the story in 1918 and 1931. In the 1918 version Elliott Dexter was the squaw man and Ann Little played the Indian maiden.

The 1931 talking version suffered mightily from miscasting. The "Mexican spitfire," Lupe Velez, was better suited for Leon Erroll comedies than playing Indian maidens.

The Plainsman (1936) is an excellent example of how De Mille rewrote history. In this picture the Indians were in as good a form as they were in dime novel days, down to and including Buffalo Bill's fight with Yellow Hand, played to form by Paul Harvey. A young Anthony Quinn, at the beginning of the "ugh" phase of his long career, played a bit as "a Cheyenne brave."

According to De Mille, all that was needed to utterly defeat the Indians were more men the likes of Wild Bill Hickok and Buffalo Bill Cody. Using the already existing myths about these two army scouts and throwing in Calamity Jane as well, he proceeded to create his own odyssey of the plains. Making tin gods of them, he has them cunningly eliminate feathered manifestations of the devil's wrath. The film runs the gamut of Western exploits, climaxing with Custer's finale at the Little Big Horn.

Many well-known authors have written film criticism, including Graham Greene (film critic for *The Spectator*, 1935-1937) whose review of this film appeared in Alistair Cooke's *Garbo and the Nightwatchman* (1937):

MR. CECIL B. DE MILLE: there has always been a touch of genius as well as absurdity in this warm-hearted sentimental salvationist. *The Crusades, The Ten Commandments* were comic and naive, but no director since Griffith has handled crowds so convincingly. How—startlingly—Mr. De Mille seems to have grown up. *The Plainsman* is certainly the finest Western since *The Virginian*: perhaps it is the finest Western in the history of film.

The story of the Indian rising after the Civil War when General Custer's forces were annihilated, with Mr. Gary Cooper as a famous scout, Wild Bill Hickok, the lover of

Calamity Jane. Mr. De Mille has never before handled stars of Mr. Cooper's and Miss Jean Arthur's quality, and another unexpected trace of sophistication, the music is by George Antheil. Indeed one might wonder whether Mr. de Mille's [sic] name had been taken in vain if it were not for the magnificent handling of the extras in the big sets: the brilliant detail, depth and solidity of the dockside scenes at St. Louis, the charge of the Indian cavalry. A few great spectacular moments in the history of the film remain as a permanent encouragement to those who believe that an art may yet emerge from a popular industry: the long shots of the Battle of Bull Run in *The Birth of a Nation*, the French attack in *All Quiet*. Some of the scenes in *The Plainsman* belong to that order.

That might have been expected, and the excellent dialogue may be a fortunate accident; what takes one by surprise in a De Mille film is the firm handling of the individual drama: the silent moments in the cleared street of the shabby frontier town where Hickok crosses the road to meet his wouldbe murderers: the final poker game he plays in the barred saloon with the white prisoners he is keeping for the military to hang, the air of doom while we wait for the inevitable shot in the back from the little treacherous bowler-hatted comic behind the bar: and most surprising of all the brilliant satirical sequence when the armament directors, whose new repeating rifle has been put on the market too late for the Civil War, discuss how to dispose of their unwanted stocks and the cynical Old Pickwickian chairman persuades them to sell to the Indians "for hunting purposes." This actor's performance, when the news of Lincoln's murder comes roaring down the street, is superb; the conventional shocked regrets, the roaming, faintly speculative eye. It is a pleasure to see Mr. Charles Bickford back in one of his rough scoundrelly parts as the trader who smuggles the rifles to the Indians. Only in the character and treatment of Buffalo Bill Cody does the dreaded softness of the traditional De Mille intrude.

Perhaps this film did impress Mr. Greene in 1936. However, for a man so exacting in his own craft, he seems to have suspended all notions of credibility. *The Plainsman*, in its treatment of the Native American, must remain a remarkably bad film.

The success of *The Plainsman* was followed by *Union Pacific* (1939), in which De Mille borrowed heavily from John Ford's *The Iron Horse* (1924), especially the Indian attack on the train.

North West Mounted Police (1940) was about the Riel Rebellion, a magnificent and stirring story rarely treated by Hollywood. However, De Mille reduced exciting history to bad soap opera, phony heroics, and cheap sentimentality.

His last Indian opus was *Unconquered* (1947). Once again De Mille rewrote history to suit his own dramatic purposes. James Agee, in the October 27, 1947, issue of *Time*, offered this estimate of De Mille's devotion to history:

> He has often been laughed at for his historical inaccuracies*; actually he has a great interest in research and knows how to use it.

De Mille's *Unconquered* (1947) Paramount. (The Museum of Modern Art/Film Stills Archive)

*One anonymous verse read:
Cecil B. De Mille,
Much against his will,
Was persuaded to keep Moses
Out of the Wars of the Roses.

In *Unconquered*, Boris Karloff played Guyasuta, a famous Seneca leader, dressed from wig to mocassins in the finest Sioux style of the 1860s, although the story takes place in the East in the 1760s. Karloff makes just as fascinating an Indian in *Unconquered* as Bela Lugosi as Uncas in a German-made *The Last of the Mohicans* (1922).

Walter Hampden, one of the great actors of the American theatre, was allowed only to grunt as the chief in *North West Mounted Police.* There's a certain fascination in watching people like Hampden, Karloff and, more recently, Dame Judith Anderson, play Indians. There is the hope that they may bring a new, different, added dimension or approach to portraying an Indian. It may all start out differently but the result always ends up the same. Marc Lawrence, best noted for his gangster roles, played the medicine man in *Unconquered* like an unhinged feathered hoodlum.

If De Mille did nothing for Native American culture, he did contribute to its meager economy. He hired so many Native Americans as extras that some Native Americans in Hollywood did try to form a new tribe. John del Valle wrote this story for the *New York Herald Tribune*, November 17, 1940:

> . . . Since De Mille set the pace with his first filming in 1912-'13 of "The Squaw Man" as Hollywood's first feature picture, the red man has had more than his share of work . . . .
>
> This offers an anthropological aspect which might not have been anticipated; Hollywood has acquired a permanent colony of representatives of almost all tribes still extant. With the cinema as their melting pot, these expatriates are taking on the semblance of a tribe all their own—perhaps the largest tribal group not on any reservation. One among them, a stalwart of Cherokee blood known professionally as Chief Thunder Cloud, who plays a Cree war chief in "North West Mounted Police," has taken the initiative. With a nucleus of eighteen, and an eligible list running into hundreds, Thunder Cloud is applying to the Bureau of Indian Affairs for recognition of the "De Mille Indians" as a new tribe composed only of Indians who work in the films . . . .

A Hollywood tribe is not beyond the imagination, for, sadly enough for most of us, the only real Indian is a Hollywood Indian.

ENTER WILLIAM S. HART: ACTOR-WRITER-DIRECTOR

The following describes some of William S. Hart's Indian films juxtaposed with the stars own self-image, purpose, and concern for "Western" purity.

Hart was interviewed by Marguerite Tazelaar for the *New York Herald Tribune*, March 29, 1938. He said, "As a boy my only playmates were Indians. I still bear the knife wounds I got in a fight with one of them."

This is from a magazine article in *Pic*, May 30, 1939: "No Hart picture was complete without Indians. They were good or bad, depending on their attitude toward the White Man as represented by Bill. 'Bad' Indians were hunted down and exterminated."

The article in the *Herald Tribune* continued with Hart saying:

> ... the pictures of my boyhood days were ingrained in my mind. I knew the West as few people knew it, and I guess I always had a kind of mission about telling people what it was like in its early days. The old West is now gone, never to return ....

In describing *The Last Card* (1915, Hart), *Film Notes—The Museum of Modern Art*, 1949, stated: "Such films outrivalled the dime novels in catering to the desire for escape and it was this quality, rather than their idealization of frontier morality, which accounted for their universal popularity."

For an article in *The American Magazine*, Hart once said: "When I saw some Western pictures they nearly bowled me over. I got mad through and through. They were crude, false, overdone. They were libels of the immortal memory of those stalwart, good-hearted men who had packed guns in the open and lived and died with their boots on. Even the costumes and sets were untrue."

In *The Primal Lure* (1916, Hart), the hero, played by Hart, is fired from his job as the manager of a trading post. Still, he returns, in the nick of time, to organize a defense against an impending Indian attack. During the flight, realizing that the post is about to be overrun, Hart offers himself to the marauding Indians as the sacrificial lamb. He is tied to a tree and is about to be burned at the stake when all of a sudden a rain storm extinguishes the flames. Meanwhile, a priest, who happened to be passing by, sees Hart's predicament and convinces

135

the Indians that the storm was sent by the great spirit as a sign of disapproval. Our hero is released.

In his interview with Miss Tazelaar, Hart said: "My first part was in 'The Bargain.' I was paid $75 a week. That was in April, 1914. Almost from the start I made a success. Three years later I had offers from every important company there was at figures

From an article about Wm. S. Hart (Theatre Collection, New York Public Library)

running into thousands a week. I say this without boasting, because it happened that I knew the West better than the directors did themselves."

In *Wagon Tracks* (1919, Lambert Hillyer), the hero, Hart, is a scout for a wagon train. Indians surround the train and threaten to attack if one white man is not surrendered up to them in retribution for one of their men who had been killed by someone in the wagon train. To save the caravan, Hart offers himself to the revengeful Indians. Needless to say, all is righted before the final reel.

In addition to making films, Hart also wrote books, including a series for boys. In his Introduction, "To My Boy Friends All Over the World," for *The Golden West Boys, "Injun" and "Whitey"* (1919), Hart wrote:

> During my Dakota boyhood I not only acquired the accomplishments of the West, but I met some of the most famous characters of frontier days—white and red men. In fact, my early days of intimate relationship with the Sioux Indians enabled me to learn their tribal traits and history nearly as well as I know our own. I speak the "silent tongue"—the sign language of the Sioux which, by the way, is understood by all Indian tribes.
> In those days the luxuries and even many of the necessities of civilization were denied us in our frontier settlements. My mother brought four children into this world, attended by Sioux squaws because a doctor could not be procured. And, when a vicious rattler nearly ended my career at the age of twelve years, a squaw officiated as the doctor, the nearest physician being engaged in punching cows at a ranch some sixty miles distant. That the Sioux squaw was a good doctor is proven by the fact that I am alive today.

The theme of the film *The Aryan* (1916, Hart) is aptly described in this subtitle which movie audiences read: "Oft written in letters of blood, deep carved in the face of destiny, that all men may read, runs the code of the Aryan race: 'Our women shall be guarded'; and a man of the white race may forget much—friends, duty, honor, but this he will not, he cannot forget."

Further on in the introduction to his book, Hart writes about his early stage appearances and the appeal of Western stories on stage and on the screen:

> As Cash Hawkins in "The Squaw Man," . . . it was my good fortune to be able to give the American public a

typical Western character. My success in this character opened up a subsequent line of Western roles for me, the emphatic success of "The Squaw Man" causing the production of many Western plays. Considerable comment was caused by my repeated successes in these characters that I knew as a boy and loved so well. Many persons who were interested in my work marveled at the realism of the interpretations. Their enthusiasm persuaded me that the entire American public loved the West and its traditions when presented with truthfulness—and the boys most of all.

Unfortunately, other sections of the United States had long been deluged with sensational "thrillers" of the West on the melodramatic stage, in dime novels and later in the early motion pictures. Many intelligent people had formed the most weird and distorted ideas of the West from the history of frontier days to the present.

In 1914 Western pictures were, to use the language of the motion-picture producers, "a drug on the market."

The following are excerpts from a review in *Wid's*, September 14, 1916, of Hart's *The Dawnmaker* (also attributed to Reginald Barker) which he also directed:

Mr. Hart is presented as a halfbreed, the son of a full-blooded Scotsman who married the daughter of an Indian chief. He was to be the leader of his tribe.

Grown to manhood, he had the queer combination of the ambition of the white man, which was held back by the native Indian lack of initiative . . . .

In advertising this I would particularly emphasize the fact that this is a unique characterization registering the struggle of a halfbreed who dreams the ambitious dreams of a white man but is unable to realize them because of the handicap of his Indian blood, which leaves him without the necessary initiative and tenacity of purpose.

Near the end of his introduction, Hart wrote:

. . . Realizing that because of my early associations of the West and my training as an actor combined, I was qualified to rectify many mistakes which were then being made in the production of Western photoplays, I decided to try my luck. To give the American public the benefit of all I knew of the West . . . became my one ambition. In turn, I would enjoy the gratification of doing something that I had longed to do all my life. And, naturally, I hoped for increased fame and financial success . . . . Nearly five years have passed since that eventful time in my career. That I have devoted this lengthy period exclusively to the production of Western pictures is the best proof that the American public possessed a love for the West that will endure for all time . . . .

THE WAR AND POST-WAR YEARS—1915-1922

SCENE XIII

As Western production decreased, so naturally did the appearance of the Indian. Yet no year has ever gone by without Indian films being made or seen. 1915 is a case in point. It was not a vintage year for Westerns; still, at least 45 of the same old Indian films were made. Among them were: *The Boundary Line, Green Backs and Red Skins, The Ghost Wagon, An Intercepted Vengeance, Son of "The Dog", Refuge, The Huron Converts, The Secret of Lost River, The Race Love, The Greater Barrier, The Indian Changeling, A Message for Help.*

CUT TO
Richard Schickel interviewing Raoul Walsh for "Good Days, Good Years," *Harper's Magazine*, October, 1970. Walsh is speaking: We loved our work. There was a sort of camaraderie. You'd get hold of a story and then you'd find some actor and say, "There's a hell of a part here for you—you get to kill eight Indians"—and then you'd get your film, enough for just one take on a scene, and then you'd make your picture.

And Tom Mix rode on.

In 1915 Douglas Fairbanks rode in. He leapt, jumped, bounded, slid, sprang, and grinned his way gallantly through innumerable predicaments for his fans, who loved every minute. In several of his films Native Americans were used in small parts and as extras when shooting on location. As caricatures they fitted in perfectly with Fairbanks' light-hearted and good-natured world. His first picture, *The Lamb* (1915, William C. Cabanne), showed how he could lick his weight in Indians with hi-jinks and acrobatics and nary a drop of sweat. In 1916

Fairbanks played the lead in *The Halfbreed* (Allan Dwan). He did not go unnoticed, as this, from a review in the *Times* of July 10, 1916, illustrates:

> Much of the action is set in the giant forest and as a half-breed who looks rather more like Peter Pan than Fairbanks even lives within one of the great trunks, although this, to any one who has lived in a suitcase, is not a great feat. Fairbanks has infrequent opportunity here for his talented smile but his muscles are starred and, from the way he bounds about, you realize that he can, whenever he leaves the movies, become a pugilist or represent us at the Olympic games. That is, if they do not kill him.

In *Wild and Woolly* (1917, John Emerson) he plays an Eastern dude who visits an all too civilized Western town. The local cowpokes decide to liven things up a bit for him and the fake Wild West becomes real as Doug smiles his way in and out of one adventure after another and, as the ads would read, into the hearts of the American public.

A perfect example of Indians and Doug in outlandish situations and plots is *The Mollycoddle* (1920, Victor Fleming). Fairbanks once more plays an American dude who is living in Europe but, as he points out to some American tourists, "All my people were cow persons in Arizona."

The plot is just absurd enough to be delightful. The young woman who is Doug's love interest is really a Secret Service agent out to get the goods on Wallace Beery, who has Hopis working a diamond mine in Arizona and smuggling the diamonds to him in Europe by a most roundabout way. Doug and his entourage finally end up in Arizona. This gives Doug a chance to have some fun talking "ugh" talk to a college educated Indian, who replies, "What the hell are you talking about?" He also joins in the Indian dance with boyish enthusiasm. But the high point is a spectacular fight between Doug and Beery, slugging it out and sliding down the entire side of a mountain. It was sensational.

CUT TO
Montage of 1915 movies including: *The Arrow Maiden, As in Days of Old, Author! Author!, Babbling Water, Big Jim's Heart, The Boundary Line, Broncho Billy's Teachings, The Cactus Blossom, The Ceremonial Turquoise, The Corporal's Daughter, A Deal in Indians, From out of the Big Snows, The Ghost Wagon, The Girl I Left*

Behind Me, The Gold Dust and the Squaw, The Greater Barrier, Green Backs and Red Skins, Ham Among the Red Skins, The Heart of a Bandit, The Heart of the Sheriff, The Huron Converts, The Indian Changeling, The Indian Trapper's Vindication, The Indian's Narrow Escape, An Intercepted Vengeance, Jack Chanty, Jerry's Celebration, The Lamb, The Legend of the Lone Tree, The Legend of the Poisoned Pool, A Message for Help, O'Garry of the Royal Mounted, The Old Code, Pals in Blue, The Race Love, Refuge, The Renegade, Satan McAllister's Heir, Saved by Her Horse, The Secret of Lost River, The Sheriff's Story, Son of "The Dog", The Taking of Luke McVane, The Trapper's Revenge, The Wanderer's Pledge, West Wind, The Western Border.

CUT TO
A theatre marquee in Hometown, USA. It reads: Latest War News From Europe—Plus—Douglas Fairbanks' Latest—*The Halfbreed*.

Well, too many Indians finally spoiled the broth. Fewer than 25 Indian films were made in 1916: *The Ancient Blood, The Stain in the Blood, The Passing of Pete, The Night Riders, Jerry's Celebration, Britton of the Seventh, The Aryan, The Bugle Call, The Dawnmaker, The Deserter, The Halfbreed, His Mother's Scarf, The Patriot, The Primal Lure, The Quarter Breed, Davy Crockett.*

Rudyard Kipling's "East is East, and West is West, and never the twain shall meet" proved false, for in *The Dawn of Freedom* (Paul Scardon) the twain did meet: "Cartwright becomes separated from his companions, and is attacked by Indians; he is shielded by Father Ambrose, a missionary, who has spent his life in India. The Indians demand Cartwright's life, and as a means of saving him, Father Ambrose tries suspended animation, an art which he learned of the Hindus."

Ramona (Donald Crisp) was remade again. Concerning Adda Gleason who played Ramona, George Blaisdell, in his April 22, 1916 *Moving Picture World* review, said: "She has the fire of youth, the light and speedy foot characteristic of the Indian, the tenderness and the affection of the white." Of Monroe Salisbury who played Allesandro: "He has the dignity of the red man, the red man broadened by the education of the white man."

In 1916 the public was given a rare opportunity to see some good documentary footage about the Native American. Filmed by the Department of the Interior and released by the Gaumont Company, these films about the Blackfoot Tribe were shot near

141

their reservation in Glacier National Park, Montana. Led by Chiefs Two Gun White Calf and Three Bears, various members of the tribe demonstrated the use of sign language, breaking and setting up camp, a courting dance, a war dance, and a ceremony in which they pray to the "Under-Water God," a term used in the movie press and promotion sheet.

Also filmed was the rare Medicine Elk ceremony. This sacred ceremony was done for the benefit of all members of the tribe who were ill. At this time, only one medicine man, Many Tail Feathers, was allowed to perform it. It had not been performed for ten years previously. Many Tail Feathers died several months later, leaving no one to carry on the ceremony and, according to the press, the cameras caught Many Tail Feathers smoking the Medicine Elk pipe for the last time as another ritual passed into history.

The Motion Picture Division of the Library of Congress has some footage from these documentaries. After days and months of Hollywood creatures on parade, what a pleasure it was to see real Native Americans do real things.

CUT TO
A montage of 1917 Indian films. The sequences include *Adventures of Buffalo Bill, A Daughter of War, The Indian's Lament, Indian Raiders, The Soul Herder, The Squaw Man's Son, Wild and Woolly, Wild Sumac, Man Above the Law, Broadway, Arizona.*

In 1917 John Ford, after a brief apprenticeship, begins directing films for Universal, leading to a long and illustrious career.

CUT TO
A montage of 1918 films which include sequences from *Blue Blazes Rawden, Hands Up, The Sign Invisible, The Squaw Man.* During the sequence from *The Law of the North,* (Irvin V. Willat), we hear this in Voice Over: The scenes where Charles Ray forced a young innocent girl into the clutches of an uncouth and lewd Indian . . . were not what his public wanted to see.

And still Tom Mix rode on.

CUT TO
A montage from *Ace High* (Lynn Reynolds) with these excerpts from *Wid's Daily* [another movie trade paper], June 24, 1918: Technically, you can pick enough holes in this to build an Australian cheese net but in this case I don't think this is going to keep the production from entertaining the great eighty per cent.

142

I might cite, as one instance, where Minnie, the old Inceville squaw, held a door closed against about forty rough-necks and in another place they had Tom talking to Minnie by Indian sign language after it had been established by several lengthy spoken titles that she could sling the English language very, very fluently for an Injun.

Indian Flapper—1920's calendar art.

143

CUT TO

The front page of *Wid's*, March 28, 1918. As the camera comes in

DISSOLVE INTO

The page containing the review of Tom Mix's *Six Shooter Andy* (C. M. and S. A. Franklin). The camera continues in until it picks up: Tom Mix should always wear his hat. As soon as he removes his chapeau he looks like most any other human being does. With a hat on, however, he looks nearly as if he means business.

CUT TO

A montage of 1919 films which include sequences from: *By Indian Post, Desert Gold, A Fight for Love, The Last of His People, Riders of Vengeance, Wagon Tracks.*

CUT TO

A clip from *The Wilderness Trail* (E. LeSainte), with the Voice Over describing the scene: . . . Tom goes out single-handed to accomplish the deed of catching the real free-traders. A half-breed is the leader and his squaw mother realizes that if he can marry the Factor's daughter all will go well with him. So the girl is lured to the cabin so as to be compelled to become the half-breed's wife. And there it is that Mix finds her and effects her rescue after a series of exciting events.

CUT TO

A montage of 1920 pictures including: *The Mollycoddle, The Moon Riders, The Phantom Foe, The Testing Block, The Last of the Mohicans.*

The world wanted to escape the horrors and headlines of World War I. Countries in Europe had been expending all their energies on the war; they had no time to make movies. Hollywood accepted the challenge and sent them a galaxy of romances, comedies, adventures, and fantasies. By 1920, six short years after the beginning of the war, a giant industry had emerged and Hollywood became a household word.

A new era was beginning. Despite war, prohibition, and the roaring twenties—the phantom horseman continued riding relentlessly across the landscape.

The Last of the Mohicans was made again (versions had been done in 1911 and 1914). This version was directed by Maurice Tourneur and Clarence Brown. Much has been written about the photographic quality, beauty, exquisite composition, and breathtaking shots in this film. All of this did not help a film which was less than inspired. Cooper's story had been transformed into a series of static tableaus. Wallace Beery, as Magua, played the creature in authentic comic strip style. His fellow

A scene from the 1920 version of *The Last of the Mohicans.* Note Wallace Beery (left) with rolled-down socks. (The Museum of Modern Art/Film Stills Archive)

Indians romped around with knives clenched in their teeth like pirates in cave man skins, their heads topped by tufted skull caps in order to simulate "shave-head" Native Americans.

The massacre scene in *Mohicans* was very carefully borrowed from Griffith. Drunken Indians rampage everywhere, while throughout the scene you glimpse the same Indians struggling with the same women again and again and again. And the two girls, our heroines, walk through the slaughter undaunted and unscathed until captured by Beery.

> CUT TO
> A montage from 1921 movies: *Across the Divide, Behold My Wife, Bob Hampton of Placer, Bring Him In, The Raiders, A Ridin' Romeo, The Sage Hen, That Girl Montana, White Oak.*
>
> CUT TO
> A sequence from *The Paleface* (1921) showing a bunch of Indians in their futile attempts to burn Buster Keaton at the stake.

The Paleface, written and directed by Buster Keaton, brought this man's great comic genius to redskin land. For the first time

Buster Keaton in *The Paleface* (1921) (The
Museum of Modern Art/Film Stills Archive)

and, perhaps the only time, a genuinely funny movie was made
involving Indians. Keaton very simply extrapolated the absurd
ingredients inherent in all Indian films and put them into their
proper perspective.

At the beginning of his film Keaton fills, lights, and smokes a
gigantic "peace pipe" very solemnly. Later on, when Indians

attempt to burn him at the stake, Keaton resorts to two simple expedients: he puts on asbestos underwear, and after being bound, picks up the large stake to which he is tied and makes his escape. The resulting chase in which the frustrated Indians are constantly foiled by our pole-carrying hero is in the best Keaton tradition. Thank you, Buster Keaton.

CUT TO

A montage from 1922 movies: *Blazing Arrows, Cardigan, The Desert's Crucible, The Great Alone, The Half Breed, One Eighth Apache, The Hate Trail, Hellhounds of the Hills, In the Days of Buffalo Bill, The Prairie Mystery, The Snowshoe Trail, Winning of the West, The Primitive Lover, Suzanna, The Mohican's Daughter, White Eagle.*

147

THE EPICS—1923-1925

SCENE XIV

CUT TO
A montage from 1923 movies: *The Courtship of Miles Standish, The Covered Wagon, The Girl of the Golden West, The Huntress, In the Days of Daniel Boone, Jamestown, The Lone Wagon, The Oregon Trail, Pioneer Trails, The Prairie Schooner, The Santa Fe Trail, The Secret of the Pueblo, The Sting of the Scorpion, The Uncovered Wagon, Vincennes.*

By 1923 the country was in a recession, as was the Indian film. William S. Hart, the old reliable, was fading. Younger and more modern heroes brought a new flashy style to the Western. *The Covered Wagon* was the first of a new genre—the epic Western. As the scope of film increased, so did its emotional appeal.

The Exhibitors Trade Review extolled on March 31:

> In many ways, "The Covered Wagon" is a great American picture. Its appeal is swift and sure, because it carries the appeal of the pioneers, with their pathos, their life in the midst of death, and their unfailing native humor.
> No American can see this picture and fail to be stirred. If he is not stirred, he is not an American. And that is only another way of saying that the picture is a great patriotic document.

Robert E. Sherwood, once a movie critic, gave it a rave in *The Best Moving Pictures of 1922-23*: "There is one glorious period of American history which is usually omitted . . . . Indeed, it had received but little recognition, except in the works of Francis Parkman, and in those humble, paper-covered dime

149

novels that used to be frowned upon by the same type of person who now sneers at the movies."

On March 23, 1923, *The Moving Picture World* published an article containing rave excerpts from 15 New York City newspapers. *The Covered Wagon* even inspired a parody. That same year Paul Parrott made *The Uncovered Wagon*, in which Indians attacked a wagon train on bicycles.

Cruze's *The Covered Wagon* was in fact long and boring, but its success changed the course of the Western.

Col. Tim McCoy had been hired as technical adviser to insure the authenticity of matters Indian and it has been said that he planned and staged much of the action involving them. The Indians attack en masse; those on foot carry and hide behind branches and shrubs. Now this is a perfectly legitimate tactic if you're in a wooded area. But not out on a flat, almost desert-like prairie.

Since Native American Indians were used in most of the picture, the appearance of white Indians in very bad makeup was jarring. More jarring still was seeing Native Americans in this very same makeup.

To quote once more from Sherwood's review: "This is the period of expansion which commenced in 1846 .... It was then that the pioneers—men, women and children—struggled across the prairies and over the mountains in their trains of covered wagons, passing through incredible hardships and cordons of belligerent Indians that they might ultimately drive their ploughs into the soil of Oregon and California .... With the presentation of 'The Covered Wagon,' I venture to say that the pioneers of the Oregon Trail will receive honorable mention on every school-boy's list, even if he flunks out on all other important dates."

Once the wagon master first shouted "Wagons Ho!" they never stopped rolling, the Indians never stopped attacking, and the wagons never stopped circling.

CUT TO

A montage from 1924 movies: *The Alaskan, America, Behind Two Guns, The Flaming Forties, The Frontier Woman, The Heritage of the Desert, The Last White Man, Leatherstocking, The Left Hand Brand, The Mine with the Iron Door, North of Nevada, North of '36, Trail Dust, Trigger Finger, The Valley of Vanishing Men, Ramshackle House, Weeping Waters.*

CUT TO

A montage from 1925 movies: *The Bad Lands, The Bloodhound, Border Justice, A Daughter of the Sioux, Galloping Vengeance, The Gold Hunters, The Golden Strain, Quicker 'n Lightin', Reckless Courage, Red Love, The Red Rider, The Scarlet West, The Thundering Herd, Tonio, Son of the Sierras, The Verdict of the Desert, Warrior Gap, The Wild Bull's Lair.*

A scene from *The Thundering Herd* (1925) Paramount. "Tom Doan (Jack Holt) while attempting to break through the Indian lines to an ammunition wagon is attacked by Nigger Horse." (Photo and caption: The Museum of Modern Art/Film Stills Archive)

Director James Cruze wanted to follow his successful *The Covered Wagon* with another winner, *The Pony Express* (1925). He only succeeded in making another dull film, completely overburdened with plots and sub-plots.

He used Native Americans once more. The air of authenticity created by their costuming and dancing was quickly dispelled by the absurd story line. In this case our white hero, played by Ricardo Cortez, carries the mail through hordes of warring redskins, dropping them left and right, and emerges triumphant.

151

Nevertheless, this from the *New York Times*, September 14, 1925: "This pictorial document, which causes one's heart to throb with delight, is another chapter in American history which is bound, as was the case with 'The Covered Wagon' and 'The Iron Horse,' to stir all audiences to a state of intense pride for the achievements of the men of yore."

Another major epic, *The Thundering Herd* (William K. Howard), was also praised by the *New York Times*. The critic implied that the slaying of the Indians was treated as "a work of art."

A postcard promoting *The Scarlet West* (1925) First National.

Besides the big pictures, there were additional potboilers such as *A Daughter of the Sioux* (Ben Wilson) and *Galloping Ven-*

geance (William James Croft). Custer was getting his come-uppance in *The Scarlet West* (John G. Adolfi) and William S. Hart appeared in his last film, *Tumbleweeds* (King Baggott), considered by many to be his greatest film and one of the best of all Western epics. This film was reissued in 1939 with a prologue in which Hart bid farewell to his fans in an emotional, melodramatic speech.

One of the most important films ever made about the Native American was Paramount's *The Vanishing American* (George B. Seitz). In light of Hollywood's attitude, the fact that this film was ever made at all is incredible. And considering the times, it was even more unusual.

We were at the height of the roaring Twenties—David Robinson's *Hollywood in the Twenties* (1968) offers a look at those days:

> The Red scare reached a peak of hysteria in the monstrous Palmer Raids, in which some 6,000 suspected Communists were rounded up, and in many cases deported, while people who visited them in prison were quite liable to be themselves arrested. Intolerance, masquerading as patriotism, grew in those years until a writer in *Harpers* in 1922 could say, "America is no longer a free country, in the old sense . . . everywhere, on every hand, free speech is choked off in one direction or another." All-American solidarity led to persecution of other minorities apart from socialists: racial hatred reached unprecedented virulence in the early Twenties, at a time when coloured Americans, returning from the war, felt a new consciousness of equality (cf. G. B. Seitz' film version of *The Vanishing American*). 1919 and 1920 saw the fatal colour riots in Chicago and Tulsa.

John Grierson, organizer of Britain's great documentary movement, wrote a series of six articles which appeared in *The Moving Picture News* in 1926. In the first "The Product of Hollywood," November 6, he analyzed *the Vanishing American:*

> THE VANISHING AMERICAN, like the Indian it recorded, started magnificently and finished miserably.
> Yet THE VANISHING AMERICAN had a great story; there is no greater story than the passing of the Indian. And it had a love theme; the impossible and tragic love of

an age-old Indian for a twentieth century white girl is a great love theme. Then think of the setting: the picture had the desert, the canyons and the plains to conjure with. It had the night rain-gods and the night luck-gods to conjure with.

It began finely. The Valley of Vanishing Men took hold of the spectator and gripped him from the beginning. The primitive races came out from the rocks, they built their cave houses; they fought and were beaten. The Indians rejoiced in their victory; the Spaniards came and the horses and the muskets; the advancing Americans of the new era came, and the soldiers, and the artillery. That was noble stuff. There was something of the wilderness of space and the infinity of time written on it, that took one's breath away. The whisper of the winds of history was on it.

But something failed at that moment. The last episode was the twentieth century story of how grafters took advantage of the Indian and stole his lands and how the twentieth century Red Man (Dix was amazing) loved the little school-mistress. But how cheap and how trivial they made the story! The punch of the picture faded, the dignity of the theme vanished, the story lost the atmosphere of the valley and the sense of fate and became like any other story of gentle, gentle heroines and nasty, nasty villains. Dix did a grand job; he caught the spirit of the thing and lived and died like a god; but he hadn't a chance.

No one could have had a chance under the circumstances. The film was burdened with a most one-sided and insipid love story. The audience was subjected to a white schoolmarm who does nothing but smile at the Indian hero, while he does nothing but moon and mope whenever he is near her. His love for her must always remain mute. She, unaware of his true feelings, ends up marrying a white Army officer.

The Vanishing American was an important film. It wasn't a great film. It certainly wasn't, as some claim, the best film ever made about the Native American. Too many things put in for the right reason had the wrong effect. Contrary to Mr. Grierson's opinion, the prologue, tracing the history of the Native American in the Southwest, was too long and too absurdly inaccurate.

Yet, for the first time, a modern feature film was made which attempted to portray the Native American as, tragically, an alien in his own homeland. It was unfortunate that a trite, saccharine sub-plot was used to enhance the tragedy. By destroying the dignity of the hero, a leader of his people, and by pitting him against unbelievable villains, the film makers might have assured the film's success at the box office, but they failed to make history.

A very mediocre remake of *The Vanishing American* was done in 1955 (Joseph Kane), which had all the faults and none of the possibilities of the original.

A scene from *The Vanishing American* (1925) Paramount Promotional caption: "The cliff dwellers are defeated by the Navajos."

MORE RAIN MAKERS

SCENE XV

Enter Tim McCoy

CUT TO

Col. Tim McCoy talking directly into the camera. The quote is from Anthony Thomas' article on McCoy in *Films in Review*, April, 1968:

"I received a call from Hollywood because they were going to make a picture called *The Covered Wagon* and they wanted 500 long-haired Indians from the Western States. They asked me if I would be interested in rounding up those Indians, which I did. I brought them to Hollywood in two special trains—Indians, squaws, papooses, teepees, dogs, everything. Because I was the only one who could talk to these Indians, who belonged to several tribes, Paramount, or Famous Players as it was called in those days, asked me if I wouldn't get up a prologue and appear on the stage at Graumen's Chinese Theatre in Hollywood with the showing of the picture. So I resigned my commission and did."

VOICE OVER: Clyde Dollar, technical adviser for *A Man Called Horse:* As a white man . . . I can move freely from one tribe to another, . . . and communicate as Indian members of the tribes usually cannot.

Written material tends to take on a reality of its own and, in time, may come to stand for truth. This has happened not only to the Native American but to screen personalities as well.

For example, William S. Hart probably didn't know as much about the West as he pretended. He once said that all tribes understood sign language. This is not so. But Hart did enjoy playing the role of "the old-timer" or "the last of the frontiersmen." Eventually he began to believe the things he was saying about himself. Other stars began to believe publicity stories written about themselves as well.

And, perhaps, the same thing can be said of Col. Tim McCoy. All sorts of claims have been made for him. Jack Spears, in "The Indian on the Screen," *Films in Review*, January, 1959, stated:

> ... McCoy had developed a fanatical interest in Indians while cowpunching in Wyoming and had become one of the world's foremost authorities on Indian culture and history, especially Indian sign language, to which he was introduced by the late General Hugh L. Scott, one of the last great Indian fighters. McCoy's proficiency in sign language and Indian dialects led to his adoption by the Arapahoes, who named him High Eagle—"one who leads the coyote." Dressed in a feathered warbonnet and full ceremonial garb, McCoy had competed in the Indian dance at the Cody Stampede in '21 and had won first place against the best dancer of the Sioux, Chief Red Wolf.

... while Anthony Thomas claims:

> In '23 he was serving as Adjutant General in Wyoming and in his free time pursuing his interest in Indian history and languages. His picture was often in newspapers and magazines of the West because of his researches and discoveries. In an Arizona valley, for example, he had located Wovoka, the Ghost Dance Messiah of the Indians, and the photograph of the two of them has become famous.

McCoy appeared in over 75 Westerns during his career and, in the beginning, his reputation as an "Indian expert" put him in good stead.

McCoy's first acting part was in *The Thundering Herd* (1925). He also acted as technical adviser. In these same capacities McCoy signed with MGM in 1926 to do a series of Westerns which were never to be very successful. His first film for MGM, *War Paint* (1926, W. S. Van Dyke), shot on location at the Wind River Reservation in Wyoming, used Shoshonis and Arapahoes, and the title is a dead giveaway for the plot. *Winners of the Wilderness* (1927, W. S. Van Dyke), concerned the French and Indian War, but had the Indians wearing 19th century Plains costumes. *The Frontiersman* (1927, Reginald Barker), dealt with a subject rarely used in films—Andrew Jackson and the Creek wars. But here again the knowledge McCoy claimed was somewhat lacking. Plains Indians of the North Central United

States and their tipis—by now almost essential to any Indian film—were not left out of this story about Southeastern tribes. *Sioux Blood* (1929, John Waters), if nothing else, was lucky enough to have actor Chief John Big Tree in it.

In 1930 McCoy made a serial for Universal, *The Indians Are Coming* (Henry Mac Rae), which had the distinction of being released in both a silent and a talkie version.

McCoy continued to star in films through the '30s and into the '40s. After World War II time had passed him by, as it had so many other Western stars. In the '50s McCoy did a series of children's programs for TV that included illustrated talks on some aspect of the West or Native American history; he also showed some of his old films. These programs were innocuous, inoffensive and, at times, informative. The material about the Native American was on a simple, elemental level—somewhat like an early "Sesame Street" or "Discovery." McCoy won several awards, including an Emmy, for this series.

The role of expert consultants or technical advisors is questionable since their advice is either ill-founded or ignored. Knowledgeable technical advisors such as David Humphreys Miller or Rodd Redwing are often ignored. "Experts" such as Tim McCoy and Clyde Dollar use their "expertise" to reinforce the already existing concept of the Hollywood Indian. They know what sells.

Anthony Thomas pointed out McCoy's pride in his knowledge of things Indian:

> ... For a time McCoy was Scott's aide and accompanied him on visits to some of the Army's foremost Western posts: Forts Riley, Sill, Snelling and, particularly, Washakie in Wyoming. After Scott retired from the Army he was appointed head of the Board of Indian Commissioners and no doubt had something to do with McCoy becoming Adjutant General in Wyoming. Scott once said, "Tim knows more about the Indians than they know about themselves." In appraising that compliment one should remember McCoy's own aphorism: "The best way to find out an Indian's history is to tell it to him."

CUT TO
Dan Jorgensen interviewing Sandy Howard, producer of *A Man Called Horse*, for his article in the *Sioux Falls Argus-Leader*, April 25, 1970. Howard is speaking: Americans do not really know the Indian, and Indians themselves do not really know their past....

RE-ENTER JOHN FORD

"When The Legend Becomes Fact, Print The Legend"

John Ford, now "the grand old man of Westerns," was 29 when he directed *The Iron Horse* in 1924. From 1917 to 1924, he directed about 50 minor films, the majority of them Westerns. The first stars he worked with were Harry Carey and Hoot Gibson at Universal. He later worked with Buck Jones and Tom Mix at Fox. Indians did not figure too prominently in these early Ford Westerns, a good many of which were part of a series starring Harry Carey. When Indians did appear in the early Ford films, they were carbon copies of all other Hollywood Indians.

There was the usual Indian raid in *The Soul Herder* (1917). In *By Indian Post* (1919) an Indian, fascinated by the handwriting or "papertalk" which he sees in a love letter, unintentionally plays Cupid. In *Riders of Vengeance* (1919) the white hero is trapped by Apaches. The Mounties have trouble with some meanies who are running whiskey to the Indians in *A Fight For Love* (1919).

Appearing in *Love* was Chief John Big Tree, who was to become one of the most outstanding Native American actors.

By the time he made *The Iron Horse* (1924), the story of the building of the transcontinental railroad, Ford was already a veteran filmmaker. The picture was much better than Cruze's *The Covered Wagon* (1923) and was much more exciting. It was just as successful and grossed over a couple of million. The *New York Times* critic praised *The Iron Horse* in this review on August 29, 1924: "This is an instructive and inspiring film, one which should make every American proud of the manner of men who were responsible for great achievements in the face of danger, sickness and fatigue. They were, as we said, true sports, who worked with a vim and got satisfaction and even fun out of the hazardous labors."

The *New York Times* critic had to ignore the role of the Indian in the film. It would have been impossible to justify the white man's manifest destiny and "the manner of men who were responsible for great achievements," from the Native American's point of view. Ford, too, glossed over the red man's plight by using him as another "hazard" to the great men of

160

progress. He had the Indians charging at them like invading hounds of hell.

The Native American did fight like hell to prevent the iron horse from coming through. The transcontinental railroad plowed through his land, dividing the enormous buffalo herd which covered the continent. Thousands of slaughtered buffalo were supplied to feed the railroad workers. Buffalo Bill was one supplier. In 1868 he agreed to supply buffalo meat to construction crews. During a period of eighteen months he is said to have killed approximately 5000 buffalo, and thus earned the nickname of "Buffalo Bill."

The East was supplied with thousands of buffalo tongues as delicacies for the rich, while the carcasses remained to rot upon the plains. And thousands more provided robes to warm the laps of luxury.

A scene from Ford's *The Iron Horse* (1924) Fox. (The Museum of Modern Art/Film Stills Archive)

The U.S. government gave or sold (for a nominal fee) enormous tracts of the Native American's land to the railroad moguls; they, in turn, gave or sold some of this land to settlers, knowing that they would have to use the railroad. The travelers, in turn, shot more buffalo by the thousands to wile the time away during their long journeys. Thus ran the real saga of the invasion of the iron horse.

In *The Iron Horse* hundreds of Sioux, Cheyennes, and Pawnees were used. The costuming was in most cases exceptional, since in those days Native Americans hired for films wore their own traditional tribal dress. There were spectacular shots of Indians riding to the warpath. The sight was powerful, as was Chief Big Tree—though Ford had him shading his eyes in the standard Indian hand-to-forehead gesture.

In 1926 Ford made the popular *Three Badmen*. It was his last silent film and his last Western until *Stagecoach*. In *Three Badmen* Indians were used as nothing more than background and atmosphere, with the standard Indian village with tipis and canoes.

1939 was the year of *Stagecoach*. A highly praised and touted film, it offered a number of firsts: it was Ford's first sound Western; he and John Wayne worked together as director and star; Ford used Monument Valley for the first time.

During a conversation between directors Burt Kennedy and Ford, which was published in *Action*, the magazine of the Directors Guild of America, Kennedy asked, "How did you happen to use Monument Valley for *Stagecoach*?" Ford replied:

> I knew this guy, Harry Goulding, who had a trading post there. Once he asked me, "Did you ever think of Monument Valley for a location?" I said, "Say, that's a good idea." He said, "The Indians are starving down here, and I'm starving. They're hocking their jewelry—the turquoise things they made—so they can eat. If a movie company came down here the Indians could make some money and be able to live." I thought that was a good idea. I remembered Monument Valley when I had driven through there. So I took the company of *Stagecoach*—the first one, not the second one—down to Monument Valley and we left $200,000 down there and the Indians ended up fat and sassy. It's a wonderful location and a wonderful place to live.

David Humphreys Miller, author of *Custer's Fall* (1957), served as technical advisor on the bad remake of *Stagecoach* (1966). He offers this explanation for the spectacular climactic chase of the stagecoach by Apaches in both films:

A scene from Ford's *Stagecoach* (1939) United Artists. Note Apache costumes.

It's necessary in order to have a menace which opposes the American progress story—the march of so-called civilization. To have this progress is an underlying conflict which may be beyond and above the personal conflict which is in the drama itself. The Indian was a good conflict always to have in the background. When you brought them into the foreground, then you had to make believable characters out of them, but as long as they were in the background, they served as a convenient threat and a convenient conflict. As in *Stagecoach*, for example, where you never personalized the Indians. It was never a personal conflict. It was simply that they were raiding. Therefore, all of these people in the stagecoach were in danger—a nebulous threat.

William S. Hart once pointed out that such a chase could never have happened since Native Americans would have shot the horses first.

Peter Bogdanovich, in his book *John Ford* (1968), quotes Ford:

163

Frank Nugent was once talking to me about that film and he said, "Only one thing I can't understand about it, Jack—in the chase, why didn't the Indians just shoot the horses pulling the stagecoach?" And I said, "In actual fact that's probably what did happen, Frank, but if they had, it would have been the end of the picture, wouldn't it?"

Drums Along the Mohawk, Ford's first color film, was released in 1939. Certain vivid impressions can be recalled: Chief Big Tree's wonderful performance as Blue Back, wearing a blanket and a three-cornered hat with a feather sticking straight up; Edna May Oliver brow-beating the Indians as they carry her out of the house, bed and all; and, of course, the unforgettable race when Henry Fonda outlasts his Indian opponents in a dash across the wilderness.

A scene from Gordon Douglas' *Stagecoach* (1966) 20th Century Fox. Note the Hollywood "Instant Plains Indian Kit."

White renegade John Carradine leads the Iroquois in the Mohawk Valley against the settlers just as he had led the Delaware in *Daniel Boone* (1936, David Howard) against those settlers. The Indian in *Drums Along the Mohawk* remains faceless and unchanged. He slaughters, he dies or, as in the case of Big Tree, becomes a friend to the whites.

Ford managed to remain impartial in his treatment of the Indian in *Fort Apache* (1948) and *She Wore a Yellow Ribbon* (1949). In *Fort Apache* there's a powerful scene in which the colonel meets the Apaches and the interpreter introduces the Apache leaders, ending up with Geronimo. It was very clear that now that the formidable Geronimo was there, the army was going to get theirs.

In *She Wore a Yellow Ribbon*, Chief John Big Tree plays a leader too old to fight or control his young men who do want to fight. John Wayne—an old army officer about to retire—and Big Tree had once been foes, yet they had always respected each other's abilities. Now old, they are friends as they agree that fighting must be left to the young. Big Tree's scene with Wayne, in which he professes his Christianity and exhorts Wayne to get drunk with him, was nothing less than beautiful.

By 1950, despite the excellence of *Wagon Master*, there seems to have been a change. Racism, sometimes subtle, sometimes not, crept into Ford's approach to the Indian. *Rio Grande* (1950) has the customary attack on a wagon train, captured white children, drunken Indians, a crooked white trader, plus a vengeful cavalry charging into an unsuspecting Indian village.

The Searchers (1956) is a film about a white girl captive among the Comanches. Natalie Wood, playing the girl, had seen her family being slaughtered by the Comanches and watched while her sister was raped. She remained a captive for many years, witnessing Ford's Indians' brutality, cruelty, and lechery. Racism, heretofore only implied by the characterization of the Indians, becomes blatant by the time she is finally discovered by John Wayne and is found to be happily wived to Chief Scar, the ruthless leader of the Comanches. That she could be in any state of happiness after witnessing so many horrors is completely repugnant to the white rescuers, who feel that death would have been preferable to becoming a squaw. At the end of the film she is swept up into Wayne's arms and we know that

165

they will live happily ever after. The old man is taking her home to family and civilization.

Sergeant Rutledge (1960) ranks as one of the worst films Ford ever made. He uses the faceless red man in order to exploit black and white relationships. Raiding Indians serve as a device for getting. a black soldier and a white woman to spend a night together in a railway station. In later scenes the Indians are again the faceless enemy who, this time, fight the black 9th and

From the *Sergeant Rutledge* pressbook.

10th Cavalries. The publicity for the picture stated that the Indians called black cavalrymen "buffalo soldiers" because of the winter coats they wore made of buffalo robes. Another reason given in school books is that the Indians honored the heroism and fierce fighting prowess of the black by bestowing the name of their sacred animal upon them. Actually, they were called "buffalo soldiers" because Native Americans thought the blacks' hair closely resembled the hair of the buffalo.

Another film *Two Rode Together* (1961) concerned the captivity of several white children among the Comanches. This, according to the film's equation, would make life as a captive several times worse than it had been in *The Searchers*. Woody Strode, black man turned red, who played Sgt. Rutledge the previous year, appeared as Stone Calf, a fierce white-hater who was given to much chest thumping and arm raising while entreating the Indians to go on the warpath. Ford's Indians were becoming cruel and horrific. Henry Brandon, a magnificently evil-looking man, played Chief Scar in *The Searchers* and Quannah Parker in *Two Rode Together*. His cold, cruel look and harsh, metallic voice chilled the marrow of our bones.

CUT TO

A page from the pressbook of *Cheyenne Autumn* (1964) which is bannered: "WORLD PRESS, FILM STARS CONVENE IN

CHEYENNE." We hear the following in Voice Over: "To coincide with the nation's observance of American Landmarks Week.., Warner Bros. staged the press premiere of 'CHEYENNE AUTUMN' in Cheyenne, Wyoming, the main urban center of the 1500-mile area traversed by the heroic Indians whose story is told in the film .... During the event, the Cheyenne Autumn Trail which the freedom-seeking Cheyenne followed, was officially dedicated as a place of national interest ...."

It does one's heart good to know that an area in which Cheyennes were hounded, frozen, and starved to death has at least been designated "a place of national interest."

Cheyenne Autumn was long and unbelievable, especially the Indian caricatures played by whites. Andrew Sarris, in *The American Cinema* (1968), offered this opinion: "*Cheyenne Autumn* is a failure simply because Ford cannot get inside the Indians he is trying to ennoble." But it was more than that. The picture proved to be nothing but a vehicle for an all-star cast: Victor Jory as Tall Tree, Gilbert Roland as Dull Knife, Ricardo Montalban as Little Wolf, Delores Del Rio as Spanish Woman, and Sal Mineo as Red Shirt.

A scene from Ford's *Cheyenne Autumn* (1964) Warner Bros.

168

Stanley Kauffman's review of the film in his *A World on Film* (1966) said in part: "The cast is beyond disbelief . . . . Sal Mineo, as a proud Cheyenne brave, acts like a reject from a road company of *West Side Story*."

The screenplay, as the official credits read, "suggested" by *Cheyenne Autumn* (1953), a touching novel by Mari Sandoz, was changed into a Hollywood grab-bag.

In Bogdanovich's book, Ford said about *Cheyenne Autumn*:

> I had wanted to make it for a long time. I've killed more Indians than Custer, Beecher and Chivington put together, and people in Europe always want to know about the Indians. There are two sides to every story, but I wanted to show their point of view for a change. Let's face it, we've treated them very badly—it's a blot on our shield; we've cheated and robbed, killed, murdered, massacred and everything else, but they kill one white man and, God, out come the troops.

The story of *Cheyenne Autumn*, as told briefly in the film's pressbook, was ". . . the heretofore obscure 1878 saga of a small, determined band of Cheyenne Indians who during an extremely bitter winter marched 1500 miles from a barren Oklahoma reservation to freedom and a better life in their own Northwest homeland."

Mari Sandoz's long involvement with and empathy for the Native American produced, among other works, *Cheyenne Autumn*. The motives, as expressed by Ford, for putting her book on film seem fine. The difference between the two creators lies primarily in the quality and depth of their perceptions. Mari Sandoz was able to identify totally with different Native Americans and deal with them as individuals of various cultures, religions, and contrasting views. Using the novel as a narrative form, she was able to translate the history of the Cheyennes into a personal tragic experience for all.

The *Times-Herald* of Alliance, Nebraska, printed in 1965 an Associated Press story on Mari Sandoz, in which she commented on *Cheyenne Autumn*:

> She said she was "terribly disappointed" with the film version. It is the story of how the remnants of the Cheyenne Indian tribe leave their reservation after U.S. government promises of help are not forthcoming and how they are pursued by soldiers trying to get them to return.
> "It was a bad picture," said Miss Sandoz. "They made it slow and dreadful, and this was a story of a great pursuit. I

169

don't see how you can make a slow story about one of the great chases of history. They made it dull."

She also complained that the movie "took great liberties with the great men of the tribe," attributing to them acts which they never did. She said the movie "besmirched their characters."

The following is from a letter received by the authors from Mrs. Hila Gilbert, an author from Sheridan, Wyoming, and a friend of Mari Sandoz who also has many close ties among the Cheyenne:

> I took a Cheyenne friend of mine to see the movie. Her great-aunt was one of those wounded at Ft. Robinson in the outbreak when the Cheyennes were attempting to go home. She does not speak English and I know very little Cheyenne. However, she made most expressive little "Nah" sounds all through the movie. Later her daughter said they were not talking Cheyenne in the movie, that the story was not true and they were not like Cheyennes.
>
> The Wild Hog family, great grandchildren and grand-children of Chief Little Wolf, asked me to see what I could do for them because they had heard the movie was "not like our mother told us." Their mother, Lydia Wild-Hog, daughter of Chief Little Wolf, was a small child of eight on the trek back from Oklahoma and told of hiding in the day and traveling at night. They are very proud people and were most unhappy at the misrepresentation in the movie, especially when Little Wolf was depicted as killing the son of Dull Knife. I wrote to Warner Brothers telling them of the family's objections and of their poverty, but never received a reply. A local lawyer agreed to consider hand-ling the suit, but after research revealed that such cases involving slander of a dead person had failed, he advised dropping it.

Ford once said in an interview, "I've always wanted to show the Indian side . . . . They are a very dignified people . . . ."

The Indians used in *Cheyenne Autumn* were Navajos. Those same Navajos were used by Ford in various films to portray every other Native American tribe. Here, they are Cheyennes who are supposed to cross the plains. However, being in Monument Valley, they cross a desert—and so it goes.

CUT TO

A group of men seated behind a table. They are there, as is the audience, to pay tribute to John Ford at the University of California in Los Angeles. One of the panelists is Ford, who is talking about *Cheyenne Autumn*:

I don't want to sound like I'm plugging it but I think it's pretty good. It's a true story about the Cheyennes and how they outwitted the whole US Army in their retreat across the middle part of this country.

I liked the story and caught Jack Warner in a weak moment. He agreed to let me do it. People in Europe and other parts of the world always ask me about the Indians—what they were really like, their culture, their history. I've long wanted to do a story that tells the truth about them and not just a picture in which they're chased by the cavalry. I think we did that in this new picture. I hope we did.

NOW YOU SEE THEM—NOW YOU HEAR THEM

SCENE XVI

1926-1950

CUT TO
A Montage from 1926 movies: *Buffalo Bill on the U. P. Trail, The Flaming Forest, The Flaming Frontier, Fort Frayne, The Frontier Trail, General Custer at Little Big Horn, Hands Up!, The Last Frontier, Moran of the Mounted, Pony Express Rider, Prisoners of the Storm, Ransom's Folly, Tom and His Pals, Under Fire, War Paint.*

Braveheart (Alan Hale) was released in 1926, as Westerns continued on the upswing. Rod La Rocque played the old reliable college-football-Indian-hero who goes back to rule his tribe.

One of the most incredible films ever made was *The Devil Horse* (Fred Jackman), produced and written by Hal Roach. It told of a boy and his colt who are separated from each other by an Indian raid on the wagon train. The colt, who is taken by the Indians, grows up to hate all Indians. The boy, escaping capture, grows up hating all Indians because his horse was taken from him. Many human prejudices and emotions are expressed by the horse, who is given all sorts of anthropomorphic characteristics. If given half a chance this horse could have exterminated the entire Indian population by itself. Roach should have stuck to intentional comedy.

George B. Seitz, capitalizing on *The Vanishing American*, came up with *The Last Frontier*, with the by then almost mandatory large scale panoramic Indian fights. *The Flaming Frontier* (Edward Sedgwick) told once again of Custer's last

173

stand. Custer had many stands to go before ever getting close to his last.

Bugeyed Frank Lackteen (in bonnet) and buckskinned William Boyd in *The Last Frontier* (1926). (The Museum of Modern Art/Film Stills Archive)

And there were Indians in: *Prisoners of the Storm, Tom and His Pals, War Feathers, War Paint,* and *Hands Up!* (Clarence Badger), where the white hero teaches his Indian captors to dance the Charleston.

CUT TO
A Montage from 1927 movies: *Arizona Nights, The Bugle Call, The Devil's Saddle, Drums of the Desert, King of the Herd, Men of Daring, Open Range, The Overland Stage, Red Clay, Red Raiders, Sitting Bull at the "Spirit Lake Massacre", Spoilers of the West, Winners of the Wilderness, The Frontiersman, The Last Trail.*

Tom Mix, starring in *The Last Trail* (Lewis Seiler), in which the Indian fight made a good "opening scene," was getting competition from Ken Maynard, while Mix's white horse, Tony, was getting stiff competition from Maynard's, Tarzan.

It was with some trepidation that we attended "The Western" special event at the 1968 Lincoln Center Film Festival, where an excerpt from Maynard's *Red Raiders* (Albert Rogell) was being shown. William K. Everson, in his program notes for the event, commented:

"Red Raiders" is that extreme rarity, a western without even a nominal white villain—not even a renegade trader selling firewater to the indians! [sic] As such, it is a perfect example of the later cliched depiction of the indian [sic] as a convenient, dehumanized *mass* villain who could be mowed down without any second thoughts, despite the brotherhood and peace-treaties espoused in the brief fadeout scene . . . .

In contrast to the good Indian, a film's tribe had to have a hot-blooded Indian renegade who wanted to war against the whites. For further conflict, the hot-blood could be the son, brother, friend, rival of the chief who wants peace, or an outcast, a rejected suitor, a wild youth. And, in some cases the hot-blood could be the chief himself, as was the case in *Red Raiders.*

CUT TO
A Montage from 1928 movies: *The Glorious Trail, Kit Carson, Orphan of the Sage, The Riding Renegade, Rose-Marie, The Water Hole, Wyoming.*

Ramona (Edwin Carewe) was remade once more. This time around we got a film and a hit song of the same name.

Sheet music cover, 1928.

Hollywood reacted to the advent of sound with turmoil, confusion, and resistance. Some studios tried to combat the inevitability of sound with other technical achievements, by experimenting with color, wide screen processes, and 3-D.

CUT TO
A Montage from 1929 movies: *False Fathers, The Invaders, The Overland Telegraph, Sioux Blood, Wolf Song.*

In 1929 Richard Dix tried to repeat his acting triumph in *The Vanishing American* with an early two-color Technicolor processed *Redskin* (Victor Schertzinger). However, the picture was greatly hampered, if not paralyzed, by an antiquated story. Wing Foot, a Navajo (Dix), loves Corn Blossom, a Pueblo (Gladys Belmont). He goes on to college and is scorned by the white students. For whatever it was worth, the only advantage this picture had to offer was that now it was possible to see the redskins' red skins.

CUT TO
A flyer for the 1970 Lincoln Center Film Festival. The camera picks out "Special Events III" and "Cinema and Color" and then zooms in on the following:
WESTERN UNION (1941)
Directed by Fritz Lang and photographed in Technicolor by Edward Cronjager and Allen M. Davey. Known as the first Western to show Indian war paint in color, this is one of Lang's personal favorites, partly because of its experimental technique, but also because, though a foreigner, he was considered to have captured the essence of the Old West . . . .

CUT TO
A Montage from 1930 movies: *The Santa Fe Trail, The Big Trail, The Silent Enemy, Spurs, Way Out West.*

In 1930 the semi-documentary *The Silent Enemy* (H. P. Carver) was released without sound. This stunning film told of the Ojibways' difficult and eternal struggle for survival. One of the leads was played by Chauncy Yellow Robe, a relative of Sitting Bull, who had voiced such strong objections to the misuse of Native Americans in Wild West Shows and movies in 1913. He also appeared in the talkie short which preceded the feature. Using excerpts, he described how *The Silent Enemy* was made.

The Big Trail (1930, Raoul Walsh) was filmed in sound and was one of the early experiments in wide-screen, 70mm projection. The audience could not only see and hear the Indians attack the wagon train but they could watch John Wayne, for the first time, give the Indians theirs on a wide screen.

Sound revolutionized the making of movies but the Indians

in them retained their filmic origins. The same DUM-dum-dum-dum, DUM-dum-dum-dum music was transferred and elaborated upon on the soundtrack; the same story line continued while now you could actually hear the warwhoops and "Ugh, me get 'um firewater. Ugh, me take 'um scalp." Such lines had previously been written in subtitles; actually hearing them made the caricature totally and irrevocable complete.

Even when attempting to do a modern story, Hollywood often uses "ugh" dialogue. *Black Gold* (1947, Phil Karlson) is the supposedly true story of a Native American-owned horse, Black Gold, who eventually runs in the Kentucky Derby. Even in this modern film, Anthony Quinn "ugs" his way through as the Indian hero.

When film makers want to steer clear of "ughing," they head directly for another rocky shore. They get bogged down in pseudo-poetic dialogue. Writers attempt to improve or embellish the simple beauty of Native American speech. Chief Joseph, leader of the Nez Perce, surrendered to Gen. O. O. Howard on October 5, 1877, after they had been pursued by the Army in a five-month, thirteen-hundred-mile running fight. Joseph and his people were hoping to reach Canada and find refuge there. His famous surrender speech will best illustrate the distinctive way in which the Native American expressed himself:

> Tell General Howard I know his heart. What he told me before I have in my heart. I am tired of fighting. Our chiefs are killed. Looking Glass is dead. The old men are all killed. It is the young men who say yes or no. He who led the young men is dead. It is cold and we have no blankets. The little children are freezing to death. My people, some of them, have run away to the hills and have no blankets, no food; no one knows where they are, perhaps freezing to death. I want time to look for my children and see how many of them I can find. Maybe I shall find them among the dead. Hear me, my chiefs, I am tired; my heart is sick and sad. From where the sun now stands, I will fight no more forever.

VOICE OVER:
This excerpt from *A Man Called Horse,* which appeared in the company's *Production Notes:*
   . . . Running Deer tells Lord John in Sioux that she knows someday he will leave her; what she is saying is: "Like the sun, my lover dazzles all who look at him. Like the moon, I reflect his shining light. But the time comes when the sun departs beyond

the mountains and the moon must wane and grow cold alone in the night sky."

Still another school of dialogue sounded more like Biblical parables: A chief might say to his hot-blooded son who wants to fight the whites, "The bear has the strength to fight many but it is the rabbit who knows when to run away." His son, thinking his father has become a coward, might retort, "The rabbit may run but it is the dog that creeps with his tail between his legs." To which his wise old father might answer, "The little pup will bark at anything but the owl hoots only when necessary." Sometimes this kind of dialogue can take up a good percentage of a picture as it did in *Mohawk* (1956, Kurt Neumann).

In many movies we hear the Indians speaking in what is supposed to be their native tongue. Cullison Cady, in his article "Return of the Redskins," the *New York Times*, April 23, 1939, tells this tale:

> ... there was the case of the director who, upon hearing a sound track of Indian dialogue on a certain strip of film, decided that it didn't sound "Indian enough." To solve the problem, he had the Indians speak English in a retake, and then ran the sound track backward. The verdict on the resultant gibberish was thoroughly acceptable.

The dialogue spoken by the Indians in *A Man Called Horse* (1970) was in the Sioux language. In order to help the non-Sioux actors to understand what they were saying, translations were provided for them. The following brief exchange took place between Dame Judith Anderson, playing Buffalo Cow Head, and her son Yellow Hand, played by Manu Tupou:

She:
   What kind of animal did you give me?
He:
   It's a horse! What did you expect, a herd of buffalo?

CUT TO
A Montage from 1931 movies: *The Rainbow Trail, Thoroughbreds, The Conquering Horde, Red Fork Range, Trails of Golden West, Cimarron, The Squaw Man, Fighting Caravans.*

De Mille, taking advantage of sound, remade *The Squaw Man* one more time. The public could now hear as well as see this "great classic." In addition to seeing and hearing Lupe Velez playing an Indian maiden once more, little Dickie Moore could also be seen as her mixed blood son—sired by Warner Baxter.

CUT TO
A Montage from 1932 movies: *The Golden West, Telegraph Trail, White Eagle, Call Her Savage, Oklahoma Jim*; and such serials as *Heroes of the West, The Last Frontier, The Last of the Mohicans.*

CUT TO
A Montage from the 1933 serials *Fighting with Kit Carson* and *Clancy of the Mounted.*

GO NAVAJO

COSTUMES: Stage a special matinee for kids who come dressed in complete Western garb . . . cowboy or Indian. Publicize the show through stores selling children's Western merchandise. Give youngsters promoted souvenirs.

GIVEAWAY: Arrange giveaway of black arrows (real or simulated) to your patrons. Each arrow has a tag which reads: *"Here's a Reminder to See 'Black Arrow,' Starting Friday at the State Theatre!"* You might also have a pretty girl distribute arrows around town.

SIGNALS: Have an Indian send out smoke signals in front of your theatre opening day of each chapter. Publicize his performance via press, radio and TV. An alternate suggestion is to have him beat out "authentic rhythms of the Navajo Indians" on a tom-tom.

BALLY: Send out a young man in typical Indian attire through town with a sign on his back reading: *"I'm Joining 'Black Arrow' Friday at the State Theatre."*

INDIAN FRONT: Lend authentic Indian atmosphere out front by transforming your boxoffice into a full-fledged tribal wigwam. This can best be accomplished by mounting an old canvas upon a framework of rods and painting tepee with colorful Indian symbols and insignias. Enhance front with display of Indian paraphernalia borrowed from local museums.

INDIAN SUITS: Children's clothing and department stores sell Indian suits which can be linked with your showing of "Black Arrow." Arrange co-op ads and windows boosting the sale of the suits and your credits.

From the pressbook for the serial *Black Arrow* (1944) Columbia.

SCARLET FOR A CHAMPION

Chapter 1

The SCARLET HORSEMAN

A UNIVERSAL SERIAL   46/4000

Exhibitors display card

Western serials began with *Perils of Pauline* (1914), reached their zenith in the '30s, and ended with *Blazing the Overland Trail* (1956). The ultimate in captive audiences was created. "Continued next week" was the snare that brought millions of children into movie theatres every week. And every week they saw yet another chapter with the most horrific Indians ever created in any medium.

CUT TO
A large city in the 1930s. A movie marquee reads: "Now Big Double Feature—Two Big Pictures for the Price of One."

The Depression hit the film industry as it did the rest of America. To get its share of the scarce buck, the industry turned to double features. And so the "B" pictures were born, many of them Westerns. They were cheaply made and brought in big profits. Saturday night at the movies became an American institution. And for the kids, there was always the Saturday matinee.

181

An ad for the last of the Western serials.

Remember? Our mothers would pack our lunches and then
pack us off at 10 AM to the Saturday matinee—an all-day ritual

of a double feature, a serial or two, and a few cartoons. We'd come home at 5 PM bleary-eyed, tired, happy, and hoarse, having booed the Indian and cheered our hero to our hearts' content. We had enough inspiration to keep us going wildly at cowboys and Indians until the following Saturday. We saw and we believed. And we learned our catechism well. The Indian was dirty, bad, evil, mean, cruel, shiftless, crafty, devilish or just not nice.

A scene from *Massacre* (1934) First National.

CUT TO
A Montage from 1934 movies: *The Star Packer, Wagon Wheels, Wheels of Destiny, West of the Pecos, The Miracle Rider.*

In 1934 a film version of Oliver LaFarge's Pulitzer prize novel, *Laughing Boy*, was made. The pressbook for *Laughing Boy* (W. S. Van Dyke) enticed the exhibitors with:

Ramon Novarro, the singing prince of romance, now a handsome, dashing Indian! And wait until your audiences hear him sing "Call of Love"!
Opposite him the magnetic, exotic and beautiful Lupe Velez in one of the finest, most beautiful and dramatic love stories ever written or filmed.

There is a very strong parallel between *Massacre* (Alan Crosland), made in 1934, and *The Vanishing American*, made in 1926. Both were highly praised; both were made for the same reasons, to champion the Indian cause; both were made in troubled times and included the same mistakes. Future sympathetic films in the '60s were to continue making these same mistakes. By showing the inhumanity of the whites, one was logically expected to feel compassion for the Indian. *The Vanishing American, Massacre, Broken Arrow, A Man Called Horse, Tell Them Willie Boy Is Here, Soldier Blue,* and *Little Big Man* were created to serve the same function—there's nothing America likes better than rooting for an underdog.

Massacre, like *The Vanishing American*, was a film that failed to achieve its desired goal. The white villains, who are officials of the federal government, are again too villainous to be believable. The films put the blame on corrupt officials instead of the government which appointed them. *Massacre*, which supposedly championed tolerance in inter-racial relationships, unwittingly revealed itself as racist. The hero, an Indian and a rodeo star, employs a black valet. The role of the valet was written, typically, for comic relief.

In 1956 another film called *Massacre* (Louis King) was released. This was not a remake of the original even though Indians were involved. The later version concerned gun-running to the redskins.

CUT TO
The movie theatre on a now almost deserted street. The marquee reads: "Big Triple Feature—See 3-Three-3-Big Pictures—Pay For One."
CUT TO
A Montage from 1935 movies: *Behold My Wife, Annie Oakley, Wanderer of the Wasteland, Custer's Last Stand, Rustlers' of Red Gap.*

Behold My Wife (Mitchell Leisen) brought the squaw man theme up-to-date by asking the question of whether an Indian maiden, Sylvia Sidney, from a little reservation out West could find true happiness as the wife of a wealthy Easterner, Gene Raymond. The Original *Behold My Wife* had been made in 1921 under George Melford's direction, but the theme seemed more timely now during the Depression. There was a popular cycle of films concerning poor but nice girls who marry into rich but haughty families.

In *Annie Oakley* (George Stevens) Barbara Stanwyck, Preston Foster, and Melvyn Douglas get star billing, but it is Chief Thunderbird, giving a very real, very warm portrayal of Sitting Bull, who walks away with the picture.

A bizarre musical routine from the 1954 remake of *Rose Marie* MGM. (Theatre Collection, New York Public Library)

CUT TO
A Montage from 1936 movies: *Daniel Boone, For the Service, The Last of the Mohicans, The Phantom Rider, The Plainsman, Ramona, Rose Marie, The Texas Rangers, Trailin' West, West of Nevada, Treachery Rides the Range, The Glory Trail, Desert Gold.*

1936 yielded a bumper crop. In addition to the serials and the "B" programmers, Nelson Eddy and Jeanette MacDonald in *Rose Marie* (W.S. Van Dyke) harmonized all over the Canadian

185

Northwest while the Mounties got their men: red or white. In 1954 Mervyn LeRoy directed a terrible remake with Ann Blyth and Howard Keel. Mounties and Indians were another winning combination, with or without music.

As with *Rose Marie*, Indians were used in musical interludes or for comic relief. The musical Western was to become a successful new genre. The two best known chanticleers associated with the West and music are Gene Autry and Roy Rogers.

Don Ameche is the one in the middle in *Ramona* (1936) 20th Century Fox. (The Museum of Modern Art/Film Stills Archive)

Hollywood, having assuaged its conscience by filming a story about the Sioux in *Massacre* in 1934, decided in 1936 to shed crocodile tears for the Cheyenne in *Treachery Rides the Range* (Frank McDonald), which featured Jim Thorpe as Chief Red Smoke. It was all about mean white buffalo hunters who stir up trouble between the Cheyennes and the cavalry so that they can continue to shoot the buffalo. In the same spirit of atonement, *Ramona* (Henry King) reared her by now familiar head for the fifth time. In this go around, Loretta Young played Ramona as a Technicolored porcelain doll. Don Ameche as Alessandro wore the funniest looking Prince Valiant fright wig imaginable, proving that a wig does an Indian make.

Another famous character also reappeared. Daniel Boone, played by George O'Brien in *Daniel Boone* (David Howard), fights the Delawares in typical heroic fashion, prompting *Variety* to state that it was "Indian opera a la mode."

And this year saw *The Last of the Mohicans* (George B. Seitz) in its third remake. In a review signed J. T. M., in the *New York Times* of September 3, 1936, it was said that technical aid was required from"...Boy Scouts to teach the modern Redskins how to whoop and holler in the accepted James Fenimore Cooper manner." Further on the review states that "the massacre of Fort William Henry is by far the bloodiest, scalpingest morsel of cinematic imagery ever produced."

orge B. Seitz's *The Last of the Mohicans* (1936) United Artists. Note similarity to illustrations from De Mille's *Unconquered* and Griffith's *America*. (The Museum of dern Art/Film Stills Archive)

Writers just loved to have the Indians attack forts. In *Daniel Boone* the Indians attack the fort for nine days and finally set fire to it with fire bundles and arrows. Then it starts to rain, putting out the fires. And the Indians? . . .Foiled again.

According to some historians in the National Parks Service, there were probably no more than six full-scale attacks on Western forts between 1850 and 1890. This is the period in which the majority of Hollywood Westerns are set. Native Americans, contrary to popular belief, avoided confrontations with the military unless directly provoked.

> CUT TO
> Rod Taylor, producer and star of *Chuka* (1967, Gordon Douglas) being interviewed for the picture's pressbook. He is speaking: "I read it (Richard Jessup's novel) and I was hooked immediately. It was a Western with no cliches, and if there's anything I can't stand, it's cliches.
>
> It was just what I wanted, a realistic account of an Indian attack on a prairie fort . . .
>
> CUT BACK TO
> The theatre marquee. It reads: "Free Dishes—To All Ladies—Free Dishes—Every Wednesday."
>
> CUT TO
> Scenes from 1937 films: *The Glory Trail, Prairie Thunder, Ride, Ranger, Ride, Riders of the Dawn, Roll Wagons Roll, Wells Fargo.*
>
> CUT BACK TO
> The theatre marquee, which now reads: "Bingo—Bingo—Bingo—Every Thursday—Win $100—Everybody Plays Bingo on Thursday."
>
> CUT TO
> Scenes from 1938 films: *Arizona Frontier, Flaming Frontier, The Great Adventures of Wild Bill Hickok, The Law West of Tombstone, Overland Express, The Texans, The Lone Ranger.*

Probably the most famous fictional Indian character in the world today is the Lone Ranger's sidekick, Tonto, whose name in Spanish means a fool, a dunce, or a dolt. The series started on radio in 1933. *The Lone Ranger* later appeared in movies and as a successful television series. Tonto became the butt of many a joke but also became synonymous with the American Indian.

In its unsuccessful campaign to improve television's depiction of the Indian, in 1960 The Association on American Indian Affairs noted that "The Lone Ranger" was one of "the most authentic portrayals of frontier life." It was also noted that the masked rider's faithful Indian companion, Tonto, is accorded "co-hero status." The present administration of the Association does not feel that such recognition should have been given to this show.

Certainly children loved the masked rider and his faithful Indian companion. But, let's face it—Tonto's a fink. He is like those faithful family retainers who remained loyal to their masters in those after-the-Civil-War pictures. At best, Tonto was an Indian Stepin Fetchit who went around saying "Me . . . White man friend," instead of "Yozzur, boss."

CUT TO
A Montage of scenes from 1939 movies: *Allegheny Uprising, Bad Lands, Drums Along the Mohawk, Frontier Marshal, Geronimo, Man of Conquest, Oregon Trail, Stagecoach, Susannah of the Mounties, Union Pacific.*

CUT BACK TO
The theatre marquee which now reads: "Shirley Temple Look-Alike Contest—Your Child May Win—Free Trip To Hollywood—Contest Saturday Nite."

Shirley Temple in *Susannah of the Mounties* (1939) 20th Century Fox.

In 1939 Shirley Temple sang and danced her way into the hearts of the Blackfoot in *Susannah of the Mounties* (William Seiter). While doing so she also managed to save Randolph Scott from being burned at the stake, kept the Blackfoot at peace with the Mounties, and acquired an Indian boyfriend.

During the Depression, the government did not forget the Native American; as a result, the Works Progress Administration (WPA) gave some of them employment. The *Brooklyn Daily Eagle*, June 4, 1939, reported:

> No circus is complete without a Wild West display and this year the WPA circus has secured the services of Chief White Cloud and his congress of full-blooded Mohawk Braves, cowboys and cowgirls. In a display titled "The Last Frontier," Chief White Cloud and his congress of Rough Riders, Indians and cowgirls recreated the sports and pastimes of the old Far West that was.

As already noted, European interest in the Native American was obsessive. In 1939 the *American Weekly* published the article "Playing Red Indian on the Blue Danube," which was about an Indian Club in Visegrad, Hungary. It has been estimated that by 1970 there were some 1200 Indian Clubs in West Germany with their own frontier towns and Indian villages. England has many Indian Clubs as well. France has some 700 such clubs. There is an Indian village near Paris called *La Vallee des Peaux Rouges*, which has become quite a tourist attraction. This explained the appearance of an Indian series on French TV called "Les Indiens." In attempting to correct Hollywood's conception of the Indian, Pierre Viallet, the writer and director, created his own Gallic myth.

CUT TO
A page in the *New York Daily News*, April 4, 1939, showing a picture of Chief Thunder Cloud, who played the title role in *Geronimo* (1939) sitting under a sun-lamp. The caption reads: "Lily-gilder?—Chief Thunder Cloud, through whose veins runs the blood of a thousand generations of Cherokee Indians, takes a sun-lamp treatment in Hollywood. It seems he's not ruddy enough to play redskin roles in films."

Geronimo (Paul H. Sloane) was a rehash of *Lives of a Bengal Lancer* which included everything: stock shots from many other

Indian pictures and dialogue from the original. East Indians became Apaches and the Bengal Lancers became U.S. Cavalry. *Bad Lands* (Lew Landers), a rehash of Ford's *The Lost Patrol*, traded the Arabian desert for Arizona and Arabs for Apaches.

The story of Wyatt Earp, *Frontier Marshal* (1939, Lew Seiler), was to be remade in 1946 by Ford as *My Darling Clementine.* In each, Earp goes into a saloon to bring out a drunken Indian and in each the Indian was played by the same Native American actor, Charles Stevens.

I'M ALL SET FOR A POW·WOW

1940's pin-up art.

Liquor was used as a means of getting Indians to go on a rampage or as a vehicle for comic relief. At no time has the problem of drinking among Native Americans been seriously explored in films.

In 1965 the Calvert Distillers Co. had a nationwide campaign planned showing an Indian in full regalia holding a glass of whisky. The caption read: "If the Sioux had a soft whisky, they couldn't have called it firewater."

The idea infuriated many people. The National Congress of the American Indian, the Association on American Indian Affairs, the Tribal Indian Land Rights Association, many Tribal Councils, and thousands of individual Native Americans and whites protested and enough pressure was exerted so that the ad was withdrawn immediately.

The word "firewater" may be amusing to some, but for the Native American its meaning was quite explicit. Traders diluted alcohol to make it go further, then added almost anything to give their concoction a kick. This would not only make Native Americans drunk but, in many cases, it would also make them dead. Bruce Nelson in *Land of the Dacotahs* (1946) gives one recipe for "firewater:"

    1 quart of alcohol
    1 pound of rank, black chewing tobacco
    1 handful red peppers
    1 bottle Jamaica Ginger
    1 quart black molasses

Water from the Missouri River *ad libitum*. Mix well until all the strength is drawn from the tobacco and peppers.

> CUT TO
> A Montage from 1940 movies: *Kit Carson, Wyoming, Pioneers of the West, North West Mounted Police, Santa Fe Trail, Wagons Westward, Young Buffalo Bill, Northwest Passage, Hi-Yo Silver, Winners of the West, Prairie Schooners, Pony Post, Brigham Young, Arizona Frontier, Colorado.*
>
> CUT TO
> A sequence from *Go West* (1940, Edward Buzzell) in which the Marx Brothers meet the Indians.
>
> CUT TO
> A Sequence from *My Little Chickadee* (1940, Edward Cline) in which W. C. Fields and Mae West meet the Indians.

Indians fared equally as well in comedies as in any other type of Indian film. Whether the Indians were impersonated by Joey

Bishop or Buddy Hackett, or were fall guys for the Three Stooges, Bob Hope, or Abbott and Costello, Hollywood's desperation to be funny about its own creations was close to derangement.

In 1940 Indians were still raiding settlers, as in *Wyoming* (Richard Thorpe). They were still attacking wagon trains, as in *Pioneers of the West* (Lester Orlebeck). This was one of the many films in the popular Three Mesquiteers series. In this movie the Mesquiteers were played by Bob Livingston, Raymond Hatton, and Duncan Renaldo. In *Kit Carson* (George B. Seitz) the Indians continued their attempt to beat the Army.

The Marx Brothers meet the Indians in *Go West* (1940)

The country was coming out of a Depression and going into a Second World War. Hollywood semingly responded to the frustration and aggression of the public by making a particularly vicious and vehemently anti-Native American film, *Northwest Passage* (King Vidor). In this film revenge for the torture and death of one white man is the sole justification given for Rogers' Rangers to wipe out an entire Native American village. The whole point of this bloody film is to justify and advocate genocide. The film was based on fact. The actual raid did all but exterminate the entire Abenaki tribe.

CUT TO
A Montage from 1941 movies: *Badlands of Dakota, Hudson's Bay, The Pioneers, The Roundup, Thunder Over the Prairie, Unconquered, Western Union, White Eagle, Go West, Young Lady, Silver Stallion.*

Hollywood continued killing the Indian in the name of patriotism. In *They Died With Their Boots On* (1941, Raoul Walsh), another story of Custer, the Indians' victory was only a minor one, a fluke. All sympathy was given to Errol Flynn as Custer. The picture had that Indian music and those Hollywood Indian costumes, too. The utter absurdity of Hollywood Indians wearing full-feathered bonnets in war was illustrated in *Boots*, as one Indian tried to hide in the grass with his feathers showing. In reality Native Americans, in order to have as much freedom as possible, wore as little as possible, while in Hollywood the Indians don piles of regalia like the colorful creatures they're supposed to be.

A shipboard scene from *This Woman is Mine* (1941). This film was re-released in 1949 as *Fury at Sea.*

The only claim to originality of *This Woman is Mine* (1941, Frank Lloyd), is that in this film, instead of attacking wagon trains, forts, et al., the Indians attack and burn a sailing ship. Rarely did writers deviate from standard Indian themes. Some other exceptions were: an Indian attack on a funeral wagon train in *The Deadly Companions* (1962, Sam Peckinpah); *Naked in the Sun* (1957, R. John Hugh) involves a subject covered, to our knowledge, only once before, in *The Romance of the Utah Pioneers* (1913)—the enslavement of the Native American. In both films it is the Spanish or Mexicans, and not the Anglo-Saxons, who are the slave traders.

Slavery, a handmaiden to genocide, flourished in the colonies. Spaniards, French, English, and Dutch all profited greatly from the sale of "savages." It should be noted that acquiring "savages" for the slave trade was always difficult. Resisting enslavement, in many cases, resulted in the total extermination of many Native American tribes. Sometimes a few Native American children survived and were easily sold into slavery. As a consequence, almost all Northeastern and Southeastern tribes no longer exist—neither do films portraying the enslavement and eradication of these and other tribes.

CUT TO
A Montage from 1942 movies: *Apache Trail, Ten Gentlemen from West Point, Lawless Plainsmen, Overland Mail, Ride 'Em Cowboy, Valley of the Sun, Dawn on the Great Divide, The Omaha Trail, King of the Stallions, Pierre of the Plains, Perils of the Royal Mounted.*

The war hampered Hollywood production somewhat. Because of the shortage of manpower, rampaging Indians were fewer and further apart.

Hubbard Keavy wrote an article about the filming of *Valley of the Sun* in Taos, New Mexico, using Taos Native Americans under their leader, Governor Juan Concha. The article appeared in the *Milwaukee Journal*, October 23, 1941:

The rate of pay agreed upon was $4 a day for braves, $3 for squaws and $2.50 for papooses. Those who furnished their own horses were paid $1.50 a day additional. Those who provided their own transportation to and from the scenes of the filming, several miles from the pueblo, were paid another $1.50 . . . .

This picture being made here is not about the Taos Indians or even the Taos artists' colony. It is "Valley in the

Sun," which has to do with the founding of Phoenix, Ariz. But here is breathtaking scenery . . . which George Marshall, the director, insisted he could not find in Arizona.

Marshall also liked the Indians. Many he saw in Arizona and elsewhere in New Mexico appeared 5 feet tall, or less. The Taos men are tall, not 6 footers by any means, such as the average moviegoer fancies all Indians are.

It amused the Taos to learn they were portraying Apaches, their deadly enemies in years gone by. It amused them also to see the assortment of headgear and other Indian regalia the movie company brought along. The Indians preferred their own—although sometimes less colorful—clothes. Nor did they like war paint from little sticks. They painted themselves with varied colored clays.

And sometimes the Taos were amusing. The agreement was that the Indians were to work until 5 p.m. Marshall had a short scene to do late one afternoon and he asked Concha if the Indians would mind working a few minutes overtime. Concha spoke to the Indians. Maintaining a poker face, one answered:

"Nope, we tired playing Indian. Go Home."

Concha laughed and shrugged. The Indians went home . . . .

It was many dollars for little work, as Concha said, but not an Indian was seen with a new blanket, new boots or a better gun.

What Gov. Concha meant was that his tribesmen would not go Hollywood. They didn't.

CUT TO
A Montage from 1943 movies: *Buckskin Frontier, Frontier Fury, In Old Oklahoma, The Law Rides Again, Wagon Tracks West, Deerslayer, Wild Horse Stampede, Daredevils of the West.*

CUT TO
A Montage from 1944 movies: *Riding West, Sonora Stagecoach, West of the Rio Grande, Black Arrow, Arizona Whirlwind.*

A series of "B" Westerns with the "Trail Blazers"—Ken Maynard, Hoot Gibson, and Bob Steel—as heroes, had been launched. In 1944 Chief Thundercloud replaced Maynard. Now an Indian really had co-hero status, as the three "pards" upheld law and order on the Western frontier in the likes of *Sonora Stagecoach* and *Outlaw Trail*.

By far the most productive series of features involving white-man-and-Indian-companion was the Red Ryder series. These stories had the added appeal of the companion being Little Beaver, an Indian boy. Wild Bill Elliott and Bobby Blake started out in the series; Allan Lane later replaced Elliott as Red Ryder with Bobby continuing as Little Beaver. Still later Jim Bannon took over as the Ryder and Don Kay "Little Brown Jug" Reynolds took over as Little Beaver.

CUT TO

A Montage from some of the Red Ryder series: (1944) *Tucson Raiders, Vigilantes of Dodge City, Cheyenne Wildcat, Marshal of Reno, San Antonio Kid;* (1945) *Colorado Pioneers, Phantom of the Plains, Lone Texas Ranger, Great Stagecoach Robbery, Texas Manhunt, Marshal of Laredo;* (1946) *Sheriff of Redwood Valley, Wagon Wheels Westward, California Gold Rush, Sun Valley Cyclone, Conquest of Cheyenne;* (1947) *Santa Fe Uprising, Rustlers of Devil's Canyon, Marshal of Cripple Creek, Stagecoach to Denver, Vigilantes of Boomtown, Homesteaders of Paradise Valley, Oregon Trail Scouts;* and *Roll, Thunder, Roll* (1949).

Buffalo Bill (1944, William Wellman), a pedestrian attempt at sanctifying him, contained a spectacular sequence in which Indians and cavalry charge at each other and meet head-on in the middle of a shallow stream. The Indians lose, but the exciting fight makes you root all the harder for them to win. This particular footage has been used in many films since. A few years ago it was used on television's "Time Tunnel" in a science fiction story about Custer at the Little Big Horn.

CUT TO

A Montage from 1946 movies: *Romance of the West, Trigger Fingers, Wild Beauty, The Phantom Rider, The Scarlet Horseman.*

The war was over. The pre-war era had Shirley Temple singing and dancing her little heart out; the post-war era had Margaret O'Brien crying her way into the hearts of the American public while Wallace Beery "aw shucks"ed his way in. In *Bad Bascomb* (1946, S. Sylvan Simon), both joined talents to survive the Indian attack on the wagon train.

In *Canyon Passage* (1946, Jacques Tourneur) the Indians attack a town, a useful but by no means frequent plot device. Perhaps production costs have prevented movie makers from having more movie Indians raiding more towns.

CUT TO

A Montage from 1947 movies: *Duel in the Sun, Last of the Redmen, The Last Round-Up, The Prairie, Renegade Girl, The Senator Was Indiscreet, Bowery Buckaroos, Buffalo Bill Rides Again, Northwest Outpost, Unconquered, Under the Tonto Rim.*

197

A myopic Linda Darnell in *Buffalo Bill* (1944) 20th Century Fox. (The Museum of Modern Art/Film Stills Archive)

After the war the production of "B" pictures declined. Their equivalent, the Western television series, began taking their place. Hollywood was forced to bolster box office receipts with the super epic which ad all-star casts, all-star color, and all-star wide screen. The Western was given this star treatment almost at once; it lent itself well to the technique. One such example was

David O. Selznick's *Duel in the Sun* (King Vidor). Such films also became another weapon in Hollywood's struggle to combat the ever-increasing threat from television. Just as in the pre-sound days, interest in 3-D and wide screen was revived. The novelty of 3-D didn't last long but Indians came in for their share of throwing spears and shooting arrows at the audience in *Fort Ti* (1953, William Castle), *The Charge at Feather River* (1953, Gordon Douglas), and *Hondo* (1953, John Farrow). One of the most successful of the wide screen processes was Cinemascope, and one of the first pictures to be done in this technique was *The Command* (1954, David Butler).

One of the few times the Indian was seen as an intelligent fighting man was in *The Command*. The last wagon of the wagon train has a hidden cannon. It takes only a couple of surprise shots, cutting a path of destruction among the pursuing redskins, for them to figure out the loading and firing procedure. The next time the cannon is ready to fire, they suddenly veer off into two separate galloping columns and the cannon is left with no Indians to shoot at. This particular scene always brought much applause and cheering. The effect on the wide screen was tremendous.

An often seen cliche. This time in *The Return of the Mohicans* (1948).

A Montage from 1948 movies: *Blood on the Moon, The Dude Goes West, Fort Apache, Fury at Furnace Creek, Montana Belle, The Paleface, The Plunderers, Rachel and the Stranger, Red River, The Return of the Mohicans, Silver River, Singing Spurs, Blazing Across the Pecos, Renegades of Sonora, Indian Agent, Yellow Sky.*

Smoke signals were puffing way back in 1911 with *The Silent Signal.*

CUT TO
A quick series of smoke signal shots from *Yellow Sky* (1948), *Winchester '73* (1950), *The Last Outpost* (1951), *Flaming Feather* (1951), *Wagons West* (1952), *Indian Uprising* (1952), *Siege at Red River* (1954), *The Last Wagon* (1956), *7th Cavalry* (1956), *Fort Dobbs* (1958), *Six Black Horses* (1962), *Texas Across the River* (1966) and, of course, *Smoke Signal* (1955, Jerry Hopper).

Another kind of communication came in after the inception of sound. Rarely does a Western go by without Indians signaling each other with bird calls, whistles, and animal barks or howls. And rarely does a Western go by without the crusty old scout or the battle-scarred sergeant or James Stewart or John Wayne knowing who's really making those sounds.

John Wayne and Walter Brennan in *Red River* (Howard Hawks) are facing a night attack by Indians. Our heroes determine the number and exact positions of the Indians by their furred and feathered cries.

William Holden in *Rachel and the Stranger* (Norman Foster) hears the sound of a male turkey and is immediately on his guard. "Gobbler call's a Shawnee signal," says he. But it turns out to be Robert Mitchum who brings word, "Signs of the Shawnee up to North."

James Stewart and Arthur Kennedy in *Bend of the River* (Andre De Toth) pinpoint five Shoshoni by their sounds. They sneak out under cover of darkness and, being knowledgeable men of the West, return after having killed five Shoshoni.

CUT TO
A quick series of bird whistle and animal call shots from *Winchester '73* (1950), *Dakota Incident* (1956), *Ride Lonesome* (1959), *Stage to Dancer's Rock* (1962), *Incident at Phantom Hill* (1966).

Indians will keep on barking, hooting, and whistling and the whites will keep on recognizing them and the Indians will keep

on getting killed until one day . . . somebody's going to change
the signal and the white man is going to be in a hell of a lot of
hot water.

CUT TO
A Montage from 1949 movies: *Apache Chief, Canadian Pacific,
Colorado Territory, The Cowboy and the Indians, Daughter of the
West, Davy Crockett—Indian Scout, Laramie, Lust for Gold, Mass-
acre River, Ranger of Cherokee Strip, Sand, She Wore a Yellow
Ribbon, Stallion Canyon, Trail of the Yukon, Tulsa.*

Apache haute couture in *Apache Chief* (1949) Lippert.

CUT TO
A montage from 1950 movies: *Ambush, Annie Get Your Gun,
Broken Arrow, California Passage, The Caribou Trail, Cherokee
Uprising, Colt .45, Comanche Territory, Devil's Doorway, The
Iroquois Trail, The Outriders, Rio Grande, Rock Island Trail, Rocky
Mountain, A Ticket to Tomahawk, Two Flags West, Wagon Master,
Winchester '73, Young Daniel Boone.*

Just a few years after the war Hollywood found itself in a
world it never made. It was forced to turn to films of awareness
and conscience. It tried to make up for all its past injustices and

sins with a rash of films with sympathetic, religious, and racial themes, such as *Gentlemen's Agreement* and *Pinky*. If Jews and blacks got this kind of attention, Indians couldn't be too far behind. They came in for this kind of treatment for better or for worse. Unfortunately for the Native American, it was for the worse.

The film that introduced the new sympathetic portrayal of the Indian—the film that was supposed to have broken the old stereotypical molds, the film that was supposed to present the Indian in a new and different light, the film that supposedly finally did justice to the Indian, the film that started a whole new generation of stereotyped-sympathetic Indian films—was *Broken Arrow* (1950, Delmer Daves).

When Hollywood makes up its mind to do something, it doesn't fool around. Audiences were grabbed by their throats and large, liberal doses of a new patent medicine were rammed down their gullets. Seeing things from the Indians' point of view was to become obsessive. These films were to be the cathartic to cleanse us all. And *Broken Arrow* was the film that started it all. Indians would now be proud, noble, decent, but oppressed people. Great emphasis would be placed on customs, culture, and traditions. These, however, remained the creations of the writer's imaginations.

The Indians in *Broken Arrow* were so damned proud and so damned noble that their leader, Cochise, played by Jeff Chandler, was indeed the noblest Roman of them all.

Although many people were taken in by this charade, some, like Bosley Crowther, were not. His review in the *Times*, July 21, 1950, was one of the few times we wholeheartedly agree with him:

> Apparently in his enthusiasm to treat the Indian with politeness and respect, Delmer Daves, the director, brought forth red men who act like denizens of the musical comedy stage. Jeff Chandler, who plays Cochise, is twice as clean and stalwart-looking as James Stewart, who plays the drawling prospector by whom the peaceful mission is embarked. Mr. Chandler carries himself with the magnificence of a decathlon champion at the Olympic Games and speaks with round and studied phrasing of the salutatorian of a graduating class . . . .
>
> No, we cannot accept this picture as either an exciting or reasonable account of the attitudes and ways of American Indians. They merit justice, but not such patronage.

The bait was eagerly snapped up, since *Broken Arrow* was highly praised by many. The Association on American Indian Affairs (a white organization) honored it by giving the film a special award. Jeff Chandler was nominated for an Academy Award and became a star. Chandler played Cochise again in *The Battle at Apache Pass* (1952, George Sherman), and appeared briefly at the beginning of *Taza, Son of Cochise* (1954, Douglas Sirk), when he is killed off, passing on his chiefdom to none other than Rock Hudson.

Broken Arrow was to become a TV series with Michael Ansara playing Cochise, out-nobling the noblest and out-wising the wisest.

Television embraced the horrific Indian to its bosom, with predictable ardor. On November 15, 1966, *The Milwaukee Journal* printed a story, "TV Replay of 'Oat Dramas' Infuriates American Indian," by Harold Heffernan. He interviewed Charlie Blackfeet, "veteran campaigner in the cause of Indian rights" who was the "self-appointed president of the IFTP (Indians for Truthful Portrayals)" Mr Blackfeet said:

> Thousands of old westerns have been sold to TV by the studios, and the whole false Indian cycle is making the rounds for new generations to absorb.
> That's why I forbid my children to watch old westerns on TV—they're liable to grow up hating Indians!

The cinematic assault upon the Native American is only comparable to the actual massacres at Sand Creek, the Washita, Summit Springs, and Wounded Knee.

Indian films after 1950 follow, essentially, in the footsteps of their predecessors. Bestowing benevolent additives is not enough to change the smell of rot so long festering in the continually resurrected seventy-seven-year-old corpse—first wounded in *Sioux Ghost Dance* in 1894.

PARADOX AND REALITY

SCENE XVII

Tribes

Historically, many tribes were involved in the death struggle to protect themselves, their homes, and their lands from the white man. To name all the tribes would result in an almost endless list of tragedy. To point out only a few would be an insult to the memory of the hundreds of thousands who died. Relations between the white man and red man are a checkerboard of paradoxes. Some tribes resisted and were nearly exterminated by the white man's guns. Some tribes did not resist and were nearly exterminated by the white man's diseases. Some tribes fought the white man and then made peace. Some tribes made peace with the white man and then fought him. The important thing to remember is that all the tribes had their own individual cultures, customs, and traditions. Each tribe was like a nation unto itself.

However, Hollywood reinforced the U.S. government's concept of a general adversary called "The Indian." By using whites to portray "Indians" and by exploiting Native Americans from several different tribes to play at being "Indians" from other tribes, Hollywood denied the Native American his individual identity.

Little Big Man (1971, Arthur Penn), was filmed, in part, on the Crow Reservation in Montana. One segment of the story deals with Custer's fall at the Little Big Horn, which is now located on the reservation. Taking into consideration whatever expediencies Hollywood might have to deal with, it is ironic that some of the roles of the Cheyennes and Sioux were played by their hereditary enemies, the Crows. In actuality, the Crows acted as scouts for Custer. To this day there are some among these tribes who have strong feelings about the past.

In the original short story *A Man Called Horse*, by Dorothy M. Johnson, the white man, "Horse," is captured by a band of Crows and the rest of the story takes place in a Crow village. Yet the press releases read ". . . members of the Rosebud Sioux Reservation appear in featured roles, and two hundred members of the tribe worked behind the scenes . . ."

The customs depicted in *A Man Called Horse* were neither Sioux nor Crow. They belonged only to the authentic Hollywood tribe called "Indian."

"If the white man speaks the truth he is our friend; if he lies he shall meet death by club and fire."

A scene from *The Great Sioux Uprising* (1953) Universal.

Although Hollywood made the pretense of depicting other tribes, there seem to be just two tribes for the writers, the Sioux and the Apache. Their popularity was probably a result of the widespread notoriety given them and their leaders during the Indian Wars and the infamous exhibition and exploitation of Geronimo and Sitting Bull.

Hollywood seized the opportunity and to this day Sioux and Apache conjure up a visual image and evoke an emotional reaction for the movie-going public.

Films have been made about the most famous leaders of the Sioux, Crazy Horse and Sitting Bull. Many pictures have been made using them as characters. None of these films, however, had anything to do with the reality of their lives. Otis Guernsey commented on *Sitting Bull* (Sidney Salkow) in the *New York Herald Tribune*, November 26, 1954.

> . . . Sitting Bull addresses a cavalry officer with the following bit of sarcasm: "When you win you call it a victory. When we win you call it a massacre."
> This testy bit of dialogue is typical of the new fad in Indian pictures, and so is "Sitting Bull." No longer do the movies relish the phrase "Another redskin bit the dust." These days the motif is "Lo! The poor Indian!" and in this latest saga of the Old West the Sioux are seen as a peace-loving people being crowded out of their homeland by ruthless gold miners . . . .

> VOICE OVER:
> Dustin Hoffman, star of *Little Big Man,* comparing the battles of the Washita and the Little Big Horn is saying: "When the whites won a battle, it was a victory. But when the Indians won, it was called a massacre."

William Zinsser said of *Chief Crazy Horse* (George Sherman) in the *New York Herald Tribune*, April 28, 1955:

> This is one of those films that take the Indian point of view—a trend that calls for some readjustment on the part of old-time movie fans. The cavalry with whom we have ridden all these Technicolored years, are suddenly the villains doing the white man's greedy business, and it's satisfying to see them routed.
> And the Indians, whose war whoops on the hilltop have chilled us with fear, are now peaceable folk, living in a sort of tepee Levittown, minding their own business, bringing up the kids and hunting buffalo the way other country dwellers play tennis. Oh, it's a crazy, mixed-up movie world . . . .

In pre-*Broken Arrow* days Indians were still being depicted as cruel and bloodthirsty. So we had Anthony Quinn, playing Crazy Horse in *They Died With Their Boots On*, as an evil wizard of UGH. Conversely, after 1950 chiefs were to become wise, noble, loyal, and reverant. Then we have J. Carrol Naish as

Sitting Bull in the film of the same name, being a wise, patient, benevolent patriarch—like a Jean Hersholt with feathers—and Victor Mature as Crazy Horse in *Chief Crazy Horse*, being a grand, noble, proud, religious Indian who keeps having visions and hearing celestial music.

The Sioux and their leaders did not fare much better on TV. CBS, on "The Great Adventure," a series designed to educate our young, presented the story of Sitting Bull, in two parts, October 4 and 11, 1963. It was an earnest attempt at dramatizing his life. The Indian movie syndrome of mixing fact and Hollywood fantasy persisted throughout, so that the real Sitting Bull remained the movie phantom he always had been.

An episode on "Time Tunnel," a science fiction series, dealt with Custer and the Sioux just before the famous battle. Sitting Bull and Crazy Horse take us through the time tunnel to the Little Big Horn, complete with phony sets, "ugh" dialogue, and drums that sound more Tahitian than Teton Sioux.

A fairly recent episode of "Hogan's Heroes," a television "comedy" series in questionable taste, concerned a prisoner of war who happened to be a Sioux. The writers used the worst type of vulgar racist humor. The prisoner's name combined a myriad of hyphenated abominations and he resorted to war-whooping histrionics in order to frighten the German guards.

CUT TO
This scene as described in John Gregory Dunne's book *The Studio* (1969):

Richard Zanuck. . .stood up as director Fred Zinnemann walked into his office. . . .The studio had signed Zinnemann to direct a $10 million Western based on Custer's last stand. . . . It was Zinnemann's first Western since he won an Academy Award for his direction of *High Noon* and he was excited about the project. Richard Zanuck's enthusiasm, however, was beginning to wane; . . .

"Is it true, Dick," he said carefully, "that you're thinking of shooting locations in Mexico?"

Zanuck nodded slowly.

"It's outrageous," Zinnemann said. "Shooting a great American folk legend in a foreign country."

"It'll save three million dollars," Zanuck replied pleasantly. "It's a factor, it's a real factor."

Zinnemann yielded the point grudgingly. He went on to the next item on his agenda. He had already won assent from the studio to cast Toshiro Mifune, the Japanese film star, in the role of Crazy Horse, and now suggested that another Oriental play

Sitting Bull. "It'll maintain an ethnic balance, Dick," Zinnemann said.

A stricken look crossed Zanuck's face. "Jesus, Freddy," he said, "you want us ostracized by the American Indian Association? Those are the two biggest heroes in the history of Indians. And you want Japs to play both of them?"

In an attempt to capitalize on the successful sympathetic style of *Broken Arrow*, *Run of the Arrow* (1957) set the Sioux back hundreds of years. It included everything: drunken and renegade Indians; heroic dialogue; some silly story about running the arrow similar to running a gauntlet; a foreign starlet, Sarita Montiel, as the maiden; a Cinderella marriage ceremony; and an Indian-hating officer. Yet, it, too, was praised. Samuel Fuller, its director, in an interview with Stig Bjorkman for *Movie* 17, Winter 1969-70, said:

> It was the first American picture where the Indians won, and I was invited by the Indian Commissioner in Washington. He ran the picture of all the senators . . . then the Indians wrote me and invited me to go to their tribes. And they like it . . . that started a little thing anyway; a lot of friends of mine who make pictures said—We'll make pictures too showing the Indians won.
> . . . I thought it would be time to show the truth that in many of the battles the Indians—particularly the Sioux— did not massacre all people (I did a lot of research for this) and often sent back survivors, with a message: —Don't make trouble! They often did that. And I was very fed up with many American movies where they're jumping around and yelling and screaming and killing. The only ones who used to do that in the old days were the beatniks of the Indians, the avant-garde of the Indians, the delin- quents. They used to do it, just like they do it today . . . .

Howard Thompson's comment in the *New York Times* on *Bugles in the Afternoon* (1952, Roy Rowland) is most appro- priate: ". . . this film should be given back to the Indians. And judging by the expressions of the contributing Sioux, they want no part of it."

The Sioux (the French form of the Chippewa word for serpent or enemy) actually called themselves the Dacotahs, the allies. The Dacotahs were comprised of various tribes and bands. All roamed the Northern Plains.

The Apache (the Spanish form of the Zuni word for enemy— a name the Spaniards bestowed on practically all Southwestern tribes) actually called themselves Shis-Indays, the people. They too were comprised of various tribes and bands. All inhabited the Southwest.

And never, never did the Sioux and the Apache meet in battle.

> CUT TO
> A sequence from *The Fight on Deadwood Trail* (1914) showing Sioux and Apaches fighting each other.
> CUT TO
> A sequence from *Buffalo Bill* (1963) showing Sioux and Apaches fighting each other.

Hollywood's favorite tribe, by far, is the Apache, probably because it is the easiest to costume with a semblance of authenticity: cotton shirt, trousers, bandana around the head, wraparound leggings, cartridge bandolier. Their film costumes were often augmented by the feathered bonnets of the Plains tribes. Despite the sympathetic treatment in *Broken Arrow* and its ilk, the Apache have always been depicted as the fiercest, cruelest and most warlike of people. By 1965, in *Apache Rifles* (William Witney), even the fierce Apaches were paid noble homage by the screen writers.

The old Spanish hot-foot. Apaches in *Duel at Diablo* (1966) United Artists.

210

CUT TO

Chief Thunder Cloud being interviewed for a newspaper article concerning the picture he is currently making—*Geronimo* (1939). He is speaking:

The script hardly does justice to an Indian military genius. I've suggested some changes to studio officials.

Geronimo was pretty cruel, but he wasn't a double-dyed villain. Yet the opening montage of this picture, as now written, shows him tomahawking a pioneer woman and her child.

I've pointed out that Geronimo began committing his depradations only after womenfolk of his own family (his mother, wife, and three children) had been massacred by renegade whites. It would be only fair, I think, to give some of this background to show why he fought so long and so hard against such great odds.

CUT TO

A segment from *Geronimo* in which Geronimo is about to scalp actress Marjorie Gateson. We hear Chief Thunder Cloud continuing the newspaper interview in Voice Over: I certainly am glad they let the cavalry arrive in time. It would have been very bad for me to have to scalp Miss Gateson. You see, I make Western pictures out at Republic, and I'm always a good Indian. The kid fans wouldn't like it if they caught me off the reservation.

For its New York engagement, the Paramount Theatre sponsored a contest for the "ideal full-blooded Indian girl" who would appear at the theatre. From the many applicants, Miss Bucki Monitowa, an "Algonquin" from Oklahoma, was chosen. Coincidentally, her grandfather, Chief Monitowa, just happened to have been a close friend of Geronimo. Or so the publicity releases claimed.

Geronimo (1962, Arnold Laven) was another incredulously fictitious biography of the leader who, in this case, was played by Chuck Connors.

Geronimo has been more than amply mistreated. It is said that the Apache chief Mangas Coloradas gave Geronimo his name as a war honor. Geronimo's boyhood name was Goyathlay, One Who Yawns. However, in *Lone Star* (1952, Vincent Sherman), Clark Gable meets an Apache boy named Geronimo who dreams of becoming a great warrior and leader of his people. In *Taza, Son of Cochise* Geronimo, played by Ian MacDonald, is a villainous second to Rock Hudson's Taza. Geronimo, we might add, never played second banana to anyone.

In *I Killed Geronimo* (1950, John Hoffman) Geronimo, played by Chief Thunder Cloud, is killed off in a fight. In reality

Geronimo died of pneumonia in 1909. He had been drinking and passed out in freezing weather at Ft. Sill, Oklahoma. He had been a prisoner of war for 23 years.

The Apaches have fared equally as well as the Sioux on television. *Broken Arrow*, as previously mentioned, was transferred to the home screen.

In 1967 *Hondo* also went the TV route but with considerably less success. Jack Gould commented in the *Times*, September 9, 1967: "If last night's premiere of 'Hondo' is an example . . . it would be a long and tiring winter for . . . the Apaches . . . ."

TV's "High Chaparral" was an insult to the memory of even the worst "B" Westerns. The series was fraught with inept acting, inept direction, and inept writing. The central character, Big John, played by Leif Erickson, wishes to live in peace and harmony with his fellow men, among whom he graciously counts the Apaches. To achieve this end, he spends much of his time killing them off.

To sum up the Apaches misfortunes in films and on TV, there is Mark Sufrin's remark in the *Saturday Review*, August 25, 1956, about the film *Walk the Proud Land* (Jesse Hibbs), with Audie Murphy playing the famous Apache agent John P. Clum to Jay Silverheel's Geronimo: "Like other 'serious' efforts, it is an earnest, dreary exercise in native anthropology, Hollywood's vulgar apology for all 'the only good injun . . .' films."

Other tribes should not feel slighted. They, too, have been used, if in name only. Some of them were: Blackfoot, Pawnee, Paiute, Shawnee, Shoshoni, Arapahoe, Comanche, Hopi, Pueblo, Modoc, Delaware, California Mission, Yuma, Piegan, Ojibway, Zuni, Pequot, Ute, Choctaw, Creek, Crow, Huron, and Ottawa.

White Feather (1955, Robert D. Webb) was based, in part, on a true and pathetic story of two Cheyennes: Headchief, age 25, and Youngmule, age 13, who worshipped his older companion. By 1890 the Native American was told to walk the white man's road or perish. Yet these two still wanted to prove their warrior status and their manhood by killing whites. Instead, they only succeeded in killing a young white boy. This mistake led them to prove themselves further by defying arrest by the military, knowing they had no chance of survival.

The Hollywood version had the two Cheyennes, played by Jeffrey Hunter and Hugh O'Brian, get shot because they refuse to be removed to a reservation. In the end, they die in a panoramic long shot, while charging at what looks like the entire U.S. Cavalry.

Massacre at Sand Creek (1956) was based on the infamous Chivington raid on Black Kettle's Cheyenne camp on November 29, 1864. It had been reported that Chivington, a minister, told his men before the raid to "kill and scalp all big and little; nits makes lice." Afterwards, Chivington boasted that some 300 Native Americans were killed, half of them women and children. In the film version Chivington is played as a vicious, psychotic, Indian-hating officer. Hollywood frequently dismisses or excuses genocide by attributing it to the whims of a few unbalanced people, i.e., General Custer in *Little Big Man*.

Concerning the Kiowas in *The War Wagon* (1967, Burt Kennedy), Robert Larkins in his article "Hollywood and the Indian," in the British magazine *Focus On Film*, No. 2, raises an interesting question: "Probably the most miscast Hollywood Indian in recent years was ... Howard Keel ... a genuine masterpiece of miscasting in which Keel, ... neither looked nor sounded like an Indian ...." Now the question is: What does an "Indian" look and sound like?

Another example of a Hollywood misconception, that of Indians being inept fighters, can be seen in *They Rode West* (1954, Phil Karlson). Here two white men hold off 30 Kiowa Indians. Similarly, the Apaches were held off in *Garden of Evil* (1954, Henry Hathaway); and the Sioux in *Bugles in the Afternoon* (1952, Roy Rowland), *Tomahawk* (1951, George Sherman), *Yellowstone Kelly* (1959, Gordon Douglas) and *Red Tomahawk* (1966, R. G. Springsteen). The list is endless.

Women, who with few exceptions are supposed to be inept fighters as well, overcome the Indians with gusto in *The Guns of Fort Petticoat* (1957, George Marshall). Their leader is, of course, ʻa man, Audie Murphy, who organizes them into an efficient fighting force.

When you come to think of it, Indians are always outfought and outsmarted. This occurs in the sympathetic Indian picture as well. The vicious enemy is now our misunderstood fellow human but he is still losing to the same superior few.

CUT TO
A film clip from *The Cariboo Trail* (1950, Edwin L. Marin). Randolph Scott is holding a jackass' head while the animal flails away with both back feet, catapulting Indians in all directions.

Occasionally Hollywood adds a little spice to the cake by putting the Indians up against some unusual adversaries. In *The Red Devils* (1911) a troupe of acrobats called the Red Devils confronts the Indians and tumble their way to victory. Indians get involved with a theatrical troupe in *Heller in Pink Tights* (1960, George Cukor), which results in much running and no fighting. In *Thunder in the Sun* (1959), Russel Rouse) Indians attack a wagon train of Basques and soon live or die to regret it. The Basques out-fight, out-leap, and out-war whoop the redskins, to the audience's great delight.

Some Eastern tribes were represented in films dealing with early settlers, the colonial period, and the American Revolution. The Iroquois ran the gamut of famous directors, from Griffith's *America* (1924), to Ford's *Drums Along the Mohawk* (1939), to De Mille's *Unconquered* (1947).

Plains blanket strip and breastplate and Woodlands breechclout adorn a New York "Mohawk Chief." Ted de Corsica in *Mohawk* (1955) 20th Century Fox.

George Montgomery, as a coonskin-capped frontiersman, starred in three French and Indian War cheapies: *Iroquois Trail* (1950, Phil Karlson), *The Pathfinder* (1952, Sidney Salkow) and *Fort Ti* (1953, William Castle), with the last having a slight edge since it was filmed in 3-D. *The Pathfinder and the Mohican* (1956), *Along the Mohawk Trail* (1956), and *The Long Rifle and the Tomahawk* (1964), with John Hart as the white hero and Lon Chaney, Jr. as the faithful red companion, were pasted-together segments from the ghastly "Hawkeye" TV series.

A scene from *Seminole* (1953) Universal. The "Seminole" is wearing the standard costume assigned to any "tribe" not listed as Plains or Apache. Note bathing trunks under breechclout.

The Iroquois Confederacy was composed of the Mohawk, Seneca, Cayuga, Onondaga, Oneida and, later, the Tuscarora tribes. Their fighting force never went beyond approximately 2200 men. For some 300 years they fought the Dutch, the French, and other enemies such as the Hurons and the Algonquins, and were outnumbered by all. The disintegration of the Iroquois Confederacy was only achieved by the division of the six tribes during the American Revolution. Some tribes sided with the Loyalists and others with the Revolutionaries. It might be well to consider that if the whole Confederacy had remained allied to the Loyalists and the British Army, there would not have been an independent United States.

The Seminoles were depicted in films as early as 1906. In *Seminole Uprising* (1955, Earl Bellamy), as in all Indian stories, the cavalry goes in and whips them. Actually, the army rarely, if ever, found the Seminoles, because they just disappeared into the impenetrable Florida Everglades. In the Second Seminole War, 1835-1842, it cost the U.S. government twenty million dollars and the lives of 1500 soldiers in an attempt to subdue them.

A Southwestern tribe, the Pima, and their fellow tribesman, Ira Hayes, were treated very fairly on a one-shot TV presentation.

In 1960 NBC-TV presented "The American," directed by John Frankenheimer and produced by Robert Alan Arthur, with Lee Marvin as Ira Hayes. Merle Miller, who wrote the script, described part of the taping in his and Evan Rhodes' *Only You, Dick Daring* (1964):

> All of the San Xavier extras were on hand for the taping of the funeral scene, the young children, the girls and boys in their teens, their parents, and the old men and women of the tribe. They were all brushed and in their Sunday-go-to-meeting clothes.
>
> Frankenheimer placed them in a *ramata*, a handmade shelter that had a beautiful simplicity. It was where the Tribal Council met.
>
> Not far away a replica of the memorial the Pimas had erected for Ira had been constructed; next to that was a flagpole. A Zuni law student dressed as a Marine stood next to the flagpole. At the end of Steve Hill's speech— Steve had got it only that morning—the Zuni boy was to run up the flag.
>
> It was late afternoon, and the orange sun brought out the strong, warm colors of the mountains in the background.
>
> Frankenheimer talked to the Indians for a while; he told them to imagine they were attending a memorial service for Ira Hayes and asked them to listen to what Steve Hill was saying, "because," said John, "it's important."
>
> Then Frankenheimer talked to Steve for a minute, went to inside the tape truck, and gave the cue to begin.
>
> Steve waited. He looked at the distant mountains and at the green fields just below. He looked at the dusty reser-

vation; he looked at the sad, small huts, and, finally, he looked at the Indians in the *ramata*.

Then with deliberation with which all Indians speak, he began.

"I once called Ira Hayes a symbol," he said, "but he was not that. He was never that. History will, I suppose, call him a hero—but he was never that either. He was a man. He had the strength of a man and the weakness of a man.

"Ira was a gentle man, a good man, a trusting man. He believed in God, in honor, in courage, and in truth. To him a promise was a sacred thing. In all his life he tried never to break a promise.

"Ira Hamilton Hayes was given a great many things, but nobody ever gave him what he wanted most. It was very little, really. He loved the land—this land. As indeed we all do. And he wanted enough water to farm this land. As indeed we all do."

Steve paused and looked at a very old man standing near the *ramata*. Tears were running down the old man's face.

Steve looked at the children, at the parents, at the old people. Many of them were crying. Steve was talking about them, about their frustrations, their tragedy.

"Ira Hamilton Hayes was promised water," Steve went on." All of us have been promised water. But the promise has been broken. It has been broken many times. It is broken still.

"Ira was one of us. He shared our dreams, our anger, our defeat, and our patience.

"Once we were all proud of Ira Hamilton Hayes. Later, some of us were ashamed of him. We shall none of us ever be ashamed again."

Steve stopped and waited for the flag to be raised.

It wasn't. The young Zuni had forgotten to act. He was crying, too.

Bob wrote about that moment, "*This* was why we had come twenty-five hundred miles. Suddenly, as we always knew it would, the original hopes for the project became fully realized. Not a play to match *Hamlet*, not even the greatest play ever done on television, but a fleeting moment of absolute truth, so rarely caught anywhere, and especially rare (and so easily lost) among the other nineteen-thousand-odd yearly hours of television."

A poignant story, the life and death of World War II hero Ira Hayes, got the Hollywood treatment in *The Outsider* (1962, Delbert Mann). Tony Curtis played Hayes and Vivian Nathan played his mother. The film was a tasteless distortion of his life as well as his tragic death.

CUT TO

The sequence from *Sands of Iwo Jima* (1949, Allan Swan) showing the flag raising with Ira Hayes re-enacting his part.

CUT TO

John Redhouse, President of the Navajo Liberation Front being interviewed on July 4, 1970. He is speaking:

> Why should we celebrate independence when the BIA [Bureau of Indian Affairs] rules as an absolute dictatorship over the Navajo Reservation? Why should we celebrate independence when the BIA tells us what to do and not what to do? And what we had better not do. What to the Navajo is your independence?
>
> You tell us Kit Carson was a patriot and that we should all be proud of him. How can we be proud of a man who killed our Grandfathers, marched them 300 miles to Fort Sumner, put them in stockades, and left them there to die? That's just like asking a little Jewish boy to celebrate Hitler's birthday because it's the patriotic thing to do.
>
> In your history books, we have to be recorded as "savages" in order to justify your theft of our land. In your movies and on television, every time the calvary [sic] wins you call it a "triumph," and every time the Indians wins you call it a "massacre." Anybody want to play Jews and Nazis?
>
> You tell us how proud we should be of our country and how much we should love it. How can we be proud of; much less love a country that made up the slogan "The Only Good Indian Is a Dead Indian" and then perpetuated it into a national policy . . . .

Kit Carson had all the makings of a folk hero. He had been a wagon train scout and army scout, mountain man, "squawman," army officer, Indian fighter, Indian agent, and prosperous rancher. His exploits followed the same path taken by such legendary "heroes" as Buffalo Bill, George Custer, and Wild Bill Hickok: from reality to dime novels to movies. Carson, as a heroic character, made his debut in films as early as *Kit Carson* (1903).

Yet this "hero" led the New Mexico Volunteers, numbering one thousand, in rounding up the Navajos in the winter of 1864. Burning their crops and villages, killing their livestock, destroying their means of survival, he compelled them to surrender. They were then herded to an uninhabitable prisoner of war reservation at the Bosque Redondo in New Mexico. While there, 2321 Navajos died of smallpox in 1865.

The mass media has finally discovered the blacks, the Chicanos, the environment and ecology, and has, upon occasion, discovered the real "Indian." None of the following films have gotten the exposure they deserve. They were either seen on television once, or else viewed by very few film buffs at festivals or in small libraries giving special showings. These films certainly could not provide for the re-education of the white man. By the same token, most of the films have not been seen by Native Americans.

In 1951 the semi-documentary *Navajo* was made. Written and directed by Norman Foster, it tells a simple and eloquent story of a young Navajo boy trying to face and understand the contradictions and conflicts of two cultures. The following, from a review of *Navajo* by Joe Pihodna in the *New York Herald Tribune*, February 21, 1952, will best illustrate how a well-made film is reviewed:

> Norman Foster, who wrote and directed the screen play, is exploring the reactions of a small boy steeped in the superstitions and traditions of his tribe, a savage nation which successfully resisted Gen. Custer . . . .

Navajos resisted Custer? Where? When?

On April 20, 1970 the NET (National Educational Television) Journal presented *The Long Walk*, an excellent documentary. Written and directed by Philip Greene, it was, to quote from a NET release, a ". . . study of the Navajo Indian— his history, his customs, and his educational efforts to break a century's cycle of neglect and apathy."

Another good documentary was done by CBS-TV on May 7, 1968. *The Forgotten American* was concerned, in part, with the poverty and disease among the Navajo.

The National Film Board of Canada has been the leader in making excellent documentaries about the Native American. *The Ballad of Crowfoot* is a superb film produced, written, and directed by a Native American, Willie Dunn.

The *Film Library Quarterly*, Winter 1969-70, contained an article, "Some Wrongs Righted on Film." In two parts, the "Vanishing American: Part I" was written by Joan Clark. This is her review of *Ballad of Crowfoot*:

> *Ballad of Crowfoot*, by a teen-age Crow Indian, William Dunn, centers around a ballad which he created. The story of his tribe is sung with guitar accompaniment and told with old photographs, paintings and early films. Dunn's personal view of the history of the Crow's degradation and current poverty is an angry poem from inside the empty barrel; a searing indictment of white genocide.

We agree with Miss Clark's final statement—but:

Willie Dunn is a Micmac from Canada.

Crowfoot was a famous chief of the Blackfeet in the 1800s in that same country.

The Crow are located in the United States.

The *Film Library Quarterly* is a publication used by hundreds of libraries, museums, colleges, and archives. This kind of misinformation is thus passed on to students, teachers, film makers, and posterity.

Other NFB Films include *Encounter with Saul Alinsky*, a film showing Alinsky trying to explain his methods of community action to a group of Native Americans at the Rama Reserve in Canada; and *These Are My People*, an examination by a Mohawk of his tribe and its laws. *You Are on Indian Land* is an excellent cinema-verite confrontation between Mohawks and Canadian police officials as the Native Americans closed the International Bridge linking the U.S. and Canada. The bridge, in part, spans the Mohawk Reservation. It was blocked, in the dead of winter, in order to demonstrate their right to control their own land.

Another NFB film, *People Might Laugh at Us*, is an impressionistic view of life in a Micmac village. *The Pride and the Shame*, made by BBC-TV, offers an objective and unbiased British view of the modern Sioux. NBC Educational Films' *Between Two Rivers* is a moving examination of the life and trial of Thomas White Hawk, a South Dakota Sioux convicted of rape and murder. It originally appeared on the network. Almost all of these films were made by Native Americans.

NBC-TV's "Project 20" did a documentary in 1960 with Gary Cooper as narrator. *The Real West* only in part touched upon the Native American, but it did so with taste. This film was so well received that in 1967 "Project 20" presented another documentary completely devoted to the Native American. Done equally as well, *The End of the Trail* was narrated by Walter Brennan. The film tells of the destruction of the Plains tribes during the white man's invasion of their lands, from the 1840s to the Battle of the Little Big Horn in 1876. The film was written by Phillip Reisman and directed by Don Hyatt.

Almost all Native Americans were, at one time or another, moved from their homes when the white man wanted their lands. As a result, survival for the Native American took precedence over the preservation of his culture. The original American's way of life had its roots in his original environment. As a result of forced migrations, much was lost or distorted. Hollywoods' constant bombardment with films offering their own versions of the Native American's history was bound to have an effect. It has.

On May 1, 1970, NET Playhouse presented *The Trail of Tears*, a good dramatization of the removal of the Cherokees from their homeland in the Southeastern United States to Oklahoma. Written, produced, and directed by Lane Slate, it featured Johnny Cash as Chief John Ross and had many Cherokees playing parts.

Unfortunately, the film failed to convey the magnitude of the tragedy. There was one touching and effective moment. In order to alleviate the anxiety of the Cherokee children who are about to leave their homes, Richard Crowe tells them a story. He tells the familiar tribal legend of the creation of the earth, making their abrupt move appear natural. It is interesting to note that Native American Richard Crowe is not a professional actor. It was beautiful and there wasn't a feather in sight.

INSTANT INDIAN KIT

SCENE XVIII

Hollywood has perpetuated what can best be described as The Instant Indian Kit, suitable for any and all Indians, which consists of wig, war bonnet or headband (beaded or otherwise), vest or shirt, breechclout, leggings or fringed pants, and moccasins. To top off the costume, include Hong Kong beadwork, plastic bear, or eagle claws with plastic beads and other geegaws. Add a few streaks of paint and Voila! . . . you're an Indian, too.

Hollywood's sense of propriety made wearing bathing trunks under breechclouts mandatory. The derriere, after all, must not be seen.

Robert Salmaggi, in his review of *Finger on the Trigger* (1965, Sidney Pink), a European made Western, in the *New York Herald Tribune*, February 5, 1966, aptly describes the costume situation:

> Like, are them Injuns for real? Here's a mangy crew of local native recruits, heavy footed, lumbering, grinning and made up like clowns. And you can just picture Wardrobe handing out the costumes: "No, ain't no more Sioux costumes. Bring out the Apache gear; and any other redskin stuff—who's gonna know anyway!" So there it is—feather headdresses, loin skins, Roman sandals, jeans and you name it.

CUT TO
The company of *A Man Called Horse* on location in Mexico. It is cold, raining, and the ground is muddy. Many Sioux actors are huddled together; their resentment is very apparent. They have just been informed that they cannot wear their own tribal clothing in the film.

During the summer of 1964, Stephen Feraca, a long-time observer of and author on Sioux customs and traditions, was interviewed by Ralph Friar at the Sioux Sun Dance on the Pine Ridge Reservation. Concerning costuming, Mr. Feraca said:

> Now those movie Indians wearing all those feathers can't come out as human beings. They're not expected to come out as human beings because I think the American people do not regard Indians as wholly human. We must remember that many, many American children believe that feathers grow out of Indians' heads. Now those same children don't believe that anything grows out of anybody else's head.

Most children are exposed to movies and television long before they can read or go to school. Their attitudes toward and opinions about the Native American have been well established by the mass media long before they begin their schooling. It cannot be emphasized enough that Native American children are faced with exactly the same problem. Remember—the only real Indian is a Hollywood Indian.

As a promotion stunt for United Artists' *Apache* (1954, Robert Aldrich), a contest was held in which the prize would be Jean Peters' "authentic Indian beaded headband." The headband was described as follows: "It consists of red, yellow, green, blue, black, gold and white beads and would make an attractive belt."

The adage "if you repeat a lie often enough, it is accepted as truth" has done much to corrode the Native American's culture. Instead of the Native American influencing Hollywood, the reverse has come true. The beaded headband, for instance, is purely a Hollywood invention which has become so commonly associated with "Indian" that even some Native Americans now wear them. It is our theory that the headband was popularized in the Wild West Shows and later in Hollywood's early days to keep the Indian wigs from falling off. It is true that Native Americans wore ornaments in their hair. But it is the invented headband that has now become part and parcel of their identities. Another case in point is the beaded "Princess" crown—nothing more than an elaboration of the Hollywood headband—which is worn today by most young Native American women at many functions.

224

CUT TO
The sequence in *A Man Called Horse* in which the Indians, before
bringing the white man into camp, prepare themselves by smearing
and streaking various colored paints indiscriminately on their bodies
and faces.
On another aspect of "war paint" Mr. Feraca had this to say:

> This movie-type paint has become so indelible in the public's
> mind that it has finally just been completely adopted by young
> and middle-aged Indians themselves.

Among Native Americans, face and body painting was extremely important. The colors and designs used were often part
of their visions or were used only by a particular society or
otherwise had great symbolic meaning. A great deal of time and
care was taken in putting the paint on properly. A warrior's
paint was his pride and his protection.

James Bear Ghost, a Mandan-Arikara Native American, is
principal of schools at the Turtle Mountain Reservation in
North Dakota. He was interviewed by Ralph Friar. Mr. Bear
Ghost talked about taking his family on a vacation to Los
Angeles:

> We did all the tourist things. I took the family to see
> Knott's Berry Farm and we were talking to this white,
> blue-eyed Indian chief in full Hollywood regalia, feather
> bonnet and all, at the Indian village there. Some tourists
> asked us to step aside so they could take some pictures of
> the Indian. Can you imagine? They wanted pictures of real
> Indians for their kids and they asked that phony just
> because he was dressed the way they thought an Indian
> should look. We sure laughed a lot over that. Those tour-
> ists couldn't tell the real Indians from the phonies. But I
> guess they got what they wanted.

Not only is the Native American subverted by the constant
avalanche of misinformation about his mode of dress in the
past, he is further degraded by the additional exploitations and
perversions of his culture created by the makers of Haute
Couture and others not so haute.

John Corry wrote "A Man Called Perry Horse" for *Harper's
Magazine*, October, 1970, which describes the life of a Kiowa in
the white man's world of today:

> Not long ago, some swells who bleed a lot in public had a
> big cocktail party for Americans for Indian Opportunity,
> which is run by Mrs. Fred Harris, who is herself part

Comanche, and is the wife of the Senator from Oklahoma. The party was held at a great big summer mansion in Southampton, Long Island, and Perry and his wife were there, along with a bunch of other Indians . . . . "The people who had the party were real nice, and they made us feel right at home, but some of the other people," Perry says, "oh, man . . . . All the Indian guys were wearing jackets and ties, and the people at the party were wearing feathers and beads and things I guess they thought were Indian. There was one lady with a long skirt with fringes all around the bottom, and one of our guys said, 'Man, that's either high fashion, or the dogs got to her on the way over.' . . ."

CUT TO

This 1939 press release which we hear in Voice Over: "Everything is grist to our Hollywood designers. The Blackfoot Indians imported by Twentieth Century-Fox for 'Susannah of the Mounties' have inspired Royer to create a series of Indian necklaces for Alice Faye to wear in her new film."

CUT TO

A series of stills showing models posed in Indian fashions as we hear, in Voice Over, the following:

The *New York Times Magazine,* February 18, 1968—ad for Celanese Fortrel: "BEST THING WE'VE GOTTEN FROM THE INDIANS SINCE THAT OTHER TOWN. (AND ALL FOR ONLY $4 MORE.) The Girltown Totem Trio, sizes 7-14; pants, about $6; windbreaker jacket, about $7; knit turtleneck, about $5. The Girltown Squaw Dress, sizes 3-6x, about $10. From the Cheyenne Group in Wamsutta Tepee Cloth, 50% Fortrel/50% cotton. Sawdust or Navaho Navy."

Look magazine, October 20, 1970—"'The Indian Style:' The Indians' inventive artistry with paint, and with feathers, furs and skins, triggered New York fashion designer Giorgio di Sant' Angelo's fall collection. The look is taking everyone's mind off skirt lengths—a hide falls more or less where it may—and has given the American women the joyful alternative of dressing like a sexy Indian instead of like a schoolmarm."

New York Times, October 24, 1970, Buffy Sainte-Marie is being interviewed by Judy Klemesrud: "'We're sick of being told that we should feel honored that people want to look like us,' she said. 'They say it's a memorial to our noble race, but that's a lot of bull. We don't want any more memorials. We need things like breakfast programs.'"

The following full-page ad appeared in the *New York Times,* February 22, 1971:

TRIBAL PLUMAGE.
What A Find For S. F. A.

Wild feathers, raw wood and silvery shine. Armies of beads, colored and dazzingly dangled. Super-sized ideas on American Indian themes worked out exclusively for us to give verve and spirit to all your body-huggy things. Borrowed perhaps from the chief of the tribe? Priced from $40 to $150, in our Costume Jewelry Collections, Street Floor.

VERY SAKS FIFTH AVENUE

INDIAN LOVE CALLS

SCENE XIX

Sexual acts in films prior to the present were consummated sans coitus. Copulation most often took the form of mouth to mouth resuscitation. This treatment, when applied to interracial involvements, found yet another special nook in Hollywood's already perverted code of morality known as the "Don'ts and Be Carefuls." "No willful offense to any nation, race or creed," "No rape," and "No miscegenation." No other race relationship has gotten as much footage as the red and the white entwined. The film industry found a variety of ways of using these "abhorrent," yet titillating and, thus, salable themes.

White men have lusted after Indian maids since the cranks started turning. Some early examples are: *How Tony Became a Hero* (1911), *The Half-Breed's Daughter* (1911), *The Ancient Bow* (1912), *His Punishment* (1912), *Justice of Manitou* (1912). To skip a generation or two: In *Canyon Passage* (1946, Jacques Tourneur) the villain, Ward Bond, discovers some lovely Indian maidens swimming naked, inciting Bond to rape and murder. This leads to a revengeful Indian uprising.

As a symbol of Hollywood's coming of age, the white man no longer has to lust or rape. Our hero is presented with a nymphomaniacal Indian maiden, Anna Hotwater, in *Dirty Dingus Magee* (1970, Burt Kennedy), played by starlet Michele Carey.

The film that led, in part, to Hollywood's more graphic use of sex in the Western was *Duel in the Sun* (1947, King Vidor), which was a big, empty epic. Jennifer Jones, as a half-breed with half-closed eyes and half-opened mouth, and Gregory Peck, as a rancher's son, pant and wheeze in a passionate confrontation and, in close-up, exchange an abundance of spittle. In the end, as is the case with most other racially-mixed sinners, they die.

Julie Newmar, with decolletage and slacks, as the Indian maid in *Mackenna's Gold* (1969) Columbia.

In "New Faces," *Look*, November 3, 1970, Ira Mothner wrote about Barbara Hershey and her boyfriend, David Carradine. Barbara spoke of *Heaven with a Gun*: "I played a half-breed and David raped me. That's how we met. Now we're together." The picture mentioned was made for TV in 1969, starring Glenn Ford as a reformed gun-slinger turned preacher. It is the very old story about sheepherders versus cattlemen. And thrown in for good measure, Barbara's Hopi shepherd father is hanged by David Carradine, the no-good son of the local cattle baron. Ford buries her father and Barbara moves in with him because of some kind of strange tribal custom which she explains in some kind of strange "ugh" dialogue. Predictably, the rotten son, David Carradine, rapes the innocent Indian maid.

Martha Hyer being molested in *Blood on the Arrow* (1964) Allied Artists.

When white men rape Indian women they usually do so with a mean scowl implying "I'm entitled." But when red men lusted after white women, a favorite shot was a tight close-up of a leering redskin ogling the terror-stricken woman just before the fatal fade. Now why did the redskin want to do this when there were Indian maidens the likes of Debra Paget or Jean Peters waiting back in the tipi?

The red man was lusting after the white girl captive as early as 1908 in *In the Days of the Pilgrims*. The Indian continued being a masher in *The Last Blockhouse* (1913). While we could see the beginnings of the primal urge as Wallace Beery leered in *The Last of the Mohicans* (1920), we could see the more blatant results of that urge in such films as *Fort Courageous* (1965, Lesley Selander). In keeping with the violence of the times, the Indians rape the daughter while her mother watches.

Although an Indian maid could give herself willingly to a white man, a white woman could not give herself willingly to an Indian man. When these films were first released, the audiences thought stories of white women captives to be racy, provocative and suggestive. Seeing a fair damsel in distress—whether tied to the stake, about to be mauled, scalped, or made love to—was guaranteed to make the heart beat faster.

By the 1940s, when innocence was lost, the white woman captive had to have been raped. If she did give herself, she was either insane or a whore. Surely, she should have killed herself rather than surrender. Once having given in, she was to be called scum, a squaw, dirt, a savage, and any other appropriate term. There could never be any sign of enjoyment or pleasure. Cohabitation and captivity had to be an ordeal. If the "white squaw" had a child, the half-breed was living proof of her sin and was to be treated accordingly.

All these taboos were brought into the open in *Northwest Passage* (1940, King Vidor). After the Abenaki village was ruthlessly and totally destroyed and its inhabitants horribly massacred by Spencer Tracy's Rogers' Rangers, those who had been captives of the Abenaki were gathered together for the journey home. Because of their captivity and the sexual depravities they were subjected to, some women were driven to insanity, acting out roles as dumb mutes or sluts. Some wanted to stay and they were as viciously abused and assaulted by the whites as the whites had claimed they had been treated by the Abenakis. Who could ever forget Isabel Jewell spitting out her hatred and contempt for those women? It was a memorable scene but the picture served as a clear guide post. There was to be no happy hanky-panky between the races.

Despite the fact that *The Scalphunters* (1968, Sidney Pollack) was not a very good movie—in fact, it was a bad one—Shelly Winters offered one bit of reality. When she was about to be captured by Indians, she gleefully shouted to her abductor: "Indian man, I don't know how many wives you have now, but you're going to have yourself the damnedest white squaw in the entire Kiowa nation!"

May Wynn eventually loses Robert Francis in *They Rode West* (1954) Columbia.

One of the most popular plots was the story of unrequited love of the Indian maiden for the white man. This simple story line may be complicated by one or any of the following:
    (1) The white man
        (a) is married
        (b) is engaged

      (c) is a widower who cherishes the memory of the
          dearly departed
      (d) has children who won't accept her
      (e) likes her but doesn't love her
      (f) vice versa
      (g) is too old or she's too young
      (h) was wounded during the Civil War
(2) She's noble, he's mean
(3) She's mean, he's noble
(4) He's disinterested because
      (a) he drinks
      (b) he gambles
      (c) he fools around
      (d) he's ambitious
      (e) he's greedy
      (f) he's corrupt
      (g) he's lazy
      (h) he's out for revenge
      (i) he was wounded during the Civil War
(5) He uses her as a plaything or a tool only to discard her
   as
      (a) a worn out shoe
      (b) a broken doll
      (c) a tramp
      (d) a piece of dirt
      (e) a whore
      (f) a squaw
(6) The Climax
      (a) she returns to the tribe
      (b) she returns to one of her kind who really loves her
      (c) he returns to civilization
      (d) she dies
      (e) he dies
      (f) he never recovers from the wound he got in the Civil
          War

    Gloria Talbott, as the Indian maiden, silently but bravely
carries her heart on her sleeve for everyone to see except for our
myopic hero, Joel McCrea in *The Oklahoman* (1957, Francis D.
Lyon). The next time around, Gloria, in a sexy decolletage
buckskin Indian maiden dress, loves the equally myopic Fred
MacMurray in *The Oregon Trail* (1959, Gene Fowler, Jr.). He is

a reporter too busy following up a story on the wagon train. She finds time to save him from being tortured by the Indians. He escapes, and in the nick of time gets the message to the fort that the Indians are about to attack. By devious devilish means the Indians manage to gain entrance to the fort. While winning they are scared off by an exploding wagon at the fort's open gate. And at this point Gloria announces, "It is because of this that I renounce my people."

In a movie made for TV, *Wild Women* (1970), some women, jailed for prostitution, get a chance for freedom if they pretend to be the wives of army men. These men are on a secret mission and will travel in covered wagons. One of the prisoners is an Indian maid. Unlike the rest of the women, she is quiet and reserved. She helps the whites by leading them to water. Later, she sleeps with one of the officers, as do all the other women with their supposed spouses. Now all the women end up being "whores with hearts of gold" and winning their men—except our Indian maid, who gives in to her hero with virginal restraint. She falls in love with him and is rejected.

By far the strongest heresy in Indian films was a marriage between an Indian man and a white woman. The subject has been rarely touched upon. *Red Deer's Devotion* (1911) and *Where the Trail Divides* (1914, Oscar Apfel) were stories of such marriages.

On the other hand there is *The Greater Barrier* (1915). The Pikes Peak movie company described it as follows: "This story concerns the much debated subject of an Indian-white girl love affair. After much hesitating, they finally decide to marry, but then the Indian's mother informs him that he is the girl's half-brother."

Another picture dealing with an Indian man marrying a white woman was *Foxfire* (1955, Joseph Pevney). This modern story takes place in Arizona with Jeff Chandler, a mixed blood Apache, as an engineer at the mines. He meets Jane Russell, the rich society girl from the East, and it's love at first sight. They marry and the rest is soap opera. So many things happen that one wonders how they can survive the picture, let alone the marriage.

Hollywood usually cops out as it did in *The Greater Barrier*. At the crucial moment the Indian man finds out he's white or the white woman finds out she's Indian and they can get married and live happily ever after. In *White Eagle* (1932, Lambert Hillyer) Buck Jones, as White Eagle, is raised as Indian but discovers he is white and can marry the paleface heroine, Barbara Weeks.

This is an excerpt from a review in the *New York Herald Tribune*, March 27, 1949, signed O. L. G., jr. [Otis Guernsey]:

> The Rialto's latest offering is a piece of Cinecolored trivia about Navahos victimized by a crooked United States agent. "Daughter of the West" casts Philip Reed as a young, Carlyle [sic]-educated leader of his people and Martha Vickers as a white school teacher who discovers that she is Ramona's daughter and therefore part Indian. Intrigue over a valuable copper mine, romance and distrust of white man's laws are the ingredients for a trashy plot, and the caricatures of Navahos to be found here are awkward and ridiculous to the point of insult. All in all, "Daughter of the West" approaches as close to absolute zero as is possible without running off an hour or so of undeveloped film.

The love of an Indian man for a white woman is a much easier theme to handle. The Indian brave or chief's love is usually unspoken. To avoid the threat of an involvement between a white woman and a red man, the Indian is usually eliminated. But the involvement of an Indian woman with a white man offers a much lesser threat to film makers.

In *Last of the Mohicans* both lovers die; the film culminates in that memorable shot of Cora's hand and Uncas' hand reaching out to each other in their last moment. Their hands clasp and they are finally united in death.

Richard Dix silently yearns for the white heroine in *The Vanishing American* (1925, George B. Seitz), and is killed off.

Cochise falls in love with a white woman captive in *Conquest of Cochise* (1953, William Castle). This really stretches the imagination.

Halliday Brand (1957, Joseph H. Lewis) tries to tell a frontier story in modern terms. The white father wants to stop the romance between his daughter and a half-breed. It has that would-you-want-your-daughter-to-marry-one kind of timelessness.

In *Devil's Doorway* (1950, Anthony Mann), Robert Taylor plays a Shoshoni, a returned Civil War veteran with the Congressional Medal of Honor who should have everything going for him. A woman lawyer, Paula Raymond, tries to help when he's in trouble. There is a love interest between the two that is barely touched upon. It is finally dismissed by Taylor with, "A hundred years from now, it might have worked."

A hundred and some years later it still doesn't work. *Run, Simon, Run* (1970) was a film made for television. This is a modern story of a Papago Indian who serves ten years after being convicted for killing his brother in a drunken brawl. He didn't do it and swears vengeance on the white man who did. While seeking revenge, he meets, falls in love with, and makes pregnant a rich, white woman. She is a social worker on the reservation searching for something meaningful to do. She finds fullfilment in her pregnancy. In the end, the Indian hero is killed off before they can marry. Of course.

There is a true and lovely moment in this film which is too quickly forgotten. At a rodeo where whites and reds sit in separate sections, a group of Indian girls stage a mock Indian dance for the entertainment of the spectators. Simon, played by Burt Reynolds, a leader among his people, to show his shame and disgust, stands and covers his face. The other Indians follow suit and the girls run off the field ashamed. The portrayal of this reality makes the rest of the film all the more profane.

What puts this pretentious movie, Hollywood and ABC-TV in proper perspective is an ad run in the *New York Times* on December 1, 1970. To repeat, the story is about a Papago who returns to the Papago Reservation in Arizona. The ad reads:

A World Premiere
RUN, SIMON, RUN
An Indian must choose between his love
for a beautiful white woman—and an ancient Apache code
that compels him to avenge his brother's murder.
... which compels us to ask: what happened to the old Papago code?

CUT TO
Sandy Howard, producer of *A Man Called Horse* (1970), being interviewed by Dan Jorgensen of the Sioux Falls, *South Dakota Argus-Leader*, April 25, 1970. Howard is speaking: I feel that since this is a story of a white man captured by the Indians, then world audiences will better be able to relate to the Indian through that white man. If a story is just about Indians, then it is hard for a Caucasian to relate to it. Every man who is white could fall in love with Running Deer in this movie, because they see it happen in the movie.

White men marrying Indian maids has long been a favorite subject in Westerns but—and there has always been a but—something must happen to prevent the couple from living happily ever after. As previously mentioned, a white man cohabiting with an Indian maid was known as a squaw man.

James Stewart married Debra Paget—no Indian picture in the '50s was complete without this brown-contact-lensed-Gidget-in-Indianland ingenue—in *Broken Arrow* (1950, Delmer Daves). Their sublime happiness is destroyed when she is killed, leaving him to roam the world unhappily alone.

Clark Gable, in *Across the Wide Missouri* (1951, William Wellman), enters into a marriage of convenience with an Indian princess played by Maria Elena Marques. But when they find true love and happiness and she has a baby, she is killed off.

Cochise (Jeff Chandler) brings James Stewart, groom-to-be, to meet Debra Paget in "full bridal array" in *Broken Arrow* (1950) 20th Century Fox.

The Last Outpost (1951, Lewis R. Foster) tells of brother against brother in the Civil War who unite against the Apaches.

A former general has married an Apache and lives with her people. He has become a sort of Indian guru chief—all knowing and all wise. The problem of intermarriage is quickly resolved when a townsman sneers, "We ain't listening to any squaw man," and kills the general.

CUT TO
A Sequence from *The Indian Fighter* (1955, Andre de Toth) in which a character says of Kirk Douglas, "Indian fighter, hell. Indian lover."

In *Colorado Territory* (1949, Raoul Walsh), Joel McCrea, a bad guy this time, is the one who gets killed in the end. His half-breed wife is played by Virginia Mayo in medium pancake.

The flaming frontier extends as far as Bruce Bennett's arm as he burns himself in a test of courage in *Flaming Frontier* (1958) 20th Century Fox.

Miscegenation has been brought peculiarly up to date and made strangely relevant in two recent films. In the absolutely

239

dreadful *The McMasters* (1970, Alf Kjellin), a "now" story, a black ex-Union soldier, Brock Peters, takes to wife an Indian maiden, Nancy Kwan. In the picture he rapes her, in long shot; they hold hands, in close-up; there is a marriage ceremony; and he finally sees her naked—the audience sees her too, from the waist up. There are two characters—a black man and an Indian maiden; there are two actors—a black man and a Eurasian woman. And never—never once—do their lips meet in a kiss.

Corinna Tsopei in *A Man Called Horse* (Elliot Silverstein), prior to her marriage to the white man, goes through a sweat lodge purification ritual (there was no such ritual before marriage among the Sioux). The audience sees her naked from the waist up. It doesn't take long to realize that this scene is only a variation of De Mille's famous heroine bathing scenes—only De Mille did it better. Although spoken of, nothing is shown in *Horse* of the mandatory purification ceremony for the man preceding his taking the Sun Vow, as it is called in the film. But, then we have already seen Harris' derriere. After the marriage, Richard and Corinna settle in for a long wedding's night. The director, shooting her naked from the waist up again, has her rotating her breasts over Harris as a prelude of things to come. She, too, is killed off but the memory of the mammaries lives on.

The wedding ceremonies in most of these films always accentuate the mystical and the magical. Part of the marriage ritual in several films involves cutting the Indian bride and the white groom and mingling their blood. This is also the ultimate unification of white and red man as they become blood brothers.

This preoccupation with blood smacks of being mid-European in origin in the best Transylvanian vampire tradition. Certain male, Teutonic-type European secret societies slashed and lashed their wrists and swore to be blood brothers to the death. To our knowledge, Native Americans did not. Nevertheless, the blood ceremony between James Stewart and Debra Paget in *Broken Arrow* does seem so romantic. To add to this, Debra Paget, dressed all in white, rides a pure white horse into the darkness of the night after the ceremony. The wedding in *A Man Called Horse*, with the night-time procession of burning torches, looks like a left-over from some South Sea island epic.

The only relevance these ceremonies have to Native American customs lies in the imagination of the script writers.

Indian rituals and ceremonies, believe it or not.

Sioux in *The Way West* (1967) United Artists.

Probably the most anti-Native American film ever made was John Huston's *The Unforgiven* (1960), particularly since it was purported to be an honest portrayal of frontier life. It is loaded with overt and covert sexual innuendo. Audrey Hepburn plays a Kiowa girl, who is raised as a daughter by a homesteading white family. The question of her being an Indian is not raised until later in the picture. It is then that her foster brother, Burt Lancaster, is accused of being an Indian lover. On the other hand, Lancaster has a younger brother, Audie Murphy, who is an Indian hater. The family's neighbors demand to know whether or not Audrey is an Indian, the reason being that the Kiowas are on the warpath to claim the girl. In fact, her real

241

brother is the Kiowa chief. The crisis comes to a head when villain Charles Bickford demands in front of the mob that Audrey be stripped naked so they can see for themselves whether she is a redskin or not. The suggestion is gleefully accepted. But Big Brother Burt comes to the rescue.

Using such phrases as "Injun lover" and "red nigger" and having characters so blatantly prejudiced does not necessarily make an honest film. There are some who might say that this is nothing more than a true expression of how some settlers felt. Granted. But what does make this such an anti-Native American film is that there is no counter-balance to all the hatred. The Kiowa's familial loyalty is not enough. The chief and his companions are still ruthless red marauders. What we are left with as a counter-weight to all this vicious spewing of hatred for the red man, is the supposedly simple purity of the relationship between an innocent Indian maiden and a stouthearted white hero.

Seven Seas to Calais (1963) MGM.

242

Naked in the Sun (1957) Allied Artists.

VOICE OVER
This excerpt from the review of *Flaming Star*, signed J. M., in the *New York Herald Tribune*, December 17, 1960, is heard:

"Oddly enough, and despite its best intentions, 'Flaming Star' indulges in some foolish racism while preaching a sermon of tolerance. Pacer, the half-breed, Elvis Presley hears things which are inaudible to white men. He seems to know that horses are approaching long before his white father and half-brother hear the merest rustle of sagebrush. His Indian mother, played by Dolores Del Rio, goes off to die in the woods, drawn back by some mysterious instinct deep within her. Elephants may do this but why can't Indians die in bed?"

The progeny of a Hollywood mixed union between red and white has its own connotation. The term "half-breed" speaks for itself. For the Hollywood scriptwriter, the half-breed is a great catch-all. Villainy, weakness, and just plain cussedness or their extreme opposites are always attributed to this character. Half-breed men seemed to have been used more often than half-breed women.

In some films an even finer blood line was drawn. In 1916 Leon Kent wrote, directed, and played in *The Quarter Breed*, "a good western showing how a quarter breed overcomes a home-

243

less love and an inherent craving for drink." And in 1922 there was *One Eighth Apache*.

Broken Lance (1954, Edward Dmytryk), a remake of *House of Strangers*, had Spencer Tracy married to Katy Jurado, in one of her many Indian roles. The pronouncement of doom comes in the conflict between the half-breed son, Robert Wagner, and his all-white older half-brother, Richard Widmark. The Freudian implications of the title are too obvious to be ignored.

Gary Cooper in *Distant Drums* (1951, Raoul Walsh) has a son by a Creek wife. It was quite all right for Cooper to have been married to an Indian because, at the beginning of the film, she's already dead, and, besides, she was a Creek princess.

The half-breed went on in *The Half-Breed* (1952, Stuart Gilmore). In *Guide to Movies on TV* (1970), edited by Howard Thompson, it was said of this movie: "Dull as it is, this pat little drama does express concern about racial prejudice, with Jack Buetel . . . as the cigar store-type Indian hero, a young man supposedly torn by conflicting loyalties . . . ."

An exhibitors display card for this 1952 film.

244

Elvis Presley, as the half-breed son in *Flaming Star* (1960, Don Siegel), had troubles with his all-white half-brother, Steve Forrest, which were similar to the ones faced by Robert Wagner, as the half-breed, and Richard Widmark, as the all-white, in *Broken Lance*. In *Reprisal* (1956, George Sherman), a half-breed, Guy Madison, denies his heritage until he is witness to blatant prejudice . . . while the half-breeds played by John Wayne in *Hondo* (1953, John Farrow), Richard Widmark in *The Last Wagon* (1956, Delmer Daves), and William Holden in *The Proud and the Profane* (1956, George Seaton), are more white than Indian.

Very few films have been made about half-breed women. Those that were, dealt with them as sex objects, brazen hussies, or hell-cats. It is easier to use a full-blooded Indian woman in order to avoid the additional complications presented by a half-white woman, which would have to result in a half happy ending.

NATIVE AMERICANS PLAYING INDIAN

SCENE XX

The Native American actor was a participant in a paradox because he did his "Indian" thing, knowing full well most often that the strange character he was told to portray had no relationship to himself as a Native American. He still knows it. This means of survival is one of the conscious games played by the Native American—that of telling the white man what he wants to hear and showing the white man what he wants to see. This is from *Geronimo His Own Story* (1971), originally edited by S. M. Barrett and newly edited by Frederic W. Turner III. Geronimo speaks:

Many people in St. Louis invited me to come to their homes, but my keeper always refused.

Every Sunday the President of the Fair [The Louisiana Purchase Exposition in 1904] sent for me to go to a Wild West Show .... There were many other Indian tribes there, ... I am glad I went to the Fair. I saw many interesting things and learned much of the white people. They are a very kind and peaceful people. [Turner's footnote: The reader should recall here that Geronimo was not without guile. His statements about white culture often have the appearance of cutting several ways.] ... I wish all my people could have attended the Fair.

CUT TO
A meeting room in 1939. Rows of folding chairs are occupied by many men and women. At one end is a long table. Some reporters are seated at the table taking notes. A man stands and raps his knuckles on the table:

I'd like to call the meeting to order. We have some reporters with us tonight. To make sure they haven't made a mistake and come to the wrong place, my name is Many Treaties or, in your tradition, Bill Hazlett, and I'm chairman of the Indian Actor's Association. Are you all in the right place? Good. We will start the meeting with our customary prayer and singing of "America." Will you all please stand? (They do. He offers a brief prayer in his native tongue, Blackfoot, and leads them in singing "America.") Thank you. You can sit down now if you want to. Before we get into the regular business of the meeting, I would like to give our visitors a little background about our association. We were organized three years ago. When they were casting *The Last of the Mohicans,* some of us noticed that Indians were underbidding each other just so they could get work. We knew it was wrong, we didn't like it but we also knew that the only way we could change things was by organizing. So Friend-of-the Tribe, L. Y. Maxwell, me, and a few others helped start the association.

Our objectives were to stop the movie producers from encouraging and allowing this price cutting and to replace non-Indians in acting jobs with Indians. Needless to say, we were very successful as can be seen by our progress since 1936. The Indian Actors' Association is affiliated with the Screen Actors' Guild. We are protected by a Closed Shop Clause even though Indians outside the Association and the Guild can and are used on location shooting. We are also protected by job preference for our members, better salaries and working conditions. Our present membership is 77—52 men and 25 women. Membership is open to any Indian, no matter where he's from and no matter whether he's a full-blood or only one-sixty-fourth Indian. We meet once a month, dues are one dollar quarterly and our five directors are elected every six months. Tribes represented in the Association are: Blackfoot, Iroquois, Sioux, Osage, Pima, Creek, Nez Perce, Wiyot, Hopi, Cherokee, Navajo, Ottawa, Mission, Pueblo, Apache, Comanche, Potawatomi, Delaware-Cherokee, Klamath, Papago, Sac-Fox, Kickapoo, Penobscot and Arapahoe. So you can see we can give producers just about any kind of tribal representation they want and we certainly try and do this whenever possible.

Our Association has had other very beneficial effects. For one thing, it has made us all even more conscious of our own Indianness. As a result, we have started classes in such things as sign language and picture writing. We will be starting others soon so that we can perpetuate our Indian heritage and better prepare us for jobs as technical advisors on Westerns.

Another paradox—According to the United States government (BIA—Bureau of Indian Affairs) an Indian is a Native American born or living on a federal reservation and thus carried on tribal rolls. Thousands of others who were not born on a reserve or who were born on state reservations which are not under federal jurisdiction are not counted tribally or racially as "Indians."

Jack D. Forbes, in his *The Indian in America's Past* (1964), wrote: "Conservatively, it would seem that at least 10,000,000 residents of the United States are part Native American, and actually the figure could easily be pushed up to 16,000,000 or more."

Samuel Eliot Morison in *The Oxford History of the American People* (1965) mentions: ". . . it has become something of distinction in the United States to claim Indian ancestry. One President of the United States (Coolidge) and one Vice-President (Curtis) had Indian blood and were proud of it."

White America's obsessive attraction to things and people native is vividly illustrated by this description of the lead in the All-Native American *Hiawatha* from *The Moving Picture News*, March 15, 1913:

> Jesse Cornplanter, Hiawatha, is one of the handsomest men ever shown in moving pictures, and can boast almost royal descent, his great-great-grandfather having been the high chief of the Senecas when Washington was president, and was Washington's friend. Young Cornplanter is a mute poet, the expression of his eyes revealing the unspoken yearnings of his nature. While on tour with the Indian players, he has always attracted a great deal of attention and admiration, in fact he is always a real matinee idol. Last summer at York Harbor he and old Nakomis had hosts of visitors before and after the performances . . . . Mr. Moore [the director] said, "At times the very frank admiration of the whites seems to be upsetting the poise of the players; when I see signs of this I change the cast and in a few days the offender is a good Indian again . . . ."

In 1911 those Native Americans who were part of the 101 Ranch Show so highly praised by Ince included William Eagleshirt, Swallow, Robert Crazy Thunder, One Feather, Pete Red Elk, White Stag, and Daddy Lone Bear. The latter's wife, Mama Lone Bear, also played in Ince films, such as *Breed of the North* (1914) and *The Village 'Neath the Sea* (1914). This story on Daddy Lone Bear appeared in *Reel Life*, a publicity sheet for the Mutual Exchange on July 18, 1914:

> One of the most picturesque figures at the New York Motion Picture studios . . . is the venerable Sioux, Daddy Lone Bear. He is the sole survivor of Custer's famous fight in the Black Hills of North [sic] Dakota in the late seventies.

Daddy Lone Bear, though a denizen of the Indian village annexed to Inceville, holds himself aloof from the hundred-and-fifty-odd other Indians. He feels their ways are not his ways. He belongs to the ancient race, in spirit and customs still unconquered. The dashing young Indians in the pictures, in their war paint and shells and elaborately beaded costumes, he looks upon with scorn. Daddy Lone Bear clings to the simple life. The camera can take him as he is—or have to leave him. He is above catering even to the movies.

Dark Cloud started his career in the early days of film. He was a model for Frederick Remington, a much sought after lecturer, worked for Griffith and made films for Pathe Freres. His career was as varied as the press releases on him.

In 1914 one press release in *The Moving Picture World* tells us that he is a Sioux and "the son of a chieftain who fought Custer," whereas in *Reel Life* he is reported to be a chief of the Abenaki tribe "of the Algonquin nation . . . aborigines of the Eastern states."

His wife, Dove Eye, appeared in such films as *The Arrow Maiden* (1915) while Dark Cloud was featured in such films as *Song of the Wildwood Flute* (1910) and *An Indian's Loyalty* (1912) under Biograph and Griffith; *The Ceremonial Turquoise* (1915), *The Huron Converts* (1915), *The Indian Trapper's Vindication* (1915), *Son of 'The Dog'* (1915) for the Reliance banner; *A Red Man's Heart* (1914), *The Severed Thong* (1914), *Meg of the Mines* (1914) for Majestic.

Griffith once said that Eagle Eye was the greatest Indian actor. In addition to this claim to fame, he was also a dare-devil stuntman who would do amazing, if not reckless, leaps. Among his films were: *The Arrow Maiden* and *The Ceremonial Turquoise* for Reliance; *The Final Verdict* (1914), *The Red Man's Heart, The Severed Thong, Big Jim's Heart* (1915) for Majestic; *Indian Fate* (1914) for Kalem; plus one with the great title *Moonshine Molly* (1914).

Two of the earliest stars, of course, were Young Deer and his renowned wife, Red Wing.

Another famous acting couple in those early days was Art Ortega and his wife, Princess Mona Darkfeather. Other actors frequently used, as previously mentioned, were Little Thunder, Big Moon, Chief Phillippi, Lone Bear, Two Feathers, Eagle Eye, Eagle Feather, and Eagle Wing.

Women did not receive the same kind of press as the men. So only a few, such as Winona, Princess Whynemah and Princess Leaping Deer, became well known, while some of the men were to become internationally famous.

Iron Eyes Cody is one of the most famous of all Native American actors. One can find his name in most books on the Western. His career has spanned almost 50 years during which he has appeared in almost that number of films from *The Iron Horse* (1924) to *A Man Called Horse* (1970).

Jay Silverheels, best known as Tonto, has played in many films, including *Broken Arrow* (1950), and played Geronimo in *The Battle at Apache Pass* (1952) and *Walk the Proud Land* (1956).

John War Eagle played in such films as *Broken Arrow* and *Tomahawk* (1951), and Rodd Redwing has made a name for himself as a technical advisor. Mr. Redwing, one of the fastest draws in the movies, has trained many Western stars in his specialty.

One actor who is so often overlooked is Charles Stevens, a grandson of Geronimo. Although his face is easily recognizable on the screen, he never got the press and recognition of Iron Eyes Cody and Jay Silverheels. Mr. Stevens had a long career. He was in just about all of Doug Fairbanks' Westerns. He was shot at by Doug in *Wild and Woolly* (1917, John Emerson) and browbeaten by Noah Beery in *The Mark of Zorro* (1920, Fred Niblo). He was usually cast in sneaky villainous roles, as in the serial, *Overland Mail* (1942, Ford Beebe and John Rawlins). One of his best roles was as the clever Diabolito in *Ambush* (1950, Sam Wood). Still, as movie tradition would have it, he died at the hands of the star, Robert Taylor.

The United States government frequently appointed Native American "Chiefs" in order to sign treaties which best suited the government's interests. Officials would often seek out a man who had little power or popularity among the people of a tribe or nation, make sure they could buy him off, and dub him "Chief." Similarly, Hollywood assigned such titles as "Chief" to many Native American actors as well as using chiefs as stock characters. If any of the actors actually were chiefs, the studio publicity departments certainly exploited this fact.

Chief Yowlachie was a familiar face whose work spanned the silents and the talkies. He appeared in such films as *Moran of the Mounted* (1926, Harry Joe Brown), *The Glorious Trail* (1928, Albert Rogell), and *The Invaders* (1929, J. P. McGowan). He also appeared in such serials as *Hawk of the Hills* (1927) and *Son of Geronimo Apache Avenger* (1952), both directed by Spencer G. Bennet. Unfortunately Iron Eyes Cody and Yowlachie had to become the Indian equivalent of baggy pants comedians in Bob Hope's *The Paleface* (1948, Norman Z. McLeod).

There have been two men with similar names: Chief Thundercloud, Scott T. Williams, played the original Tonto on radio, while Chief Thunder Cloud, Victor Daniels, played in *Ramona* (1936); he also played Tonto in *The Lone Ranger* (1938, William Witney and John English, serial); he had the title role in *Geronimo* (1939) and again played Geronimo in *I Killed Geronimo* (1950).

Another famous actor was Chief Nipo Strongheart, a Yakima Native American. He acted as technical advisor for many Westerns and he appeared in such films as *Across the Wide Missouri* (1951, William Wellman), *Westward the Women* (1951, William Wellman), *Lone Star* (1952, Vincent Sherman), and *Pony Soldier* (1952, Joseph M. Newman).

Others who acted in films were: Chief Standing Bear, who appeared with Tom Mix in *The Miracle Rider* (1935, B. Reeves Eason and Armand Schaefar, serial); Chief Yellow Calf, who was in *The Covered Wagon* (1923); Chief White Horse, who appeared with Tim McCoy in *Winners of the Wilderness* (1927, W. S. Van Dyke).

Chief John Big Tree appeared in many of Ford's films. He began his career in 1915. For over a quarter of a century he was to give substantial performances with some of his best work done for Ford. Some of his other films include: *The Cactus Blossom* (1915), *The Frontier Trail* (1926, Scott R. Dunlop), *Ransom's Folly* (1926, Sidney Olcott), *The Frontiersman* (1927, Reginald Barker), *The Overland Telegraph* (1929, John Waters), *Sioux Blood* (1929, John Waters), *Susannah of the Mounties* (1939, William Seiter), *Brigham Young* 1940, Henry Hathaway), *Western Union* (1941, Fritz Lang), and *Devil's Doorway* (1950, Anthony Mann).

Jim Thorpe, considered by many to be the greatest athlete of the 20th century, retired from professional sports in 1929 at the age of 41. Although too old for sports but still comparatively young, he soon learned that this country has no room for ex-heroes. To eke out a living during the Depression, Thorpe played the carnival circuit and made a few movies. After all, the name Jim Thorpe still has some value, even if it only meant playing a feathered creature ughing and mugging for the camera. Some of the films Thorpe appeared in were: *White Eagle* (1932, Lambert Hillyer), *Telegraph Trail* (1933, Tenny Wright), *Behold My Wife* (1935), *Wanderer of the Wasteland* (1935, Otho Lovering), *Treachery Rides the Range* (1936, *Arizona Frontier* (1940, Al Herman), *Prairie Schooners* (1940, Sam Nelson), *Outlaw Trail* (1944, Robert Tansey), and *Black Arrow* (1944, Lew Landers).

CUT TO
A well appointed executive's office on the Warner Brothers lot. A press conference has been called by Jack Warner to announce their one million dollar production of *Jim Thorpe—All American*. Jim Thorpe himself is there and is presented with a $25,000 check for the screen rights to his life story. The director, Michael Curtiz, and the stars, Burt Lancaster, Charles Bickford, Steve Cochran, and Phyllis Thaxter, are there as well and as each is introduced, there is much smiling, talking, hand-shaking with Mr. Warner and Mr. Thorpe. Several shots of the men in groups and in pairs with their arms around each other's shoulders are taken. There is one pose of Jack Warner, Jim Thorpe, and Burt Lancaster, arms on shoulders, big smiles, hugging each other as Mr. Warner happily shouts to the newspeople: Jim Thorpe is all American. His story is all American. It is the kind of story that could have happened only here, in our country.

Eddie Little Sky has been active in Hollywood since the 1950s. Some of his more recent films have been *The Way West* (1967, Andrew V. McLaglen), *A Man Called Horse*, and *Run, Simon, Run* (1970).

As of 1971, SAG (Screen Actors Guild) listed these people as members in the following categories:

"American Indian-Speaking Males"	*"American Indian-Speaking Females"*
Jack Bighead	Joanne C. Johnson
Abel Fernandez	Dawn Little-Sky
Jerado De Cordovier	Constance Marlow
Pete Hernandez	Princess Lois Red Elk
Pat Hogan	Buffy Sainte-Marie
Chief Geronimo Kuth-Le	Pablita Verde Hardin
Henry O'Brien	
George Little-Buffalo	

Bill Little-Owl
Eddie Little-Sky
Vincent St. Cyr
John St. Pierre
(John War Eagle)
Sun Bear
Ed Sunrise
Felix Walking-Wolf
Carlos Manteca
Don Fisher
Semu Haute
Joseph Seaboy
Chief Dan George
Jim Spurgin
Grenade Curran
Jon Dalke
Cody Bearpaw
Arthur S. Junaluska

We assume that "American Indian-Speaking" means that these are Native American actors who speak one or more of the many Native American languages.

CUT BACK TO
The meeting in 1939. The chairman, Bill Hazlett, is still speaking:
As far as pay is concerned, we've had a lot of success there, too. We used to get $5.50 a day if we wore studio costumes. Non-Indian actors got $11 a day for the same work. Now that's no longer true. If we wear a studio costume and are on foot, we get $8.25 a day, on horseback $11 and if we supply our own costumes, $13.75 a day. By the way, to show what it means to be a member, on the *Man of Conquest* set some of our people were using sign language and wanted full speaking part pay for this. The producers refused and we took the matter to the Screen Actors' Guild and they ruled in our favor and our people got paid what they deserved.
Now we are pushing for $16.50 a day if we wear our own costumes. And we're going to get it, too, because we've already got that rate for *Union Pacific*.

By 1970s, extras were to receive from $35.65 to $91.12 a day.

CUT BACK TO
The company of *A Man Called Horse* on location in Mexico. Many Sioux families are standing huddled together in the rain. They are waiting for that day's filming to begin for which they will receive $12 a day for each male adult and $2.50 for each child.

CUT TO
Robert Redford, one of the stars of *Tell Them Willie Boy Is Here*, speaking: They had originally offered me the part of the Indian, but I felt Willie should be a real Indian—then they couldn't find one.

254

CUT TO

The former Miss Greece and Miss Universe of 1964, Corinna Tsopei, one of the stars of *A Man Called Horse*, speaking:

This is my first major part in a film, I enjoyed it thoroughly. I had never met an Indian prior to the filming, and I met some Sioux girls who would make excellent actresses. The only problem is that they are very shy until you get to know them.

I found the Indians very strong and proud, but some were not friendly because they felt that an Indian girl should have held the part that I had in the movie. I felt that if an Indian girl had tried out for the part and was good enough, she would have won the role.

CUT TO

Katharine Ross, one of the stars of *Tell Them Willie Boy Is Here*, speaking: There are qualities in the part that I'm like but don't look like. I wanted to play the part but I was worried about the physical thing of playing an Indian girl. I didn't want to make her another Hollywood Indian.

The fact that Miss Ross, a white actress, was cast in the role of an Indian maiden makes her just that—another Hollywood Indian.

Dan George, who played Old Lodge Skins in *Little Big Man*, according to the bio in Cinema Center Films' *PRELIMINARY PRODUCTION NOTES "LITTLE BIG MAN:"*

. . . is a hereditary chief of Canada's Squamish Indians and president of their tribal council in Vancouver, B.C., where he makes his home. He is an actor of considerable repute in Canada, a star of the TV series, "Cariboo Country." He has also appeared on the stage in Vancouver, and in 1968 the Disney Studio imported him to Hollywood to make his screen debut in *Smith*, starring Glenn Ford. In the court-room scene of that film he recites the famous speech with which the Nez Perce chief, Joseph, surrendered to U.S. troops in 1877. When he finished, the whole company was in tears—grips, technicians, himself included—and a rare thing occurred: the others spontaneously lined up as he walked from the set, to shake his hand. With the release of the picture, he affected audiences the same way and is now being hailed as a find with a future. He is 70.

Dan George's performance in *Little Big Man* is very reminiscent of the warm quality inherent in the performances of John Big Tree. The character of Old Lodge Skins, though beautifully conceived by author Thomas Berger in his novel *Little Big Man*, suffers badly when reinterpreted for the screen. While the

255

screenwriter, Calder Willingham, and director, Arthur Penn, were able to visualize the whites with some degree of accuracy and to satirize them with ease, they did not attribute the same lunacy and lack of virtues to the Cheyennes. Now Berger's people, white as well as red, and their relationships to each other are funny as hell with vice and virtue common to all. The Cheyennes in the novel are not a bunch of noble innocents in isolation, just as the whites are not an isolated bunch of corrupt individuals. All of them are individuals who, in their own way, do all the things people are liable to do in the midst of war, poverty, corruption, greed, and ignorance.

Old Lodge Skins, instead of being the character created by Berger, becomes on the screen like the Cochise of *Broken Arrow* fame—a noble, innocent patriarch who speaks in a quaint manner supposedly conveying an "Indian" attitude. Berger was able to make the red man quite distinct without such condescension. Since the film is treated, in part, as a historical documentation of the times, it behooved those responsible to show the Cheyennes in proper perspective.

It was a time of many battles, so survival for the Native American had long since taken a different shape. The white adversary was a constant reality and threat. To view him simply as "crazy" would have been impossible for the Native American.

Crazy Horse was a well-known visionary. It was his war cry, as he led the Cheyennes and the Sioux, "It is a good day to die," that is given to the peaceful Old Lodge Skins to say repeatedly. Sitting Bull, a great medicine man, was also a visionary. He foresaw the Battle of the Greasy Grass in a dream. The difference between Old Lodge Skins and the real Crazy Horse and Sitting Bull is that the latter two did not have the time for a quaint life in a tipi. They planned; they fought for their lives; they challenged and beat the white man many, many times prior to the Custer affair. While, in the film, the Cheyennes' costumes and customs were fairly authentic, they remained characters, not human beings.

This is from a letter from Mrs. Gilbert, who has many friends among the Cheyenne on their reservation at Lame Deer, Montana:

> Yesterday I was visiting on the Cheyenne Reservation and talked to William Tallbull. He said he had been to see

LITTLE BIG MAN, but could only stand about fifteen minutes of it. His grandfather, Lame White Man, was killed in the Custer Battle and he had heard too much to be able to endure the travesty of history as portrayed by movies.

It would seem that the producers of *Little Big Man* really did intend to treat the Native American fairly. Why, then, did they choose a satirical novel, which makes good fun of all, to make a film presumably as an atonement? Satire can only be appreciated by those already familiar with the subject being satirized. It is for this reason that they could not caricature the Cheyennes as they did the whites.

CUT TO

A Russian reporter typing a story which was to appear in newspapers in the United States during September of 1965. We hear the story in Voice Over:

The government newspaper *Izvestia* has charged that Indian reservations in the United States are "America's internal colonies."

"American propaganda depicts the reservations as exotic sites where one can see original dancing and photograph 'the last of the Mohicans,' can even touch their decorations of bright feathers and smoke a pipe of forest tobacco," *Izvestia* said.

"Yes, there are such villages, where dancing and smiles can be ordered. But these are on tourist routes. The reservations in which the Indians live have nothing in common with this publicity circus.

"They are veritable colonies, colonies on the territory of a country which is boasting of 'equal opportunities' for all citizens."

Since this story is unfortunately true, it is understandable that Native Americans are available en masse in such "colonies" to play Indians for the moving picture, i.e.: the Navajos in Ford's films, the Sioux in *A Man Called Horse*, the Crows in *Little Big Man*. Most Native Americans, who have participated in these films have done so mostly for economic reasons.

Is it the purpose of making such "authentic" films, to bring the world stories of the past and avoid dealing with the "colonies" of the present?

Dustin Hoffman, star of the film, commented in the *Times*, October 1, 1969: "I was interested in this picture because it presents the Indian in a different light. I've seen a lot of movies but never one that presented the Indian fairly. Most of them go along with the 'Indians are savages' theme. They really have a lot of culture."

Survival for the Native American is now rooted, primarily, to the reservation. There, in most cases, he lives in abject poverty while attempting to maintain contact with his culture. The conclusion we must draw is that this depressing authenticity does not lend itself to exciting Technicolor productions for the screen.

CUT TO

The Winter Soldier Investigation in Detroit, Michigan, December 31-January 2, 1971. These investigations were organized and conducted by Vietnam Veterans Against the War. A Native American Vietnam veteran is testifying: If you compare the War in Vietnam and the Indian Wars, you'll see they are the same . . . broken treaties, massacres, destruction of the land, and mass relocation.

CUT TO

Another veteran testifying: The Vietnamese will never again regain their culture as it was. We changed their ways of living by making them depend on our dollar and not on the land which they lived off previously.

Despairingly soon the silver screen may recreate the former Vietnamese "Indians" for us, as they once were. For this, too, the makers of film will have to hire experts so that, if necessary, any Oriental could play the part authentically—and be told how it "really was."

PROTEST AND DEFEAT

SCENE XXI

Ezra Goodman in *The Fifty Year Decline and Fall of Hollywood* (1962) reports: "And television has influenced the movies in other ways. One movie director I know, a specialist in horse operas, sits in front of his television set for hours, industriously scanning TV westerns for cinematic inspiration. Three good television oater episodes combined, he said, add up to a good feature-length horse opera. This is ironic because the makers of TV westerns get most of their ideas from old Hollywood horse operas."

The years spanning the '30s, '40s, and '50s were witness to a cross-pollenation. The phantom horseman, like a rocking horse gone mad, leaped from comic strip, to comic book, to radio, to movies, to television; from "Red Ryder," to "Renfrew of the Royal Mounted," to "Brave Eagle," to "Sergeant Preston of the Yukon," to "The Lone Ranger."

> An American journalist who had spent several years in India, and whose small children had come to love the Indians, came home in 1958. Shortly thereafter he found the boys crying as they watched a TV "Western" because, as one moaned, "They're killing *Indians*!" Papa had to explain that they were not Indians of India but Red Indians, and that to kill them was part of the American Way of Life. (From Samuel Eliot Morison's *The Oxford History of the American People* [1965]).

In 1960, at the instigation of the many tribes within the state, the Oklahoma legislature passed a strongly-worded resolution denouncing the television industry. The Native American population of Oklahoma is about 64,000, or 2.5% of the state's total. The tribes represented by the signatories of the resolution included the Osage, Oto, Choctaw, Caddo, Kickapoo, Sac and Fox, Creek, Pawnee, Tonkawa, Wyandotte, Arapahoe, Shawnee, Chippewa, Kiowa, Comanche, Apache, Cherokee, Miami, Delaware, Iowa, and Cheyenne.

The purpose of the resolution was summed up by the then State Representative and Principal Chief of the Choctaw Nation, Harry J. W. Belvin: "There is no excuse for TV producers to ignore the harm that may be done the children of America by repetitious distortion of historical facts pertaining to the way of life of any race or creed, including the American Indian. Many TV programs show Indians as blood-thirsty marauders and murderers."

These Native Americans emphasized that their ancestors had only been defending their homelands against the white invasion. They were particularly concerned about the fact that these distortions have had an adverse effect on their own children.

After the resolution's adoption, the Association on American Indian Affairs, a white organization, launched an intensive follow-up campaign endorsing the Native Americans' stand. For several months the Association's campaign received a great deal of play in the nation's press. Most of the stories pretty much followed the press releases. LaVerne Madigan, Executive Director of the Association at that time, said:

> Accurate portrayal of frontier history and the Indian wars does not require that the white man be presented as a ruthless invader; he was that—and yet he was more, because he built a democracy when he could have built a tyranny. Accurate portrayal, however, does require that the American Indian be presented as a brave defender of his homeland and of a way of life as good and free and reverent as the life dreamed of by the immigrants who swarmed to these shores.
>
> It will be in the spirit of our We Shake Hands program to conduct a national public education campaign to cause the TV and motion picture industries to drop the vicious stereotype of the Indian as unprofitable business and to encourage them to show frontier history as the brave if bloody history shared in common by the Indian and non-Indian American citizen who live in that area today.

Show business personalities who were members of the AAIA, including Groucho Marx, Tallulah Bankhead, Roy Rogers,

Ralph Bellamy, Joel McCrea, and Eric Sevareid, supported the campaign.

Among the prominent Native Americans combating the "war whoop" image was Allie Reynolds, one-time star pitcher for the New York Yankees. Reynolds, who is part Creek, said that he was "happy to be part of any movement to raise the TV standards and create the right impressions."

Some of the shows cited as not creating the right impression were:

"Wagon Train"—"In many episodes, Indians are shown as drunken, cowardly outlaws. Indians are usually attacking wagon trains. Curiously, the Indians hardly, if ever, score a hit on the white men, whereas they are mowed down with ease. The resultant portrait indicates that the Indians are poor, inept fighters."

"Riverboat"—"This show depicts the Indians as inhuman fiends. One of its episodes showed a village being burned and pillaged by Indians. The other side of the story is never told."

"Wanted—Dead or Alive"—"A typical program showed Apaches massacring a group of whites in the desert. The reverse is never shown, though it actually happened."

"Laramie"—"This program often portrays Indians holding white girls captive, in addition to other brutal action."

"Overland Trail"—"Portrays our original Americans as unbelievably stupid savages, believing in the most ridiculous witchcraft. Example: in one episode, two whites face twenty Indians on the opposite ridge. 'The Indians will be scared of us if we jump up and down and throw sand at each other,' one of the white men says. They performed this bit of mumbo-jumbo and lo! the simple-minded Indians flee."

Part of the AAIA's plan was that its Public Education Committee under the chairmanship of Arthur Ochs Sulzberger, President and Publisher of the *New York Times*, would offer consultation services to TV and film producers to insure accuracy in the portrayal of the "Indian." In a news letter Mr. Sulzberger "... asked members of the AAIA to monitor TV Westerns, noting both offensive and accurate portrayals of frontier life. By reporting their findings to the Association, members will aid the committee [to] form an objective picture of the actual amount of distortions emanating from home screens." This phase was a dismal failure since the response from AAIA members was negligible. By 1961, one short year later, the Association's campaign had apathetically ground to a halt. The protest that was born with a bang died with something less than a whimper.

Mr. Earl Boyd Pierce, General Counsel for the Cherokee Nation and one of the activists in the tribal protest, said: "It is my considered judgement that this timely protest was most effective and resulted in the noticeable quick change of policy in attitude of the three systems [the TV networks] regarding the portrayal of the facts of American Indian history. All of us down here were satisfied with the results."

> CUT TO
> A hearing room; it is 1960 and the FCC is conducting hearings on the extent of control that sponsors exert over their programs. A FCC staffer has just introduced four letters from General Mills, Liggett & Myers, Miles Labs, and Coca-Cola, to producers, containing the do's and don't's in the production of shows they sponsor. The letter from General Mills elaborates on 22 separate points including the Indian: ". . . any material dealing with Indians should be scrutinized carefully to insure its presentation of the Indians themselves, their life, customs and costumes in a true light . . . . Any scripts dealing with Indians . . . must present them in an impartial light . . . ."

The "Great Adventure," a CBS-TV series, dedicated to our education, presented stories of individuals who either influenced or changed the course of American history. On February 14, 1964, this program presented "The Special Courage of Captain Pratt." He was instrumental in founding the Carlisle Indian School. The story told of Captain Pratt, who, through a lack of knowledge and understanding, was, at first, prejudiced against the Native American. But because of insights gained while commanding a military party escorting Native American leaders to prison, he emerged a great champion of human rights—a beloved benefactor in the welfare, care, and education of the Native American. A sort of military saint with faithful and loving Indian followers, Pappa Pratt knew best—put them into a school uniform, teach them to walk the white man's road and there will only be good Indians.

> CUT TO
> A copy of the resolution passed by the State Legislature of Kentucky, March 2, 1966, Native American population 391, deploring the distortions of "The Adventures of Daniel Boone" on NBC. The

262

camera moves about to pick these statements concerning the series: "A historical farce; an inaccurate portrayal of historical events; an insult to the intelligence of millions of people, including school children; proper accuracy, sequence, or order of time, place, characters, and events have been disregarded by the television producer; one episode . . . had Boone encounter Inca Indians; the House goes on record as showing its displeasure with the NBC-TV network because of the way it has assaulted Kentucky history in its weekly series, 'The Adventures of Daniel Boone' and that a copy of this resolution be sent to General Mills, Colgate Palmolive Company and The Makers of Issodetts, the Kentucky Historical Society . . . and the Daughters of the American Revolution; if these companies should tolerate the lack of truth and fact in their advertising as they do in the historical drama they sponsor the general public would be afraid to use the products they produce."

CUT TO

Ernest Kinoy, president of the Writers Guild of America-East, as he testifies before the New York City Commission on Human Rights on March 22, 1968. The commission is investigating alleged discrimination by broadcasters and advertisers against minority groups. Mr. Kinoy is speaking: Content in TV is, and has always been, under the direct control of the corporations who pay the bills: the networks, the advertising agencies and sponsors. All of us, the writers, the producers, the independent packagers, are employees of these companies. Essentially we write to order. We think to order.

That American television has presented a falsified image of our country and people is a truth so obvious that only those capable of infinite self-delusion could deny it.

When it was discovered that the hearings being conducted by the New York City Commission on Human Rights were not to include the testimony of Native Americans, we called them to find out why they had been excluded. An official of the Commission, who refused to give his name, laughingly said that they had not forgotten the "Indian" but that they did not know where they could possibly park their horses.

The commission began holding hearings at the beginning of March, 1968. It confined the scope of its investigation to black and Spanish-speaking people. We should note that the commission had spent seven months researching and preparing for the hearings.

During the hearings, a group of Native Americans confronted the commission and demanded to be heard. The chairman of the commission, William H. Booth, apologized to the group for having overlooked the Native American. John Belindo, a Kiowa

-Navajo, executive director of the National Congress of American Indians, was invited to testify on March 21, 1968.

He condemned the "false, untruthful and distorted" portrayal of Native Americans in all mass media—radio, television, movies, advertising, and newspapers, and declared that such portrayals resulted in severe economic problems for Native Americans as well as loss of self-esteem.

He went on to say that "the enhancement and perpetuation of stereotype motifs of the Indian as drunken, savage, or treacherous, unreliable or childlike, produces impeding effects on employability of the Indian or his opportunities for education to a state of employability. It also leads itself to the generation of self-righteous justifications on the part of the non-Indian in application of commercial activities which have direct social and economic impact on the Indian. The Indian's situation is not unlike that of the American Negro and the possibility of his response paralleling that of the Negro is considerable."

After his testimony, Mr. Belindo was interviewed by reporters. He said that the Native American is consistently "portrayed as something opposite good, as an omnipresent threat to civilization. An example of this is a recent TV commercial for a children's breakfast food in which an Indian appeared in war paint, wearing a buffalo hat with horns, jumping up and down and screaming. This is the only picture the non-Indian gets of the Indian."

CUT TO
Sakokwenonkwas, a member of the Mohawk Nation's White Roots of Peace (a Native American action group), talking to a group of white students:

Indians are savage. How do we know? We know because we see it on TV, we see it in comic books and we see it in history books. We see it in the movies . . . .
I have never seen Indians go like this with their hands on their mouths. It is not true. It is not true that Indians are savages. They don't like to kill. Even our own children are afraid of their grandpas because of what they see on TV.

After the hearings, the Commission on Human Rights did absolutely nothing. What followed this "investigation" was a near saturation in the media of "Indian" motifs. Newspapers were filled with ads for fringes, headbands, beads, and moccasins for the "Now" look; Indians made smoke signals for cigarettes and pushed ball point pens and other products . . . and they pushed and pushed and pushed. In television commercials airlines show inflight movies of Indians versus the cavalry ; ketchup bottles are animated to DUM-dum-dum-dum soundtrack and a voice over "ugh 'em" dialogue; stockings also DUM-dummed their way on a horde of strangely clad, headbanded women coming down that famous hill; color TV could best be appreciated if you saw a full headdress on a war painted Indian in color and Tonto, Jay Silverheels, could better survive and enjoy his sandwiches wrapped in plastic. And the genocide goes on and on and on.

On January 16, 1970, NBC-TV's "Bracken's World" presented "Meanwhile, Back at the Studio." The story was about the filming of a Western and to make it authentic the director wanted to use real Indians with authentic costumes, telling a true story. In reality, actors used to portray these "authentic" Indians were Hollywood non-Indians wearing Instant Indian Kits. It had to be seen to be believed.

At one point, the director in the story explains his reasons for making the film to the Indian playing a lead, and ends his speech with, "I speak with straight tongue." To which the character replies, "Please don't use an ethnic expression. It's condescending." At another point, the director is trying to justify his use of "real Indians." According to the script, he has been out on location and has had contact with real Indians. At the same time, we see on the screen a bunch of Hollywood Indians with their pancake makeup showing. And the director says, "I like what I saw. I saw real Indians, not Hollywood imitations." Now, that's clever satire, we thought. But they were in dead ernest.

Flap (1970) was a film in a modern setting, about supposedly real Indians. This "farcical comedy" about drunken Indians was so bad that distributors sneaked it in and out of neighborhood movie theatres faster than a speeding arrow. Its claims to fame were few: Anthony Quinn starred as Flapping Eagle; and it was British director Carol Reed's (*Odd Man Out*) latest picture and the first he made in the United States.

An angry Native American, R. Black Buffalo of the National Indian Youth Council, reviewed *Flap* in the January-February, 1971, issue of *Akwesasne Notes* (a Native American monthly newspaper from the Mohawk Nation). In the closing paragraph he said:

War Party

What do Indians think of their Hollywood imqge? Using the toma-hawk to show relative merit, here are the results of an informal poll of young Indians. One tomahawk denotes fair to good, two tomahawks poor, three terrible, and four—a massacre.

-**"Soldier Blue" (1970)**

"The only good part of this picture was the massacre of the Indians by the cavalry. That saved it because it showed the truth. The rest was junk."

-**"A Man Called Horse" (1970)**

"Same old savage stereotype. White actors, playing cigar-store Indians."

-**"Little Big Man" (1970)**

"Chief Dan George was great and Dustin Hoffman was bad. But the picture actually showed some things realistically."

-**"The Last Hunt" (1956)**

"Showed the white man wiping out the buffalo and it depicted something of Indian values and religion. Pretty good picture for the time it was made."

-**"Tell Them Willie Boy Is Here" (1969)**

"The producer said he couldn't find any real Indians to play in this one. He couldn't find them because he apparently didn't look."

-**"The Stalking Moon" (1967)**

"The Indian was shown as a totally primitive animal who'd kill anything."

-**"Broken Arrow" (1950)**

"It showed what the Indians were mad about — namely, white people hunting them for scalps."

-**"Flap" (Original title: "Nobody Loves a Drunken Indian") (1970)**

"This picture made a joke of Indian rights. We don't mind a laugh at ourselves but this picture made us look like idiots." •

From the May, 1971 issue of Akwesasne Notes, published by The White Roots of Peace, Mohawk Nation.

The Warner Brothers press hand-out announces, with curious self-congratulatory glee, that they spent "$6,000,000-plus" on this film. While hard to discern the results on screen, we are not going to argue with them; the only problem is that the news might be somewhat hard to swallow for the number of our tribal brothers who haven't had enough to eat this week.

What can one say: Perhaps the only possible comment lies in the lines of an 1890 Arapaho chant for the Ghost Dance:

"I'yehe: my children — Uhi'yeye'he'he:
The whites are crazy: — Ahe'yuhe'yu:"

If *Flap* is anything to go by, that advice still stands.

CUSTER STILL LIVES

SCENE XXII

VOICE OVER
But I say unto you, Ye shall inherit their land, and I will give it unto you to possess it, a land that floweth with milk and honey: ... Leviticus: Chapter 20: Verse 24.

VOICE OVER
We hear the famous battle cry of Crazy Horse: This is a good day to die .... Hoka Hey!

From *Chief Crazy Horse* (1955) Universal.

Milo Milton Quaife in his introduction to Custer's *My Life on the Plains* (1962) wrote:

269

Friction, followed by warfare and forcible conquest of the Indians, was thus inevitable. However much one may deplore such wrongs as were committed against them, the broad fact is clear that in taking forcible possession of the continent the white race was following a practice as old as human history. But for it there would be today no United States, since every square league of our national domain was forcibly wrested, at one time or another, from the original possessors.

From *Sitting Bull* (1954) United Artists.

CUT TO

Floyd Westerman concert. He introduces and sings the title song from his album "Custer Died for Your Sins," as we

DISSOLVE INTO

A montage of clips from some Custer films: *Custer's Last Stand* (1909), *The Massacre* (1912, Griffith), *Custer's Last Fight* (1912, Ince), *The Scarlet West* (1925, J. G. Adolfi), *The Flaming Frontier* (1926, Edward Sedgwick), *Custer's Last Stand* (serial, 1936, Elmer Clifton), *They Died With Their Boots On* (1941, Raoul Walsh), *Little Big Horn* (1951, Charles Marquis Warren), *Warpath* (1951, Byron Haskin), *Bugles in the Afternoon* (1952, Roy Rowland),

Sitting Bull (1954, Sidney Salkow), *Chief Crazy Horse* (1955, George Sherman), *Tonka* (1958, Lewis R. Foster), *The Great Sioux Massacre* (1965, Sidney Salkow), *Custer of the West* (1968, Robert Siodmak), *Little Big Man* (1971, Arthur Penn).

As we see the above, we hear the following from Mr. Quaife's Introduction in Voice Over:

General George A. Custer was perhaps the most brilliant cavalry leader America has produced. His solid claim to military fame rests upon his achievements in the Civil War, yet paradoxically he is chiefly remembered by reason of his death in the minor action of the Little Big Horn in June, 1876 . . . .

Although Custer came to the Plains as a veteran soldier, he had yet to learn the methods of Indian warfare. Despite early mistakes his progress was rapid; he presently acquired the reputation of being the country's best Indian fighter and the regiment whose character he moulded became renowned throughout the Army . . . .

Always a showman with a pronounced theatrical bent, he proceeded to devise for himself a uniform such as had never been seen in the United States Army . . . . In his new apparel, set off by his shoulder-length golden curls, he looked "as if he had just stepped out of Van Dyke's pictures, the image of the 17th century."

A Sioux drawing of the battle. The figure on the white horse in the center shows Crazy Horse wearing his protective hailstone medicine paint. (New York Public Library)

George N. Fenin and William K. Everson in *The Western* (1962) offer this bit of Custermania:

One wonders now whether or not movie traditions sometimes have a more lasting effect than the authentic traditions they copy. For example, Custer's famed Seventh Cavalry . . . was subsequently reformed as a cavalry unit and retained as a permanent force in the United States Army. The Seventh Cavalry is still in action today and, like Custer himself, it utilizes flamboyant accessories to glamorize a regulation uniform—including cavalry boots, a western-style neckerchief and, among the officers, cavalry sabres. From several first-hand accounts, it seems that these "descendants" of Custer adopt a swaggering behavior more than casually related to, although somewhat enlarged upon, the behavior of the cavalry officers in a John Ford super-Western.

A most popular film subject has been Custer and his massacre, last stand, last fight, the Battle of the Little Big Horn or, as referred to by Native Americans, the Battle of the Greasy Grass. You can see as many different versions of the battle as there are movies about it—none of which are true or accurate.

Two thinly disguised Custer stories were Ford's *Fort Apache* (1948) and *The Glory Guys* (1965, Arnold Laven).

Hollywood's blatant disregard for simple historical fact is typified in *Custer of the West* (1968) and *Sitting Bull* (1954). In *Custer of the West* he actually meets with the Indians just before the battle and tries to talk them out of it. In *Sitting Bull* J. Carrol Naish, playing—or rather posing—the title role, comes to the fort after the battle to save Dale Robertson from execution. There he meets President Grant. The dialogue between the president and the medicine man ends with Grant saying, "To peace," and Sitting Bull replying, "To friendship." This scene took place, you must remember, after thousands of Indians had just wiped out Custer and his command. And then—Naish rides off into the proverbial sunset. The battle itself in *Custer* and *Chief Crazy Horse* consisted of a handful of men on each side shooting at one another.

CUT TO
Ladies night at a local veteran's meeting hall, somewhere in the midwest in 1970. Their drum and bugle corps, dressed in the uniform of the 7th Cavalry, is presenting a show. The drum major, made up and dressed to look like Custer, is standing stage center,

reciting the following from Frederick Whittaker's *Complete Life of Gen. George A. Custer* (1876):

"Were you ever in a charge, you who read this now, by the winter fireside, long after the bones of the slain have turned to dust, when peace covers the land? If not, you have never known the fiercest pleasure of life. The chase is nothing to it, the most headlong hunt is tame in comparison. In the chase, the game flees and you shoot: here the game shoots back, and every leap of the charging steed is a peril escaped or dashed aside. The sense of power and audacity that possesses the cavalier, the unity with his steed, both are perfect. The horse is as wild as the man: with glaring eyeballs and red nostrils he rushes frantically forward at the very top of his speed, with huge bounds, as different from the rhythmic precision of the gallop as the sweep of the hurricane is from the rustle of the breeze. Horse and rider are drunk with excitement, feeling and seeing nothing but the cloud of dust, the scattered flying figures, conscious of only one mad desire, to reach them, to smite, smite, smite!"

The legend of Custer and those in his command, like old soldiers, never die. One of Custer's comrades in arms was acclaimed at the premiere of *The Flaming Frontier* (1926, Edward Sedgwick), as reported in the review in the *Times*, April 5, 1926. This film was yet another version of Custer's last stand:

Prior to the presentation of "The Flaming Frontier" at the Colony Theatre at midnight on Saturday, Brig. Gen. Edward S. Godfrey, U.S.A., retired, who fought off the Indians after the Custer massacre, was introduced. General Godfrey, who is 85 years old, arose and bowed to the throng of spectators. In the course of his introduction it was explained that General Godfrey after the massacre held the redskins at bay for two days until General Terry arrived with relief troops. It was General Godfrey who found General Custer's body, and it was the same venerable fighter—there in a theatre box at midnight—who while on the Faculty at West Point wrote the official history of the massacre. The same old warrior commanded Troop K, Seventh Cavalry, under Custer at the Battle of Little Big Horn, June 24, 1876. After listening to this information scores in the audience stood up and many would have liked to have shaken the veteran's hand. It was a stirring moment.

CUT TO
A page from the *Times*, May 6, 1969, showing this banner, "Hope Has Little Meaning for Blackfoot Indians," an article by Steven V.

273

Roberts. As the camera zooms in on the article, Floyd Westerman continues to play "Custer Died For Your Sins" in the background. We hear this from the article in

VOICE OVER

"But the plight of Blackfeet youngsters goes even deeper. What pervades this town is a feeling of shame, to the point of self-loathing.

"'The popular culture is always telling them that Indians are dirty and shiftless, and we tend to see ourselves as others see us,' said Darrel Armentrout, a guidance counsellor at the high school. 'These kids watch TV and keep asking me why the hell can't the Indian win once in a while. Boy, it sure tickles them when you talk about Custer.'"

CUT TO

Custer in his command tent. He is writing an article for *Galaxy* magazine. We hear the following in Voice Over:

It is to be regretted that the character of the Indian as described in Cooper's interesting novels is not the true one . . . .

Stripped of the beautiful romance with which we have been so long willing to envelop him, transferred from the inviting pages of the novelist to the localities where we are compelled to meet with him, in his native village, on the war path, and when raiding upon our frontier settlements and lines of travel, the Indian forfeits his claim to the appellation of the *noble* red man. We see him as he is, and, so far as all knowledge goes, as he ever has been, a *savage* in every sense of the word; . . . one whose cruel and ferocious nature far exceeds that of any wild beast on the desert.

For its Fall 1967 television season, the American Broadcasting Company announced a new series based on Custer. Almost immediately Native Americans throughout the country protested. And just as quickly ABC rebutted. A spokesman for the network and the show told the press: "If the network felt it was doing something detrimental to the Indians of America, obviously the show would never be put on the air."

A. A. Hopkins-Duke, a Kiowa, who is director of the Tribal Indian Land Rights Association, declared at a press conference which received wide coverage: "General Custer was the Indian's worst enemy. Glamorizing Custer is like glamorizing Billy the Kid. The Tribal Indian Land Rights Association is planning to petition the federal courts for an injunction restraining the series.

"We are lodging a complaint to ABC, petitioning sponsors of the series to boycot it.

"We hope the nation's 600,000 Indians and all persons interested in the welfare of Indians will protest the Custer series.

General Custer endorsed a policy of genocide and massacred village after village of Indians.

"We think it's about time a true picture of the American Indian be portrayed on the American film and T.V. screen. The industry continues to build its unrealistic image of my people because of the phenomenal success of cowboy versus Indian films.

"This Custer this is the last straw."

Two days later, ABC announced it still planned to go ahead with the series despite all the protests. Another spokesman for the network said that the Indian in the series was treated "sympathetically and realistically." At the same time, he denied that the network had received "thousands of letters" protesting the series. He said, "It's just not true."

The *Pittsburgh Post-Gazette* ran an editorial on August 6, 1967. This was the paper's reaction to the announcement that Native Americans would seek redress through the courts:

> Frankly, we are disappointed. We should be relieved, of course, that the Indian groups are resorting to the courts rather than to the tomahawk. But somehow we can't conceive of Cochise slapping an injunction on a television network. Neither can we imagine Geronimo consulting his mouthpiece. We hate to say it, but we think red man talks with forked tongue.

The next day, August 7, *Newsweek* covered the story:

> Custer at Bay Again—Gen. George Custer was court-martialed twice, once left his men to die, discarded a son squired through Indian wenching and had a reputation for cruelty. But to many Western buffs, this has failed to dim the glow of a man who made major general at 25 and symbolized the frontier Indian fighter. Indeed, ABC producer Frank Glicksman maintains that Custer is a "much maligned man," . . . . Says Glicksman: "He lends himself to the TV medium . . ."

When the series finally got on the air, Jack Gould reviewed it in the *New York Times*, September 7, 1967:

> The National Congress of the American Indian demanded in advance equal time to reply to the American Broadcasting Company series "Custer," which opened last night . . . . The plea was misguided; the white man and the red man are entitled to an equal rebate for wasted electricity in turning on the receiver . . . . The Indians may find their organized protest will be superfluous; probably they can

put their faith in A. C. Nielsen, Inc., when the research company announces its ratings of the season's new shows.

While the show remained on the air, Native American protests continued. The New York City-based Young American Indian Council had printed a day-glo poster which read: "This Program Is a Lie and an Insult to the American Indian." They pasted it up on buildings housing the network's executive offices and studios and the series' sponsors.

In a few short months, according to Mr. Gould's prediction, the series was killed—not by Native Americans but by its own poor Nielson rating.

CUT TO
Ralph Friar talking to August Little Soldier, a Mandan-Arikara, Tribal Chairman of the Mandan, Arikara and Hidasta Tribes, Ft. Berthold Reservation, North Dakota (1967). Mr. Little Soldier is speaking:

> We don't like these pictures because they aren't true. They don't tell the real story. The movies always show the Indians massacring whites—like Custer. That happened only once. But they never show how whites massacred the Indians. They'd attack a village while the men were away and massacre the women, children, and old folks. That happened all the time, but the movies never show that.
> What's the use of us Indians protesting against the way they show Indians in movies and television. It wouldn't do us any good. Nobody would listen to us.

Custer in *Little Big Man* is a fool, a foppish, vain idiot who eventually goes insane. His men react to him with resigned tolerance. The real Custer, we have been told, was vain, arrogant, full of boyish dreams, and a liar. But he was no idiot and certainly not insane. He received the utmost love, respect, and loyalty from his men. He envisioned himself a musketeer, a chevalier who dared both man and beast to escape his chase—a man who took joy in killing and being reckless.

Nothing of this is shown in the film; nothing of his brother who remained with him until the end; nothing of his female cooks and the various "Indian maidens" with whom he "went a-wenching." These things might have made him real. He did lead and participate in numerous massacres of innocent people. He was called "squaw killer" by Native Americans. He rationalized his conduct by maintaining that many tribes, above all the

Cheyenne and the Sioux, had perpetrated attacks on white settlers. We know that the Cheyenne had had many encounters with the white man's soldiers. The "Cheyenne" in *Little Big Man* seem only to hunt, occasionally skirmish with the Pawnees and get massacred by Custer.

This film suffers from the Mylai syndrome, Custer's massacre of the Cheyenne camp on the Washita, like the one at Mylai, is made to remain an isolated incident, committed by a psychotic few.

CUT TO
Arthur Penn, director of *Little Big Man*, talking to the senior editor of *Look*, Gerald Astor, for an article in the magazine, December 1, 1970: *Little Big Man* is slanted. When Custer attacked, he was right out of his gourd. No one in his right mind would have gone at that many Indians, unless he was so infatuated with his capacity to win, so racially assured that he belonged to a superior breed.

Custer definitely was "racially assured" and did feel that he belonged to "a superior breed." But his decision to attack at the Little Big Horn was also based on Gen. Crook's "strategic mistake of not ascertaining the strength of his enemy . . . and the further mistake, which has unhorsed so many other white commanders, of underestimating the fighting capacity of the Indians. His [Crook's] only fear was the Sitting Bull's forces might run and escape before he could pin them down." (From *The American Indian Wars* [1960] by John Tebbel and Keith Jennison.)

The "insanity" which Mr. Penn attributes to Custer can be attributed to all white commanders whose strategies are almost always based on the overestimation of the white man's fighting strength. On June 17, 1876, five days prior to Custer's demise, 1200 Oglalas and Cheyennes, led by Crazy Horse, attacked Gen. Crook's force of 1300 at the Rosebud River. Crook suffered many losses and withdrew. This was Crook's second defeat at the hands of Crazy Horse (so we might say that Crook was twice as crazy as Custer). He did not know that Crazy Horse and his followers hurried North, after defeating him, to join Sitting Bull with the main body of Sioux and Cheyenne in the valley of the Little Big Horn.

CUT TO
Custer still in his tent and still writing his memoirs. This is heard in Voice Over:

I have yet to make the acquaintance of that officer of the army who, in time of undisturbed peace, desired a war with the Indians. On the contrary, the army is the Indian's best friend so long as the latter deserves to maintain friendship . . . . As to the frontiersman, he has everything to lose, even to life, and nothing to gain by an Indian war . . . .

The only ground upon which the frontiersman can be accused of inspiring or inciting a war with the Indian is, that when applied to by the latter to surrender his life, family, and property, scalp thrown in, he stoutly refuses, and sometimes employs force to maintain this refusal.

CUT TO

A page in *Newsweek*, April 13, 1970, which is headed "The War in Vietnam." The camera comes in on a section entitled "Through Indian Country" and picks out the following:

"... Kevin Buckley set out by car from Phnom Penh last week on a trip that carried him through Prey Veng and Svay Rieng provinces, right up to the border with Tay Ninh, South Vietnam. Buckley's report:

From the outset of the trip, it was obvious that a scare was on. All the main roads were snarled by roadblocks, and much of my time was consumed in red tape—haggling with local police for permission to drive on. This, supposedly, was 'Indian country.' But if so, the Indians seemed quiet . . . ."

CUT TO

The Winter Soldier Investigation in Detroit. The Native American veteran is speaking: When I was a kid, I watched TV with Indians and the cavalry. I would cheer for the cavalry—that's how bad it was.

CUT BACK TO

Col. Visscher's chapter "The End of the Trail" as he quotes from Short Bull talking about Buffalo Bill: "He killed us because we were bad and because we fought against what he knew was best for us."

The two "heroes," William F. Cody and George A. Custer, were linked in a common brotherhood through films. Both long-haired and buck-skinned killers, they symbolize the end of an era—the end of the Native American's freedom. Their helpful friends, the army, continued to annihilate the red man on the screen into the 1970s.

The boys in blue had their red turncoat brothers as well: the Indian Scout, Indian Police, and the Indian soldier, all of whom participated in the genocide of their brothers. Though fictionalized in films as man's best friend, they did exist in those capacities.

Colonial policy—be it British, French or any other colonizer —usually follows standard practices. In order to avoid using a large army of its own and in order to divide the conquered, the conquerors have always used natives to do their dirty work. They are recruited through bribery, intimidation, or threat. The Native American was no exception. Sitting Bull was killed by Sioux Police sent by whites to arrest him. Crazy Horse was killed with the aid of many friends, including his best friend, a Sioux named Little Big Man, for refusing to be put behind bars. This is from *Crazy Horse, the Strange Man of the Ogiala* (1961) by Mari Sandoz:

> . . . Little Big Man grabbed his arms from behind. Trying to wrench free, Crazy Horse struggled into the open, dragging the stocky Indian through the door, his warriors crying out the warning: "He is holding the arms, the arms!" while on the other side the scouts raised their guns, Red Cloud and American Horse ordering: "Shoot in the middle, shoot to kill!" the officer of the day knocking the scout guns down with his sword as fast as they came up. And between them the Indian, like a trapped animal, was heaving, plunging to get free, growling: "Let me go! Let me go!" as the angry bear growls, the knife flashing in the late sun. Then with a mighty jerk he threw himself sideways and Little Big Man had to drop one hand, blood running from a slash across his arm. But Swift Bear and other old Brule friendlies already had Crazy Horse, held him while the officer of the day tried to use his sword against him, yelling: "Stab him! Kill the son of a bitch!" The guard came running up, lunged with his bayonet and, hitting the door, jerked the weapon free and lunged twice more. At the redness of the steel a noise of alarm, of warning arose from the watching Indians. Crazy Horse pulled at his old captors once more. "Let me go, my friends," he panted. "You have got me hurt enough." And at these soft words, all the Indians suddenly dropped their hands from him as though very much afraid. Released, Crazy Horse staggered backward, turned half around, and sank to the ground, his shirt and leggings already wet and blood-darkened.

VOICE OVER
But this people is a people robbed and spoiled; they are all of them snared in holes, they are hid in prison houses; they are for a prey . . . .
   —*Isaiah*: Chapter 42: Verse 22.

279

CUT BACK TO

The Winter Soldier Investigation. The Native American Vietnam veteran is still speaking: Many Indians get drafted and a lot usually join. Indians need warrior status to regain their dignity and to remember. But things are changing. We won't go anymore. We will go to prison first. We will go to Alcatraz . . . . The Indian is thinking now about the old ways. Way back the people here had it good. Then the white man came and we made treaties to last as long as the grass will grow and as long as the rivers will flow. But the way things are going now, one day soon the grass isn't going to grow and the rivers aren't going to flow . . . .

. . . . and his voice broke and he cried . . . .

VOICE OVER

Who among you will give ear to this? Who will hearken and hear for the time to come?
   —*Isaiah*: Chapter 42: Verse 23.

ACTORS IN REDSKIN

Rodolfo Acosta
Claude Akins
Mario Alcalde
Norman Alden
Don Ameche
Broncho Billy Anderson
Dame Judith Anderson
Morris Ankrum
Michael Ansara
Marco Antonio
Tsura Aoki
Camille Astor

Rolinda Bainbridge
Sherman Bainbridge
Suzan Ball
Rex Ballard
Anne Bancroft
George Bancroft
Lex Barker
Robert Barrat
Richard Barthelmess
Warner Baxter
Noah Beery
Noah Beery, Jr.
Wallace Beery
Charles Bell
Gladys Belmont
Vedah Bertam

Tony Bill
Joey Bishop
Bobby Blake
Robert Blake
Adrian Booth
Hobart Bosworth
Clara Bow
Scott Brady
Neville Brand
Henry Brandon
Pierre Brice
Charles Bronson
Robert Brower
Jack Brown
Winnie Brown
Frank Bruno
Yul Brynner
Jack Buetel

Bruce Cabot
Susan Cabot
Joseph Calleia

Rafael Campos
Harry Carey
Michelle Carey
David Carradine
Anthony Caruso
William Cavanaugh
George Chakiris
Larry Chance
Jeff Chandler
Lon Chaney, Jr.
Sydney Chaplin
Cyd Charisse
Angela Clark
Marguerite Clayton
Steve Cochran
Chuck Connors
Mara Corday
George Cowl
Buster Crabbe
Ralph E. Cummings
Lester Cuneo
Alan Curtis
Tony Curtis

Bebe Daniels
Michael Dante
Ray Danton
Carmen D'Antonio
Nancy Deaver
Yvonne De Carlo
Ted de Corsica
Frank De Kova
Katherine DeMille
Herlinda Del Carmen
Dolores Del Rio
William Desmond
Kamala Devi
Richard Dix
Ellen Drew
Yvette Dugaty
Ann Dvorak

Ammy Eccles
Vince Edwards
Chad Everett

Douglas Fairbanks, Sr.
George Field
Margarita Fisher
Stanley Fitz
Paul Fix
Rhoda Fleming

Jay C. Flippen
Francis Ford
Victoria Forde
Robert Forster
Eduard Franz
Robert Frazer
Charles K. French
Lance Fuller

Rita Gam
George Gebhart
Joanne Gilbert
Adda Gleason
Paulette Godard
Thomas Gomez
Michael Granger
Kathryn Grant
Paul Guilfoyle

Buddy Hackett
Frank Hagney
Walter Hampden
Paul Harvey
William S. Hart
Sessue Hayakawa
Russell Hayden
Audrey Hepburn
Barbara Hershey
Fernando Hilbeck
John Hodiak
William Holden
Jack Holt
Jack Hoxie
John Hoyt
John Hudson
Rock Hudson
Gladys Hulette
Jeffrey Hunter
Paul C. Hurst

Eugene Iglesias
Miguel Inclan
Charles Inslee
Arthur Johnson
Noble Johnson
Lamar Johnstone
Jennifer Jones
Nick Jordan
Victor Jory
Lucile Joy
Max Julien
Katy Jurado

Boris Karloff
F. Serrano Keating

Howard Keel
Michael Keep
James Kirkwood
Susan Kohner
Nancy Kwan

Frank Lackteen
Burt Lancaster
Martin Landau
Harry Landers
Frank Lanning
Rod La Rocque
Keith Larson
Daliah Lavi
Florence Lawrence
Jody Lawrence
Marc Lawrence
Freidrich Ledeba
Marion Leonard
Sheldon Leonard
George J. Lewis
Mitchell Lewis
Ann Little
John Lowell
Bela Lugosi

Arthur Mackley
Guy Madison
Ian MacDonald
Jeanie MacPherson
Janet Margolin
Tina Marquand
Ross Martin
Elsa Martinelli
Maria Elena Marques
Victor Mature
Virginia Mayo
Francis J. McDonald
Claire McDowell
Steve McQueen
Burgess Meredith
John Miljan
Sal Mineo
Cameron Mitchell
Ricardo Montalban
Frank Montgomery
Sorita Montiel
Ralph Moody
Carlyle Moore, Jr.
Clayton Moore
Dickie Moore
Kieron Moore
Antonio Moreno
Rita Moreno
Myrtle Morse

Maurice Moscovich
Audie Murphy

J. Carrol Naish
Vivian Nathan
Richard Neil
Julie Newmar
Alejandro Nilo
Ramon Novarro

Simon Oakland
Wheeler Oakman
Hugh O'Brien
Joy Page
Debra Paget
Jack Palance
Larry Parks
Michael Pate
Marisa Pavan
Jean Peters
Dan Peterson
Mary Pickford
Donald Porter
Tyrone Power, Sr.
Jack Pratt
Elvis Presley

Anthony Quinn

Ford Rainey
Stuart Randall
George Ralph
George Regas
Donna Reed
Philip Reed
Wallace Reid
Francisco Reyguera
Steve Rich
Ziva Rodann
Gilbert Roland
Albert Roscoe
Katharine Ross
Barbara Rush
Evangeline Russell
John Russell

Marin Sais
Monroe Salisbury
Betta St. John
John Saxon
Robert Scott

Evelyn Selbie
Edgar Selwyn
William Shatner
Sylvia Sidney
Bernard Siegel
Henry Silva
Armando Silvestre
Joseph E. Singleton
Mortimer Snow
William H. Stratton
Woody Strode

Gloria Talbott
Akim Tamiroff
Joan Taylor
Robert Taylor
Ken Terrell
Nick Thompson
Elizabeth Threatt
Carol Thurston
Michael Tolan
Mabel Trunnell
Corrina Tsopei
Manu Tupou
Tom Tyler

Rick Vallin
Lee Van Cleef
Victor Varconi
Lupe Velez
Martha Vickers
Joseph A Vitale
Harry Von Meter
Alfred D. Vosburgh

Robert Wagner
Wende Wagner
Robert Walker, Jr.
Henry B. Walthall
Robert Warwick
John Wayne
Billie West
William H. West
Pearl White
Richard Widmark
Robert J. Wilke
Hank Worden
H. M. Wynant

Loretta Young

ANATOMY OF THE INDIAN

There were several thousand Indian films made prior to publication of the book. On the following pages is our selective listing of some of those films by subject category.

INDIANS IN TITLE

Indian War Council (1894)
Indian Day School (1898)
Procession of Mounted Indians and Cowboys (1898)
Serving Rations to the Indians (1898)
Wand Dance, Pueblo Indians (1898)
Eagle Dance, Pueblo Indians (1898)
Moki Snake Dance by Wolpi Indians (1901)
Rescue of Child from Indians (1903)
Brush Between Cowboys and Indians (1904)
Indian Revenge (1905)
The Indian's Revenge (1906)
The Indian's Revenge or Osceola, the Last of the Seminoles (1906)
Cowboys and Indians (1907)
An Indian's Honor (1908)
An Indian Wife's Devotion (1909)
The True Heart of an Indian (1909)
The Indian (1909)
The Indian Runner's Romance (1909)
The Indian Trailer (1909)
An Indian's Gratitude (1910)
Indian Blood (1910)
Indian Girl's Awakening (1910)
The Indian Girl's Romance (1910)
The Indian Land Grab (1910)
An Indian Maiden's Choice (1910)
Indian Pete's Gratitude (1910)
The Indian Raiders (1910)
The Indian Scout's Revenge (1910)
Stolen by Indians (1910)
White Man's Money—The Indian's Curse (1910)
Her Indian Mother (1910)
His Indian Bride (1910)
The Indian and the Cowgirl (1910)
The Indian and the Maid (1910)

Lo! The Poor Indian (1910)
Elder Alden's Indian Ward (1910)
Glimpses of an Indian Village (1910)
Brave Hearts United or Saved from the Indians by a Woman's Wits (1910)
An Indian Legend (1911)
Old Indian Days (1911)
Puritans and Indians (1911)
The Rebuked Indian (1911)
The Story of the Indian Ledge (1911)
An Indian Brave's Conversion (1911)
The Indian Brothers (1911)
Too Much Injun (1911)
Trailed by an Indian (1911)
Incendiary Indians (1911)
Little Ingin (1911)
Maiden of the Pieface Indians (1911)
The Faithful Indian (1911)
A Branded Indian (1911)
The Hair Restorer and the Indians (1911)
Heart of an Indian Girl (1911)
The Heart of an Indian Mother (1911)
The Indian Flute (1911)
The Indian Fortune Teller (1911)
An Indian Hero (1911)
An Indian Love Story (1911)
The Indian Maid's Sacrifice (1911)
An Indian Martyr (1911)
The Indian Rustlers (1911)
An Indian Trapper's Prize (1911)
An Indian Vestal (1911)
An Indian's Elopement (1911)
An Indian's Love (1911)
An Indian's Sacrifice (1911) (Essanay)
The Indian's Sacrifice (1911) (Lubin)
What the Indians Did (1911)

287

A Brave Little Indian (1912)
The Indian Massacre (1912)
Her Indian Guardian (1912)
Indian Dances and Pastimes (1912)
An Indian Idyl (1912)
An Indian Sunbeam (1912)
Indian Romeo and Juilet (1912)
Indian Raiders (1912)
Indian Jealousy (1912)
An Indian Ishmael (1912)
Her Indian Hero (1912)
His Little Indian Model (1912)
How the Boys Fought the Indians
  (1912)
The Indian and the Child (1912)
Isleta, N. M. Indian City (1912)
Life and Customs of the Winnebago
  Indians (1912)
The Little Indian Martyr (1912)
Kidnapped by Indians (1912)
Pueblo Indians, Albuquerque, N. M.
  (1912)
The Indian Uprising at Santa Fe,
  New Mexico (1912)
An Indian's Gratitude (1912)
An Indian's Friendship (1912)
An Indian's Loyalty (1912)
Brocho Billy and the Indian Maid
  (1912)
A White Indian (1912)
An Indian Maid's Strategy (1913)
The Indian Maid's Warning (1913)
My Indian Hero (1913)
Maya—Just an Indian (1913)
Commencement at Indian School,
  Carlyle, Pa. (1913)
The Indian Servant (1913)
The Friendless Indian (1913)
Grease Paint Indians (1913)
Her Indian Brother (1913)
The Indian's Secret (1913)
Broncho Billy's Indian Romance
  (1914)
An Indian Eclipse (1914)
The Indian Suffragettes (1914)
Indian Blood (1914)
The Indian (1914)
The Indian Agent (1914)
The Indian Ambuscade (1914)
Indian Fate (1914)
Lo, the Poor Indian (1914)

His Indian Nemesis (1914)
Slim and the Indians (1914)
The Indian Wars (1914)
An Indian's Honor (1914)
A Deal in Indians (1915)
The Indian Changeling (1915)
The Indian Trapper's Vindication
  (1915)
The Indian's Narrow Escape (1915)
The Indian's Lament (1917)
By Indian Post (1919)
The Indians are Coming (1930)
  (serial)
Indian Agent (1948)
The Cowboy and the Indians (1949)
Davy Crockett—Indian Scout
  (1949)
Indian Uprising (1952)
The Indian Fighter (1955)
Indian Paint (1967)

RED MEN IN TITLE

The Redmen and the Child (1908)
Red Man's Revenge (1908)
The Red Man (1909)
The Redman's View (1909)
Saved from the Redmen (1910)
The Way of the Red Man (1910)
The Curse of the Red Man (1911)
A Noble Red Man (1911)
The Redman's Dog (1911)
The Red Man's Penalty (1911)
Red Man's Wrath (1911)
The Way of the Red Man (1911)
The White Red Man (1911)
Battle of the Red Men (1912)
The Heart of the Red Man
  (Gaumont, 1912)
The Heart of the Red Man
  (Bison, 1912)
The Redman's Burden (1912)
Red Man's Honor (1912)
A Redman's Friendship (1912)
A Redman's Love (1912)
A Redman's Loyalty (1912)
The Red Man's Country (1913)
The Lust of the Red Man (1914)
The Red Man's Heart (1914)
The Way of the Redman (1914)
Last of the Redman (1947)

Justice of a Redskin (1908)
Romantic Redskins (1910)
The Trapper and the Redskin (1910)
The Redskin's Secret (1911)
Robbie and the Redskins (1911)
A Daughter of the Redskins (1912)
The Redskin Raiders (1912)
A Redskin's Appeal (1912)
A Redskin's Mercy (1913)
Broncho Billy and the Redskin (1914)
A Daughter of the Redskins (1914)
The Redskins and the Renegades (1914)
Ham Among the Redskins (1915)
Redskin (1929)
When Redskins Rode (1951)

RED IN TITLE

The Red Girl (1908)
The Red Girl and the Child (1910)
A Red Girl's Heart (1911)
The Raid of the Red Marauders (1914)
The Red Rider (1925)
Red Love (1925)
Red Raiders (1927)

INDIAN NAMES IN TITLE

The Bride of Tabaiva (1909)
Onawanda (1909)
Red Wing's Gratitude (1909)
Dove Eye's Gratitude (1909)
Comata, the Sioux (1909)
Iona, the White Squaw (1909)
Spotted Snake's Schooling (1910)
Starlight's Devotion (1910)
Wenonah (1910)
The Legend of Scar Face (1910)
Onoko's Vow (1910)
Red Eagle's Love Affair (1910)
Red Fern and the Kid (1910)
Red Hawk's Last Raid (1910)
Red Wing's Constancy (1910)
Red Wing's Loyalty (1910)
The Return of Ta-Wa-Wa (1910)

White-Doe's Lovers (1910)
White Fawn's Devotion (1910)
Young Deer's Gratitude (1910)
Chief Blackfoot's Vindication (1910)
Iron Arm's Remorse (1910)
Black Cloud's Debt (1911)
Brave Swift Eagle's Peril (1911)
Grey Wolf's Grief (1911)
Grey Wolf's Squaw (1911)
Sacrifice of Silver Cloud (1911)
Silver Leaf's Heart (1911)
Silver Tail and His Squaw (1911)
Starlight the Squaw (1911)
Starlight's Necklace (1911)
Wenona's Broken Promise (1911)
Lean Wolf's End (1911)
Little Dove's Gratitude (1911)
Little Dove's Romance (1911)
Lone Eagle's Trust (1911)
The Passing of Dapple Fawn (1911)
White Fawn's Escape (1911)
Lone Star's Return (1911)
Owanee's Great Love (1911)
Red Deer's Devotion (1911)
Red Eagle (1911)
Red Feather's Friendship (1911)
Red Star's Honor (1911)
White Fawn's Peril (1911)
The Winning of Wonega (1911)
Chief Fire Eye's Game (1911)
Crow Chief's Defeat (1911)
Flight of Redwing (1911)
Running Fawn's Chief (1911)
Anona's Baptism (1912)
Big Rock's Last Stand (1912)
Darkfeather's Strategy (1912)
Maarea the Half Breed (1912)
Chief White Eagle (1912)
Iola's Promise (1912)
The Redemption of White Hawk (1912)
Silver Moon's Rescue (1912)
Silver Wing's Two Suitors (1912)
Waneta's Sacrifice (1912)
White Cloud's Secret (1912)
White Dove's Sacrifice (1912)
White Fawn (1912)
Winona (1912)
Swift Wind's Heroism (1912)

The Wooing of Wathena (1912)
The Wooing of White Fawn (1912)
Yellow Bird (1912)
Darkfeather's Sacrifice (1913)
Dorothea and Chief Razamataz
   (1913)
Hiawanda's Cross (1913)
Maya—Just an Indian (1913)
Mona (1913)
The Pride of Angry Bear (1913)
The Snake (1913)
Wynona's Vengeance (1913)
The Coming of Lone Wolf (1914)
Fatty and Minnie He-Haw (1914)
Grey Eagle's Revenge (1914)
Grey Eagle's Last Stand (1914)
Lame Dog's Treachery (1914)
Red Hawk's Sacrifice (1914)
The Sea-Gull (1914)
Some Bull's Daughter (1914)
Star of the North (1914)
Strongheart (1914)
The Vengeance of Winona (1914)
White Wolf (1914)
Yellow Flame (1914)
Son of "The Dog" (1915)
White Eagle (1922, 1932, 1941)
Braveheart (1926)
Johnny Tiger (1966)

COWBOYS AND INDIANS

Brush Between Cowboys and
   Indians (1904)
Cowboy Justice (1904)
Cowboy's Narrow Escape (1904)
Cowboys and Indians (1907)
The Cowboy's Baby (1908)
A Round-Up in Oklahoma (1908)
Forced into Marriage (1908)
The Pony Express (1909)
The Cowboy and the Squaw (1910)
The Cowboy's Devotion (1910)
Cowpuncher's Sweetheart (1910)
The Heart of a Cowboy (1910)
White-Doe's Lovers (1910)
The Girl from Arizona (1910)
Flight of Redwing (1911)
In the Days of Gold (1911)
Rescued in Time (1911)

The Apache Renegade (1912)
A Heroine of Pioneer Days (1912)
Orphans of the Plains (1912)
Oklahoma Jim (1932)
Red River (1948)
The Cowboy and the Indians
   (1949)
Cowboy (1958)
The Raiders (1963)
Bullet for a Badman (1964)
The McMasters (1970)

GOLD; INDIANS VS. MINERS, PROSPECTORS, TREASURE SEEKERS

The Redman and the Child (1908)
The Gold Prospectors (1909)
The Indian Runner's Romance
   (1909)
Apache Gold (1910)
The Golden Secret (1910)
Indian Blood (1910)
The Law of the West (1910)
Red Wing's Loyalty (1910)
In the Day of Gold (1911)
The Disputed Claim (1912)
The Half-Breed's Treachery (1912)
In the Nick of Time (1912)
Lucky Jim (1912)
Man's Lust for Gold (1912)
The Seal of Time (1912)
The Story of the Savage Modock
   Mine (1912)
A Temporary Truce (1912)
A False Accusation (1913)
The Mystery of Yellow Aster Mine
   (1913)
The Secret Treasure (1913)
When the Blood Calls (1913)
At the End of the Rope (1914)
Broncho Billy and the Redskin
   (1914)
The Counterfeit (1914)
Dan Morgan's Way (1914)
The Fight on Deadwood Trail
   (1914)
The First Nugget (1914)
The Fuse of Death (1914)
The Ghost of the Mine (1914)

Indian Ambuscade (1914)
Love's Sacrifice (1914)
Meg of the Mines (1914)
As in Days of Old (1915)
The Ghost Wagon (1915)
The Gold Dust and the Squaw
   (1915)
The Passing of Pete (1916)
The Sting of the Scorpion (1923)
The Mine with the Iron Door
   (1924)
The Gold Hunters (1925)
The Verdict of the Desert (1925)
Arizona Nights (1927)
The Devil's Saddle (1927)
Renegades of Sonora (1948)
Lust for Gold (1949)
The Outriders (1950)
Bugles in the Afternoon (1952)
The Tall Texan (1953)   ·
Garden of Evil (1954)
Drums Across the River (1954)
Great Day in the Morning (1956)
The Secret of Treasure Mountain
   (1956)
Ride out for Revenge (1957)
War Drums (1957)
The Law and Jake Wade (1958)
Blood Arrow (1958)
Young Guns of Texas (1962)
Apache Rifles (1965)
Finger on the Trigger (1965)
Incident at Phantom Hill (1966)
Kid Rodelo (1966)
Massacre at Marble City (1966)
The War Wagon (1967)

OIL

Drums of the Desert (1927)
Black Gold (1947)
Tulsa (1949)
The FBI Story (1959)
Black Gold (1963)

LAND GRABBERS

The Half Breed (1922)
The Heritage of the Desert (1924)

The Red Rider (1925)
Spoilers of the West (1927)
Buffalo Bill Rides Again (1947)
Ranger of Cherokee Strip (1949)
The Vanishing American (1955)
The FBI Story (1959)

INDIANS VS. SETTLERS

In Old Arizona (1909)
On the Warpath (1909)
Onawanda (1909)
Outcast or Heroine (1909)
The Redman's View (1909)
A Mohawk's Way (1910)
Perils of the Plains (1910)
Early Settlers (1910)
Red Hawk's Last Raid (1910)
The Rescue of the Pioneer's
   Daughter (1910)
The Trapper and the Redskin
   (1910)
Days of the Early West (1910)
Fighting the Iroquois (1910)
Robbie and the Redskins (1911)
A Romance of the Rio Grande
   (1911)
Tangled Lives (1911)
The Pioneer's Mistake (1911)
As Things Used to Be (1911)
The Broken Trail (1911)
By the Aid of a Lariat (1911)
Fighting Blood (1911)
The Flaming Arrows (1911)
Incendiary Indians (1911)
Life on the Border (1911)
The Plains Across (1911)
The Deserter (1912)
The Sergeant's Boy (1912)
The Trail Thru the Hills (1912)
A Western Child's Heroism (1912)
The Indian Massacre (1912)
Peril of the Plains (1912)
Blazing the Trail (1912)
The Crisis (1912)
The Forest Rose (1912)
Her Indian Guardian (1912)
The Lonesome Trail Pioneers
   (1912)
In God's Care (1912)

On the Brink of the Chasm (1912)
The Redskin Raiders (1912)
Trapped by Fire (1912)
A Frontier Providence (1913)
The Skeleton in the Closet (1913)
When the Blood Calls (1913)
The White Vaquero (1913)
The Battle of Elderbush Gulch
  (1913)
The Land of Dead Things (1913)
The Ranger's Romance (1914)
Under Arizona Skies (1914)
When We Were Young (1914)
The Death Sign at High Noon
  (1914)
Eagle's Nest (1914)
A Daughter of the Plains (1914)
The Trapper's Revenge (1915)
The Sheriff's Story (1915)
The Stain in the Blood (1916)
The Primal Lure (1916)
The Soul Herder (1917)
Bob Hampton of Placer (1921)
The Sage Hen (1921)
The Prairie Mystery (1922)
Winning of the West (1922)
Pioneer Trails (1923)
The Lone Wagon (1923)
America (1924)
The Frontier Woman (1924)
The Flaming Forties (1924)
Trail Dust (1924)
Quicker 'n Lightin' (1925)
A Daughter of the Sioux (1925)
Spoilers of the West (1927)
The Last Trail (1927)
Wyoming (1928)
The Glorious Trail (1928)
The Golden West (1932)
West of the Pecos (1934)
Allegheny Uprising (1939)
Drums Along the Mohawk (1939)
The Roundup (1941)
The Pioneers (1941)
The Prairie (1947)
Buffalo Bill Rides Again (1947)
Rachel and the Stranger (1948)
Young Daniel Boone (1950)
River of No Return (1954)
Four Guns to the Border (1954)
The Battle of Rogue River (1954)

Southwest Passage (1954)
Thunder Pass (1954)
Yellow Tomahawk (1954)
Drum Beat (1954)
Many Rivers to Cross (1955)
Backlash (1956)
Dragoon Wells Massacre (1957)
Apache Territory (1958)
Blood Arrow (1958)
The Rawhide Trail (1958)
Escort West (1959)
The Unforgiven (1960)
Frontier Uprising (1961)
The Raiders (1963)
McLintock (1963)
He Rides Tall (1964)

INDIANS VS. CATTLE DRIVE,
RANCHERS, RUSTLERS;
STAMPEDE

North of '36 (1924)
The Thundering Herd (1925)
  (buffalo)
The Wild Bull's Lair (1925)
The Santa Fe Trail (1930) (sheep)
The Conquering Horde (1931)
Red River (1948)
The Cariboo Trail (1950)
Cattle Queen of Montana (1954)
The Tall Men (1955)
Canyon River (1956)
Cowboy (1958)
The Raiders (1963)

ATTACK ON WAGON TRAIN

The Cowboy's Baby (1908)
Pioneer Crossing the Plains in '49
  (1908)
Children of the Plains (1909)
The Indian (1909)
Across the Plains (1910)
The Flaming Arrows (1911)
A Frontier Girl's Courage (1911)
The Last Drop of Water (1911)
The Arrow of Defiance (1912)
The Apache Renegade (1912)
A Frontier Soldier of Fortune
  (1912)

292

After the Massacre (1913)
A Frontier Mother (1914)
The Hills of Silence (1914)
In the Days of the Thundering Herd (1914)
The Indian Agent (1914)
The Indian Ambuscade (1914)
Love's Sacrifice (1914)
Orphans of the Wild (1914)
Out of the Valley (1914)
The Tigers of the Hills (1914)
Wagon Tracks (1919)
White Oak (1921)
Hellhounds of the West (1922)
The Covered Wagon (1923)
The Prairie Schooner (1923)
Pioneer Trails (1923)
Way of a Man (1924, serial)
The Bad Lands (1925)
The Devil Horse (1926)
The Last Frontier (1926)
Men of Daring (1927)
The Overland Stage (1927)
Red Raiders (1927)
Orphan of the Sage (1928)
Wyoming (1928)
The Invaders (1929)
The Big Trail (1930)
Trails of Golden West (1931)
Wagon Wheels (1934)
Wheels of Destiny (1934)
The Glory Trail (1936)
Prairie Schooners (1940)
Kit Carson (1940)
Pioneers of the West (1940)
Wagons Westward (1940)
The Pioneers (1941)
Lawless Plainsmen (1942)
Wagon Tracks (1943)
Bad Bascomb (1946)
Red River (1948)
Davy Crockett—Indian Scout (1949)
Devil's Doorway (1950)
The Outriders (1950)
Rio Grande (1950)
Wagon Master (1950)
Westward the Women (1951)
Fort Osage (1952)
Bend of the River (1952)
Rose of Cimarron (1952)

Wagons West (1952)
Fort Vengeance (1953)
Tumbleweed (1953)
Arrow in the Dust (1954)
The Command (1954)
Santa Fe Passage (1955)
Westward Ho the Wagons (1956)
The Last Wagon (1956)
Fort Dobbs (1958)
Thunder in the Sun (1959)
How the West Was Won (1960)
Frontier Uprising (1961)
The Tall Women (1967)

ATTACK ON PONY EXPRESS RIDER A/O STATION

The Pony Express (1909)
The Pony Express (1925)
Pony Express Rider (1926)
Pony Post (1940)
Riding West (1944)
Pony Express (1953)

ATTACK ON TOWN

Captain Junior (1914)
The Heritage of the Desert (1924)
The Pony Express (1925)
Open Range (1927)
False Fathers (1929)
Prairie Thunder (1937)
Badlands of Dakota (1941)
Canyon Passage (1946)
Apache Drums (1951)
The Last Outpost (1951)
Indian Uprising (1952)
Last of the Comanches (1953)
Ambush at Tomahawk Gap (1953)
Comanche (1956)
The Rawhide Trail (1958)

ATTACK ON STAGECOACH A/O STATION

A Western Hero (1909)
Company D to the Rescue (1910)
Captain Brand's Wife (1911)

In the Early Days (1911)
The Bugle Call (1912)
Orphans of the Plains (1912)
For the Peace of Bear Valley
  (1913)
Red Raiders (1927)
Red Fork Range (1931)
Wells Fargo (1937)
Stagecoach (1939, 1966)
Geronimo (1939)
Apache Trail (1942)
Arizona Whirlwind (1944)
Sonora Stagecoach (1944)
Indian Agent (1948)
Laramie (1949)
Rocky Mountain (1950)
Fort Defiance (1951)
Apache War Smoke (1952)
Bugles in the Afternoon (1952)
Last of the Comanches (1953)
Stand at Apache River (1953)
Ghost Town (1955)
Dakota Incident (1956)
Ride Lonesome (1959)
The Deadly Companions (1962)
Stagecoach to Dancer's Rock
  (1962)
Stage to Thunder Rock (1964)
Convict Stage (1965)
Fury of the Apaches (1965)
White Comanche (1967)

ATTACK ON TRAIN, STATION A/O RAILROAD

An Hour of Terror (1912)
The Iron Trail (1913)
The Iron Horse (1924)
The Golden West (1932)
Union Pacific (1939)
My Little Chickadee (1940)
Dawn on the Great Divide (1942)
Wild Horse Stampede (1943)
Canadian Pacific (1949)
Rock Island Trail (1950)
Last of the Comanches (1953)
Overland Pacific (1954)
Around the World in 80 Days
  (1956)
Sergeant Rutledge (1960)

ATTACK ON FORT A/O BLOCKHOUSES

Attack on Fort Boonesboro (1906)
Daniel Boone or Pioneer Days in
  America (1907)
The Attack on Fort Ridgely (1910)
In the Dark Valley (1910)
The Mohawk's Way (1910)
Kit Carson (1910)
For the Sake of the Tribe (1911)
Daniel Boone's Bravery (1911)
Incendiary Indians (1911)
The Battle of the Long Sault
  (1912)
The Arrow of Defiance (1912)
The Penalty (1912)
The Post Telegrapher (1912)
A Redman's Love (1912)
A Tale of the Wilderness (1912)
The White Lie (1912)
The Battle of Fort Laramie (1913)
The Last Blockhouse (1913)
The Brand of His Tribe (1914)
Captain Junior (1914)
The Raid of the Red Marauders
  (1914)
The Word of His People (1914)
The Girl I Left Behind Me (1915)
The Last White Man (1924)
The Bad Lands (1925)
Fort Frayne (1926)
War Paint (1926)
The Invaders (1929)
Drums Along the Mohawk (1939)
The Iroquois Trail (1950)
Two Flags West (1950)
Slaughter Trail (1951)
Taza, Son of Cochise (1954)
They Rode West (1954)
Siege at Red River (1954)
The Indian Fighter (1955)
Mohawk (1956)
Flaming Frontier (1958)
Fort Bowie (1958)
Fort Dobbs (1958)
The Oregon Trail (1959)
Buffalo Bill (1963)
Taggart (1964)
Fort Courageous (1965)
Chuka (1967)

CHIEFS

The White Chief (1908)
In the Days of the Pilgrims (1908)
Red Cloud (1908)
Chief Blackfoot's Vindication
   (1910)
The Exiled Chief (1910)
The Navajo's Bride (1910)
Chief Fire Eye's Game (1911)
The Chief's Daughter (1911)
The Chief's Talisman (1911)
Crow Chief's Defeat (1911)
Flight of Redwing (1911)
For the Tribe (1911)
Grey Wolf's Squaw (1911)
How Tony Became a Hero (1911)
The Indian Brothers (1911)
Kit Carson's Wooing (1911)
Lone Star's Return (1911)
A Noble Red Man (1911)
The Passing of Dapple Fawn
   (1911)
Running Fawn's Chief (1911)
The Story of the Indian Ledge
   (1911)
The Tribe's Penalty (1911)
When the West was Wild (1911)
The White Medicine Man (1911)
Chief White Eagle (1912)
The Chief's Blanket (1912)
Her Indian Guardian (1912)
Her Indian Hero (1912)
The Price He Paid (1912)
Silver Moon's Rescue (1912)
Young Wild West Cornered by
   Apaches (1912)
The Call of the Blood (1913)
Dorothea and Chief Razamataz
   (1913)
An Indian Maid's Strategy (1913)
Mona (1913)
The Pale-Face Squaw (1913)
Wynona's Vengeance (1913)
A Daughter of the Redskins (1914)
The Daughter of the Tribe (1914)
Defying the Chief (1914)
In the Days of the Thundering
   Herd (1914)
Last of the Line (1914)
The Legend of the Amulet (1914)

The Navajo Blanket (1914)
The Vanishing Tribe (1914)
The Boundary Line (1915)
The Ceremonial Turquoise (1915)
White Oak (1921)
The Mohican's Daughter (1922)
The Primitive Lover (1922)
The Red Rider (1925)
The Scarlet West (1925)
War Paint (1926)
The Frontier Trail (1926)
Drums of the Desert (1927)
Red Clay (1927)
The Riding Renegade (1928)
Wyoming (1928)
The Silent Enemy (1930)
Wheels of Destiny (1934)
Desert Gold (1936)
Prairie Schooners (1940)
Arizona Frontier (1940)
Valley of the Sun (1942)
Frontier Fury (1943)
Black Arrow (1944, serial)
Renegades of Sonora (1948)
Apache Chief (1949)
Pony Soldier (1952)
War Paint (1953)
Seminole (1953)
Fort Vengeance (1953)
The Nebraskan (1953)
Fort Yuma (1955)
Santa Fe Passage (1955)
Mohawk (1956)
Comanche (1956)
Tonka (1958)
Blood Arrow (1958)
Johnny Tiger (1966)
Little Big Man (1971)

PRINCESSES

Pocahontas (1908)
The Navajo's Bride (1910)
The Paleface Princess (1910)
The White Princess (1910)
The Black Chasm (1911)
The Call of the Wilderness (1911)
The Indian Flute (1911)
An Indian Legend (1911)
Sacrifice of Silver Cloud (1911)

The Totem Mark (1911)
The Price He Paid (1912)
The Unwilling Bride (1912)
A Waif of the Plains (1914)
Jamestown (1923)
The Red Rider (1925)
Distant Drums (1951)
The Big Sky (1952)
*Captain John Smith and
    Pocahontas* (1953)
Mohawk (1956)

MAIDS AND MAIDENS

The Maid of Niagara (1910)
The Indian and the Maid (1910)
An Indian Maiden's Choice (1910)
The Indian Maid's Sacrifice (1911)
Broncho Billy and the Indian Maid
    (1912)
Broncho Billy and the Navajo Maid
    (1913)
An Indian Maid's Strategy (1913)
The Indian Maid's Warning (1913)
The Legend of the Amulet (1914)
The Last Arrow or The Lost Arrow
    (1914)
The Cave of Death (1914)
Grey Eagle's Revenge (1914)
Grey Eagle's Last Stand (1914)
Broncho Billy's Indian Romance
    (1914)
The Arrow Maiden (1915)
Broncho Billy's Teachings (1915)
The Legend of the Lone Tree
    (1915)
Broken Arrow (1950)
Across the Wide Missouri (1951)
The Wild North (1952)
Ambush at Tomahawk Gap (1953)
Apache (1954)
The Far Horizons (1955)
The Last Hunt (1956)
The Oklahoman (1957)
Gunman's Walk (1958)
The Oregon Trail (1959)
Tell Them Willie Boy is Here
    (1969)
A Man Called Horse (1970)

BRAVES AND WARRIORS

A Football Warrior (1908)
The Warrior's Sacrifice (1909)
A Cheyenne Brave (1910)
An Indian Brave's Conversion
    (1911)
A Warrior's Faith (1911)
The Warrior's Squaw (1911)
A Warrior's Treachery (1911)
The Paleface Brave (1914)
Brave Warrior (1952)
Apache Warrior (1957)

MEDICINE MEN A/O WOMEN

The Cheyenne Medicine Man
    (1911)
The Medicine Woman (1911)
The White Medicine Man
    (Nestor, 1911)
The White Medicine Man
    (Selig, 1911)
The Parson and the Medicine Man
    (1912)
The Witch's Necklace (1912)
Before the White Man Came
    (1912)
In the Long Ago (1913)
The Medicine Man's Vengeance
    (1914)
The Charmed Arrow (1914)
The New Medicine Man (1914)
White Wolf (1914)
The Arrow Maiden (1915)
The Legend of the Lone Tree
    (1915)
The Mohican's Daughter (1922)
War Paint (1926)
The Silent Enemy (1930)
Way Out West (1930)
Wagon Tracks West (1943)

SQUAWS

A Squaw's Revenge (1909)
The Squaw's Sacrifice (1909)
The Cowboy and the Squaw (1910)
For the Squaw (1911)

Grey Wolf's Squaw (1911)
Only a Squaw (1911)
Silver Tail and His Squaw (1911)
The Squaw and the Man (1911)
A Squaw's Bravery (1911)
The Squaw's Devotion (1911)
The Squaw's Love (1911)
The Squaw's Mistaken Love (1911)
Starlight the Squaw (1911)
The Warrior's Squaw (1911)
An Up-To-Date Squaw (1911)
The Twin Squaws (1911)
The Pale-Face Squaw (1913)
The White Squaw (1913)
The Fate of a Squaw (1914)
The Squaw's Revenge (1914)
The Gold Dust and the Squaw
  (1915)
The White Squaw (1956)

INDIAN HOT-BLOODS

Red Raiders (1927)
Wyoming (1928)
Last of the Redmen (1947)
Broken Arrow (1950)
Pony Soldier (1952)
Brave Warrior (1952)
Arrowhead (1953)
Conquest of Cochise (1953)
Taza, Son of Cochise (1954)
Sitting Bull (1954)
Cattle Queen of Montana (1954)
The Gun That Won the West
  (1955)
Chief Crazy Horse (1955)
The Indian Fighter (1955)
Comanche (1956)
Apache Woman (1955)
Mohawk (1956)
Yellowstone Kelly (1959)
Oklahoma Territory (1960)
Two Rode Together (1961)
Buffalo Bill (1963)
A Distant Trumpet (1964)
White Comanche (1967)

RENEGADE AND/OR NO GOOD INDIANS

The Cattle Rustlers (1908)

Red Cloud (1908)
The Heart of a Cowboy (1910)
The Long Trail (1910)
Nevada (1910)
Arizona Bill (1911)
The Desert Well (1911)
The Half-Breed's Plans (1911)
The Indian Brothers (1911)
The Message of the Arrow (1911)
The Apache Renegade (1912)
For the Honor of the Tribe (1912)
The Renegades (1912)
The Trade Gun Bullet (1912)
The Last Blockhouse (1913)
The Snake (1913)
The Waif (1913)
The Water War (1913)
The Angel of Contention (1914)
The Blood Test (1914)
The Final Verdict (1914)
The Half-Breed (1914)
The Line Rider (1914)
Pierre of the Plains (1914)
The Sea-Gull (1914)
The Squatter (1914)
A Tale of the Desert (1914)
The Test of Western Love (1914)
The Unlawful Trade (1914)
Yellow Flame (1914)
West Wind (1915)
The Heart of a Bandit (1915)
North of Nevada (1924)
The Wild Bull's Lair (1925)
War Paint (1926)
Red Raiders (1927)
The Water Hole (1928)
Flaming Feather (1951)
The Hawk of Wild River (1952)
Three Young Texans (1954)
The Vanishing American (1955)
The Bravados (1958)
Day of the Outlaw (1959)

DRUNKEN INDIANS

The Call of the Wild (1908)
A Close Call (1909)
The Flag of Company H (1910)
The Curse of the Red Man (1911)
Love in a Tepee (1911)

The Hair Restorer and the Indians
(1911)
A Romance of the Rio Grande
(1911)
The White Lie (1912)
The Frenzey of Firewater (1912)
The Half-Breed's Treachery
(1912)
In the Nick of Time (1912)
A Plucky Ranch Girl (1912)
The Redman's Burden (1912)
The Renegades (1912)
Past Redemption (1913)
Fifty Miles from Tombstone
(1913)
The Squaw Man (1913, 1918, 1931)
The Counterfeit (1914)
Last of the Line (1914)
Hopi Raiders (1914)
The Ranger's Romance (1914)
The Whiskey Runners (1914)
Satan McAllister's Heir (1915)
The Quarter Breed (1916)
A Fight for Love (1919)
The Last of the Mohicans (1920)
Winning of The West (1922)
Frontier Marshall (1939)
Northwest Passage (1940)
Western Union (1941)
Pierre of the Plains (1942)
My Darling Clementine (1946)
Yellow Sky (1948)
Fort Apache (1948)
Rio Grande (1950)
The Big Sky (1952)
The Great Sioux Uprising (1953)
Drums Across the River (1954)
Cattle Queen of Montana (1955)
The Indian Fighter (1955)
Run of the Arrow (1957)
The Wild and the Innocent (1959)
The Comancheros (1961)
The Outsider (1962)
Buffalo Bill (1963)
Cat Ballou (1965)
The Hallelujah Trail (1965)
The Way West (1967)
Stay Away, Joe (1968)
Shalako (1968)
Tell Theme Willie Boy Is Here
(1969)

Flap (1970)

TURNCOATS—INDIANS WHO
HELP WHITES AGAINST
THEIR OWN

Boots and Saddles (1909)
The Broken Trap (1911)
The Mission Waif (1911)
The Message of the Arrow (1911)
Sacrifice of Silver Cloud (1911)
The Silent Signal (1911)
An Apache's Father's Vengeance
(1912)
A Brave Little Indian (1912)
A Redman's Loyalty (1912)
An Apache's Gratitude (1913)
The Arrow's Tongue (1914)
Grey Eagle's Last Stand (1914)
The Scarlet West (1925)
War Paint (1926)
Wyoming (1928)
Taza, Son of Cochise (1954)
The Oregon Trail (1959)
The Unforgiven (1960)

INDIANS DO GOOD DEEDS
AND BECOME GOOD INDIANS

An Indian's Honor (1908)
The Squaw's Sacrifice (1909)
Dove Eye's Gratitude (1909)
Red Wing's Gratitude (1909)
The Cowboy and the Squaw (1910)
The Debt Repaid (1910)
The Girl from Triple X (1910)
The Indian and the Cowgirl (1910)
The Indian and the Maid (1910)
Justice in the Far North (1910)
The Red Girl and the Child (1910)
Red Wing's Loyalty (1910)
The Sheriff (1910)
A Shot in Time (1910)
Wenonah (1910)
Western Justice (1910)
Young Deer's Gratitude (1910)
The American Insurrecto (1911)
George Warrington's Escape
(1911)

The Horse Thief (1911)
The Half-Breed's Atonement (1911)
The Redman's Dog (1911)
Trailed by an Indian (1911)
The Trapper's Fatal Shot (1911)
Prisoner of the Mohicans (1911)
Swift Wind's Heroism (1912)
At Cripple Creek (1912)
Captain King's Rescue (1912)
The Indian and the Child (1912)
An Indian's Gratitude (1912)
The Little Indian Martyr (1912)
The Mortgage (1912)
The Rights of a Savage (1912)
The Seal of Time (1912)
A White Indian (1912)
An Apache's Gratitude (1913)
The Branded Six-Shooter (1913)
A Dangerous Wager (1913)
The Friendless Indian (1913)
A Matter of Honor (1913)
Over the Cliffs (1913)
Partners (1913)
A Redskin's Mercy (1913)
The Stolen Moccasins (1913)
The Water War (1913)
When the West Was Young (1913)
The Yaqui Cur (1913, 1916)
The Arms of Vengeance (1914)
At the End of the Rope (1914)
The Cross on the Cacti (1914)
The Desert's Sting (1914)
The Eleventh Hour (1914)
The Last Ghost Dance (1914)
The Panther (1914)
A Romance of the Pueblo (1914)
Shorty and the Fortune Teller (1914)
The Silent Way (1914)
Broncho Billy's Teachings (1915)
The Indian Trapper's Vindication (1915)
The Indian's Narrow Escape (1915)
O'Garry of the Royal Mounted (1915)
The Old Code (1915)
The Night Riders (1916, 1923)
By Indian Post (1919)
The Sting of the Scorpion (1923)

The Mine with the Iron Door (1924)
The Valley of Vanishing Men (1924)
Trigger Finger (1924)
Ramshackle House (1924)
Reckless Courage (1925)
The Red Rider (1925)
War Paint (1926)
Red Clay (1927)
The Riding Renegade (1928)
Way out West (1930)
The Rainbow Trail (1931)

INDIANS EDUCATED AT
COLLEGE, CARLISLE OR
MISSION SCHOOL, A/O
FOOTBALL HEROES

The Call of the Wild (1908)
A Football Warrior (1908)
A Daughter of the Sioux (1910)
Red Eagle's Love Affair (1910)
The Blackfoot Halfbreed (1911)
The Empty Tepee (1911)
For the Tribe (1911)
A Sacrifice to Civilization (1911)
Wenona's Broken Promise (1911)
Chief White Eagle (1912)
The Colonel's Ward (1912)
A Daughter of the Redskins (1912)
White Cloud's Secret (1912)
Wynona's Vengeance (1913)
The Call of the Tribe (1914)
The Death Sign at High Noon (1914)
Indian Blood (1914)
The New Medicine Man (1914)
Strongheart (1914)
Son of "The Dog" (1915)
The Ceermonial Turquoise (1915)
The Great Alone (1922)
Blazing Arrows (1922)
The Half Breed (1922)
The Mine with the Iron Door (1924)
North of Nevada (1924)
Red Love (1925)
The Scarlet West (1925)
The Wild Bull's Lair (1925)

Braveheart (1926)
Red Clay (1927)
Redskin (1929)
Massacre (1934)
Wagon Tracks West (1943)
Daughter of the West (1949)
Jim Thorpe-All American (1951)
Arrowhead (1953)
Apache Woman (1955)

INDIANS STIRRED UP BY WHITE RENEGADES A/O TROUBLED BY WHITE MEANIES, CORRUPT TRADERS AND WHISKEY RUNNERS

The Battle of Redwood (1911)
The Desert Well (1911)
Return of Company D (1911)
The Rival Stage Lines (1911)
The Invaders (1912)
The Cowboy's Mother (1912)
Justice of Manitou (1912)
Silver Moon's Rescue (1912)
The Buckskin Coat (1913)
Hopi Raiders (1914)
A Tale of the Northwest Mounted (1914)
The Whiskey Runners (1914)
An Indian's Honor (1914)
Red Hawk's Sacrifice (1914)
The Redskins and the Renegades (1914)
A Fight for Love (1919)
The Raiders (1921)
The Last White Man (1924)
The Overland Stage (1927)
Men of Daring (1927)
The Glorious Trail (1928)
The Invaders (1929)
Massacre (1934)
Wagons Wheels (1934)
Daniel Boone (1936)
Treachery Rides the Range (1936)
The Plainsman (1936, 1966)
Prairie Thunder (1937)
Allegheny Uprising (1939)
Geronimo (1939)
Drums Along the Mohawk (1939)
Apache Trail (1942)

The Omaha Trail (1942)
Valley of the Sun (1942)
Lawless Plainsmen (1942)
Wagon Tracks West (1943)
The Law Rides Again (1943)
Romance of the West (1946)
Blazing Across the Pecos (1948)
Indian Agent (1948)
Laramie (1949)
Daughter of the West (1949)
Rio Grande (1950)
Devil's Doorway (1950)
Two Flags West (1950)
Tomahawk (1951)
Brave Warrior (1952)
The Battle at Apache Pass (1952)
The Half-Breed (1952)
Indian Uprising (1952)
Wagons West (1952)
Fort Osage (1952)
The Black Dakotas (1954)
Siege of Red River (1954)
The Battle of Rogue River (1954)
Arrow in the Dust (1954)
Sitting Bull (1954)
The Vanishing American (1955)
The Man from Laramie (1955)
Cattle Queen of Montana (1955)
Apache Woman (1955)
The Indian Fighter (1955)
The Last Frontier (1956)
The Lone Ranger (1956)
The Oklahoman (1957)
Flaming Frontier (1958)
Oklahoma Territory (1960)
Six Black Horses (1962)

HALF-BREED FEMALE

Ramona (1910, 1914 [reissue], 1916, 1928, 1936)
Indian Blood (1910)
Kit Carson's Wooing (1911)
The Blackfoot Halfbreed (1911)
The Apache Kind (1913)
The Desert's Sting (1914)
The Gambler's Reformation (1914)
The Ghost of the Mine (1914)
Jack Chanty (1915)
The Indian Changeling (1915)

300

The Ancient Blood (1916)
The Great Alone (1922)
The Mohican's Daughter (1922)
The Heritage of the Desert (1924)
Red Love (1925)
Call Her Savage (1932)
Duel in the Sun (1947)
Colorado Territory (1949)
Daughter of the West (1949)
The Hawk of Wild River (1952)
Shotgun (1955)
Apache Woman (1955)
War Drums (1957)
Bullwhip (1958)
Last Train from Gun Hill (1959)
Gunman's Walk (1959)
Heaven with a Gun (1969)

HALF-BREED MALE

The Cattle Rustlers (1908)
The Red Girl (1908)
Half Breed's Treachery (1909)
The Heart of a Cowboy (1910)
The Indian Girl's Romance (1910)
Red Wing's Constancy (1910)
Red Wing's Loyalty (1910)
The Dumb Half-Breed's Defense
    (1910)
The Seminole Halfbreeds (1910)
The White Medicine Man (1911)
A Branded Indian (1911)
The Half-Breed's Atonement
    (1911)
The Half-Breed's Plans (1911)
An Indian's Love (1911)
A Half Breed's Courage (1911)
The Half-Breed's Daughter (1911)
An Indian Hero (1911)
The Half-Breed's Treachery (1912)
The Half-Breed's Sacrifice (1912)
The Half-Breed's Way (1912)
At the Half-Breed's Mercy (1913)
The Barrier of Blood (1913)
Breed of the North (1913)
Bred in the Bone (1913)
The Half-Breed Parson (1913)

The Half-Breed Sheriff (1913)
The Last Blockhouse (1913)
Trooper Billy (1913)
The Waif (1913)
The Arrow's Tongue (1914)
The Half-Breed (1914)
Indian Blood (1914)
Indian Fate (1914)
The Line Rider (1914)
Pierre of the Plains (1914)
The Squatter (1914)
The Unlawful Trade (1914)
Big Jim's Heart (1915)
From out of the Big Snows (1915)
The Ghost Wagon (1915)
The Heart of a Bandit (1915)
The Wanderer's Pledge (1915)
The Western Border (1915)
West Wind (1915)
The Dawnmaker (1916)
The Halfbreed (1916)
The Night Riders (1916, 1923)
The Quarter Breed (1916)
The Wilderness Trail (1919)
Across the Divide (1921)
Bring Him In (1921)
The Desert's Crucible (1922)
The Great Alone (1922)
The Half Breed (1922)
One Eighth Apache (1922)
The Bad Lands (1925)
The Bloodhound (1925)
The Verdict of the Desert (1925)
The Flaming Forest (1926)
Wagon Wheels (1934)
Distant Drums (1951)
The Half-Breed (1952)
Pony Soldier (1952)
Hondo (1953)
Broken Lance (1954)
Foxfire (1955)
The Last Wagon (1956)
Reprisal (1956)
The Proud and the Profane (1956)
Halliday Brand (1957)
Trooper Hook (1957)
Flaming Frontier (1958)
Day of the Outlaw (1959)
Flaming Star (1960)
Nevada Smith (1966)
Duel at Diablo (1966)

301

INDIAN TORTURE — BURNING AT THE STAKE, ETC.

Cowboys and Indians (1907)
In the Days of Gold (1911)
Blazing the Trail (1912)
The Way of the Redman (1914)
The Primal Lure (1916)
The Paleface (1921)
Cardigan (1922)
In the Days of Buffalo Bill (1922)
The Red Rider (1925)
The Frontiersman (1927)
Daniel Boone (1936)
Susannah of the Mounties (1939)
Northwest Passage (1940)
Unconquered (1947)
The Paleface (1948)
Run of the Arrow (1957)
Duel at Diablo (1966)

INDIAN CALAMITY — STARVATION, EPIDEMIC, FIRE

The Famine in the Forest (1909)
Government Rations (1910)
Lo! The Poor Indian (1910)
For the Sake of the Tribe (1911)
The Battle of Redwood (1911)
Cholera on the Plains (1912)
Children of the Forest (1913)
The Legend of the Amulet (1914)
Indian Agent (1948)
They Rode West (1954)
Blood Arrow (1958)
Chuka (1967)

HORSES

Peggy and the Old Scout (1913)
Saved by His Horse (1913)
Saved by Her Horse (1915)
The Devil Horse (1926)
Arizona Nnights (1927)
King of the Herd (1927)
Silver Stallion (1941)
King of the Stallions (1942)
Wild Beauty (1946)
Black Gold (1947)

King of the Wild Horses (1947)
Sand (1949)
Stallion Canyon (1949)
Old Overland Trail (1952)
Tonka (1958)
Indian Paint (1967)

DESERT STORIES

The Desert Well (1911)
Romance of the Desert (1911)
The Land of Dead Things (1913)
Desert Thieves (1914)
The Desert's Sting (1914)
A Tale of the Desert (1914)
Desert Gold (1919, 1936)
The Desert's Crucible (1922)
The Heritage of the Desert (1924)
The Verdict of the Desert (1925)
Drums of the Desert (1927)
Desert Gold (1936)

INDIAN RAISED AS WHITE A/O ADOPTED BY WHITES

The Call of the Blood (1910)
Elder Alden's Indian Ward (1910)
For the Tribe (1911)
The Rebuked Indian (1911)
A Sacrifice to Civilization (1911)
A Redskin's Appeal (1912)
Reprisal (1956)
The Unforgiven (1960)

WHITES LIVED WITH AND/OR RAISED BY INDIANS

Deerslayer (1911, 1913, 1943, 1957)
The Faithless Friend (1913)
The Flower of No Man's Land (1916)
The Girl Montana (1921)
Blazing Arrows (1922)
The Huntress (1923)
Leatherstocking (1924, serial)
A Daughter of the Sioux (1925)
The Red Rider (1925)

The Invaders (1929)
Sioux Blood (1929)
White Eagle (1932)
Arizona Frontier (1940)
Navajo Kid (1945)
Across the Wide Missouri (1951)
The Last Outpost (1951)
The Savage (1952)
The Big Sky (1952)
Rose of Cimarron (1952)
The Pathfinder (1952)
Run of the Arrow (1957)
Pawnee (1957)

MISSIONARIES, MINISTERS, CONVERSION

The Priest of the Wilderness (1909)
Onawanda (1909)
The Missionary's Gratitude (1911)
The Mission Waif (1911)
A Warrior's Faith (1911)
Anona's Baptism (1912)
The Parson and the Medicine Man (1912)
The White Brother's Text (1912)
Broncho Billy's Teachings (1915)
The Secret of Lost River (1915)
The Huron Converts (1915)
Refuge (1915)
The Primal Lure (1916)
The Dawn of Freedom (1916)
The Twinkle in God's Eyes (1955)
Pillars of the Sky (1956)

INDIAN AGENTS, COMMISSIONERS A/O OTHERWISE

The Battle of Redwood (1911)
The Red Man's Penalty (1911)
The Barrier (1913)
The Final Reckoning (1914)
The Golden Strain (1925)
The Vanishing American (1925, 1955)
The Flaming Frontier (1926)
Massacre (1934)

Valley of the Sun (1942)
The Law Rides Again (1943)
Wagon Tracks West (1943)
Fort Apache (1948)
Indian Agent (1948)
Daughter of the West (1949)
The Battle at Apache Pass (1952)
The Half-Breed (1952)
Taza, Son of Cochise (1954)

INDIANS SEEK REVENGE

The Seminole's Revenge (1909)
The Half-Breed's Daughter (1911)
The Indian Brothers (1911)
Poisoned Arrows (1911)
Red Man's Wrath (1911)
The Way of the Red Man (1911)
The Apache Father's Vengeance (1912)
Justice of Manitou (1912)
Wynona's Vengeance (1913)
The Desert's Sting (1914)
Grey Eagle's Revenge (1914)
His Indian Nemesis (1914)
Yellow Flame (1914)
The Lure of the Windigo (1914)
The Medicine Man's Vengeance (1914)
The Renegade's Sister (1914)
Slim and the Indians (1914)
The Vengeance of Winona (1914)
Gold and Woman (1916)
The Wild Bull's Lair (1925)
War Paint (1926)

INDIAN LOYAL FRIEND OF WHITES

Pocahontas (1909)
Leather Stocking (1909)
Red Feather's Friendship (1911)
Red Star's Honor (1911)
A Western Postmistress (1911)
The Last of the Mohicans (1911, 1914, 1920, 1932, 1936)
The Pathfinder (1911, 1952)
The Half-Breed's Way (1912)
The Secret-Treasure (1913)

Dan Morgan's Way (1914)
Jamestown (1923)
Leatherstocking (1924, serial)
Behind Two Guns (1924)
War Paint (1926)
Daniel Boone (1936)
The Lone Ranger (1938, serial)
Drums Along the Mohawk (1939)
Hi-Yo Silver (1940, feature made
   from the 1938 The Lone Ranger
   serial)
Last of the Redman (1947)
The Iroquois Trail (1950)
Captain John Smith and
   Pocahontas (1953)
The Lone Ranger (1956)
Along the Mohawk Trail (1956)
The Pathfinder and the Mohican
   1956)
The Redmen and the Renegades
   (1956)
The Long Rifle and the Tomahawk
   (1964)
The Lone Ranger and the Lost City
   of Gold (1958)
Shatterhand (1964)
Apache Gold (1965)
Rampage at Apache Wells (1966)
Last of the Renegades (1966)
Frontier Hellcat (1966)

SUPPOSED LEGENDS

The Legend of Scar Face (1910)
The Maid of Niagara (1910)
The Legend of Lake Desolation
   (1911)
The Devil Fox of the North (1914)
The War Bonnet (1914)
The Legend of the Amulet (1914)
The Legend of the Lone Tree
   (1915)
The Legend of the Poisoned Pool
   (1915)

WHITE MALE CAPTIVES

The Cowboy's Devotion (1910)
The Voice of Blood (1910)

Kit Carson's Wooing (1911)
Tangled Lives (1911)
White Brave's Heritage (1911)
A Child of the Wilderness (1912)
The Redemption of White Hawk
   (1912)
Across the Chasm (1913)
The Indian's Secret (1913)
A Prisoner of the Apaches (1913)
The Brand of His Tribe (1914)
The Gambler of the West (1914)
In the Days of the Thundering
   Herd (1914)
The Dawn of Freedom (1916)
Sioux Blood (1929)
The Golden West (1932)
Pony Soldier (1952)
The Light in the Forest (1958)
Blood on the Arrow (1964)
Hombre (1967)
A Man Called Horse (1970)
Little Big Man (1971)

WHITE FEMALE CAPTIVES

Rescue of Child from Indians
   (1903)
Pioneer Crossing the Plains in '49
   (1908)
A Child in the Forest (1909)
Children of the Plains (1909)
A Colonial Romance (1909)
A Friend in the Enemies' Camp
   (1909)
Iona, the White Squaw (1909)
Hannah Dusten (1910)
A Frontier Hero (1910)
Company D to the Rescue (1910)
The Paleface Princess (1910)
Charlie's Buttie (1911)
The Chief's Daughter (1911)
Fighting Blood (1911)
An Indian Hero (1911)
An Indian Vestal (1911)
The Mascot of Troop "C" (1911)
Only a Squaw (1911)
Daniel Boone's Bravery (1911)
The Trapper's Fatal Shot (1911)
The Tribe's Penalty (1911)
The Peril of the Plains (1911)

Prisoner of the Mohicans (1911)
Blazing the Trail (1912)
The Fall of Black Hawk (1912)
The Forest Rose (1912)
Her Indian Guardian (1912)
An Indian Sunbeam (1912)
The Squawman's Sweetheart
(1912)
The Price of Gratitude (1912)
When the Heart Calls (1912)
The Wooing of Wathena (1912)
After the Massacre (1913)
The Call of the Blood (1913)
Camping With Custer (1913)
For the Peace of Bear Valley
(1913)
The Squawman's Awakening
(1913)
The Pale-Face Squaw (1913)
The White Squaw (1913)
*Broncho Billy and the Settler's
Daughter* (1914)
*In the Days of the Thundering
Herd* (1914)
Love's Sacrifice (1914)
The Medicine Bag (1914)
A Romance of the Pueblo (1914)
A Tale of the Desert (1914)
A Waif of the Plains (1914)
The Ceremonial Turquoise (1915)
The Heart of the Sheriff (1915)
Winning of the West (1922)
The Secret of the Pueblo (1923)
Quicker'n Lightin' (1925)
The Frontiersman (1927)
Northwest Passage (1940)
Ambush (1950)
Flaming Feather (1951)
The Charge at Feather River
(1953)
Conquest of Cochise (1953)
Fort Ti (1953)
Comanche (1956)
The Searchers (1956)
Trooper Hook (1957)
Comanche Station (1960)
The Canadians (1961)
Two Rode Together (1961)
Buffalo Bill (1963)
The Last Tomahawk (1965)
Duel At Diablo (1966)

Day of the Evil Gun (1968)
The Stalking Moon (1969)
Soldier Blue (1970)

EARLY INDIANS — 16th, 17th,
18th CENTURIES

The Discoverers (1908)
For Love of Country (1908)
In the Days of the Pilgrims (1908)
Pocahontas (1908)
Buying Manhattan (1909)
Onawanda (1909)
Leather Stocking (1909)
The Priest of the Wilderness
(1909)
A Colonial Romance (1909)
Hannah Dusten (1910)
Fighting the Iroquois (1910)
A Mohawk's Way (1910)
Prisoner of the Mohicans (1911)
Puritans and Indians (1911)
The Rebuked Indian (1911)
In the Days of the Six Nations
(1911)
*Gathering of the Council of the
Six Nations* (1911)
An Indian Legend (1911)
The Conspiracy of Pontiac (1911)
The Last of the Mohicans (1911,
1914, 1920, 1932 [serial], 1936)
Deerslayer (1911, 1913, 1943,
1957)
Priscilla and the Pequot (1911)
The Pathfinder (1911, 1952)
The Battle of the Long Sault
(1912)
The Fall of Black Hawk (1912)
The Quakeress (1913)
Wolfe, of the Conquest of Quebec
(1914)
When Broadway Was a Trail
(1914)
The Huron Converts (1915)
Cardigan (1922)
The Mohican's Daughter (1922)
The Courtship of Miles Standish
(1923)
Vincennes (1923)
Jamestown (1923)

America (1924)
Leatherstocking (1924, serial)
The Frontiersman (1927)
Winners of the Wilderness (1927)
Drums Along the Mohawk (1939)
Northwest Passage (1940)
Ten Gentlemen from West Point (1942)
Unconquered (1947)
The Last of the Redman (1947)
The Return of the Mohicans (1948)
The Iroquois Trail (1950)
When Redskins Rode (1951)
Brave Warrior (1952)
Battles of Chief Pontiac (1952)
Captain John Smith and Pocahontas (1953)
Fort Ti (1953)
Seven Cities of Gold (1955)
The Far Horizons (1955)
Kiss of Fire (1955)
Mohawk (1956)
The Light in the Forest (1958)
Kings of the Sun (1963)
Seven Seas to Calais (1963)

MODERN INDIANS — 20th CENTURY

Ramshackle House (1924)
Reckless Courage (1925)
Red Clay (1927)
Call Her Savage (1932)
Behold My Wife (1921, 1935)
Black Gold (1947)
The Last Round-Up (1947)
Bowery Buckaroos (1947)
Tulsa (1949)
Sand (1949)
Jim Thorpe—All American (1951)
Dangerous Mission (1954)
Foxfire (1955)
Battle Cry (1955)
The Proud and the Profane (1956)
The FBI Story (1959)
All the Young Men (1960)
The Outsider (1962)
Johnny Tiger (1966)
Stay Away, Joe (1968)
The Savage Seven (1968)

Tell Them Willie Boy is Here (1969)
Run, Simon, Run (1970)
Flap (1970)

BUFFALO BILL

Parade of Buffalo Bill's Wild West Show (1898)
Buffalo Bill's Wild West Parade (1901)
The Buffalo Bill's Wild West Show and the Pawnee Bill's Far East (1910)
The Life of Buffalo Bill (1912)
The Indian Wars (1914)
Adventures of Buffalo Bill (1917)
In the Days of Buffalo Bill (1922, serial)
The Iron Horse (1924)
Buffalo Bill on the U.P. Trail (1926)
The Last Frontier (1926)
Fighting with Buffalo Bill (1926, serial)
Wyoming (1928)
Battling with Buffalo Bill (1931, serial)
Annie Oakley (1935)
The Plainsman (1936, 1966)
Custer's Last Stand (1936, serial)
Young Buffalo Bill (1940)
Buffalo Bill (1944)
Buffalo Bill Rides Again (1947)
Annie Get Your Gun (1950)
Cody of the Pony Express (1951, serial)
Buffalo Bill in Tomahawk Territory (1952)
The Pony Express (1953)
Riding With Buffalo Bill (1954, serial)
Badman's Country (1958)
Buffalo Bill (1963)
The Raiders (1963)

KIT CARSON

Kit Carson (1903)
Kit Carson (1910, 1928)

Kit Carson's Wooing (1911)
Fighting with Kit Carson (1933, serial)
Kit Carson (1940)
Lawless Plainsmen (1942)

DAVY CROCKETT

Davy Crockett (1916)
Davy Crockett—Indian Scout (1949)
Davy Crockett, King of the Wild Frontier (1955)

DANIEL BOONE

Daniel Boone or Pioneer Days in America (1907)
The Chief's Daughter (1911)
In the Days of Daniel Boone (1923, serial)
Daniel Boone (1936)
Young Daniel Boone (1950)
Daniel Boone, Trail Blazer (1956)

FRONTIERSMEN, TRAILBLAZERS, TRAPPERS, MOUNTAN MEN, HISTORIC FIGURES

Wolf Song (1929)
Annie Oakley (1935)
The Plainsman (1936, 1966)
Frontier Marshall (1939)
Prairie Schooners (1940)
My Darling Clementine (1946)
Comanche Territory (1950)
Across the Wide Missouri (1951)
Tomahawk (1951)
The Big Sky (1952)
Pony Express (1953)
Masterson of Kansas (1954)
The Far Horizons (1955)
The Gun That Won the West (1955)
The Indian Fighter (1955)
The Wild and the Innocent (1959)

Yellowstone Kelly (1959)
Cheyenne Autumn (1964)

SERIALS

Perils of Pauline (1914)
The Lass of the Lumberlands (1916)
Hands Up (1918)
The Moon Riders (1920)
The Phantom Foe (1920)
In the Days of Buffalo Bill (1922)
In the Days of Daniel Boone (1923)
The Oregon Trail (1923)
The Santa Fe Trail (1923)
Way of a Man (1924)
Leatherstocking (1924)
Hawk of the Hills (1927)
The Vanishing West (1928)
The Indians Are Coming (1930)
Battling with Buffalo Bill (1931)
The Last of the Mohicans (1932)
The Last Frontier (1932)
Heroes of the West (1932)
Fighting with Kit Carson (1933)
Clancy of the Mounted (1933)
The Miracle Rider (1935)
Rustlers of Red Gap (1935)
Custer's Last Stand (1936)
The Phantom Rider (1936)
Hawk of the Wilderness (1938)
Flaming Frontiers (1938)
The Great Adventures of Wild Bill Hickok (1938)
The Lone Ranger (1938)
Oregon Trail (1939)
Winners of the West (1940)
White Eagle (1941)
Perils of the Royal Mounted (1942)
Overland Mail (1942)
Daredevils of the West (1943)
Black Arrow (1944)
The Phantom Rider (1946)
The Scarlet Horseman (1946)
Cody of the Pony Express (1951)
Roar of the Iron Horse (1951)
Son of Geronimo Apache Avenger (1952)
Man With the Steel Whip (1954)
Perils of the Wilderness (1955)
Blazing the Overland Trail (1956)

307

MUSICALS

Rose Marie (1936, 1954)
Ride, Ranger, Ride (1937)
Riders of the Dawn (1937)
Young Buffalo Bill (1940)
Young Bill Hickok (1940)
Go West, Young Lady (1941)
Colorado (1940)
Romance of the West (1946)
The Last Round-Up (1947)
Northwest Outpost (1947)
Singing Spurs (1948)
The Cowboy and the Indians (1949)
Annie Get Your Gun (1950)
A Ticket to Tomahawk (1950)
Snake River Desperadoes (1951)
Buffalo Gun (1962)
The Fastest Guitar Alive (1968)

COMEDIES

Yiddisher Cowboy (1909)
The Hair Restorer and the Indian (1911)
Little Ingin (1911)
Maiden of the Pieface Indians (1911)
Percy and His Squaw (1911)
Too Much Injun (1911)
An Up-To-Date Squaw (1911)
The Westerner and the Girl (1911)
The White Medicine Man (1911)
General Bunko's Victory (1912)
A Picnic in Dakota (1912)
The Tourists (1912)
Dorothea and Chief Razamataz (1913)
Grease Paint Indians (1913)
A Hair Raising Affair (1913)
The Indian Servant (1913)
Andy and the Redskins (1914)
Colonel Custard's Last Stand (1914)
Fatty and Minne He-Haw (1914)
The Indian Suffragettes (1914)
Lo, the Poor Indian (1914)
Reggie, the Squaw Man (1914)
Some Bull's Daughter (1914)
Author! Author! (1915)

A Deal in Indians (1915)
Green Backs and Red Skins (1915)
Ham Among the Redskins (1915)
Jerry's Celebration (1915)
Wild and Woolly (1917)
The Mollycoddle (1920)
A Ridin' Romeo (1921)
The Paleface (1921)
The Primitive Lover (1922)
Suzanna (1922)
The Uncovered Wagon (1923)
Hands Up! (1926)
My Little Chickadee (1940)
Go West (1940)
Go West, Young Lady (1941)
Ride 'Em Cowboy (1942)
Bowery Buckaroos (1947)
The Senator Was Indiscreet (1947)
The Paleface (1948)
The Dude Goes West (1948)
The Traveling Saleswoman (1950)
The Son of Paleface (1952)
Many Rivers to Cross (1955)
Around the World in 80 Days (1956)
Alias Jesse James (1959)
The Sheriff of Fractured Jaw (1959)
All Hands on Deck (1961)
Days of Thrills and Laughter (1961)
Sergeants 3 (1962)
Man's Favorite Sport? (1964)
The Hallelujah Trail (1965)
Texas Across the River (1966)
The Scalphunters (1968)
The Shakiest Gun in the West (1968)

CHILDREN OR FAMILY-TYPE PICTURES

Susannah of the Mounties (1939)
Wild Beauty (1946)
Davy Crockett, King of the Wild Frontier (1955)
Around the World in 80 Days (1956)
Westward Ho the Wagons! (1956)
The Light in the Forest (1958)

308

Tonka (1958)
How the West Was Won (1960)
For the Love of Mike (1960)
Savage Sam (1963)
Island of the Blue Dolphins (1964)
Run, Appaloosa, Run (1965)
Indian Paint (1967)
The Shakiest Gun in the West
(1968)

FULL-LENGTH DOCUMENTARIES OR SEMI-DOCUMENTARIES

Eagle Dance, Pueblo Indians
(1898)
Indian Day School (1898)
Serving Rations to the Indians
(1898)
Sham Battle at the Pan-American
Exposition (1901)
Moki Snake Dance by Wolpi
Indians (1901)
Glimpses of an Indian Village
(1910)
Cheyenne Frontier Days (1911)
Indian Dances and Pastimes (1912)
Isleta, N. M. Indian City (1912)
Life and Customs of the Winnebago
Indians (1912)
Pueblo Indians, Albuquerque,
N. M. (1912)
Camping With the Blackfeet
(1913)
Commencement at Indian School
Carlyle, Pa. (1913)
Piegan Indians (1913)
Weeping Waters (1924)
The Silent Enemy (1930)
Navajo (1951)

MADE IN EUROPE

Cowboys and Indians (1907)
Justice of a Redskin (1908)
Texas Tex (1908)
Red Man's Revenge (1908)
The Prairie on Fire (1912)
Battles of Chief Pontiac (1952)

The Cry of the Wild Geese (1963)
Buffalo Bill (1963)
Seven Seas to Calais (1963)
Shatterhand (1964)
The Treasure of Silver Lake
(1965)
Finger on the Trigger (1965)
Fury of the Apaches (1965)
Apache Gold (1965)
The Last Tomahawk (1965)
Mutiny at Fort Sharpe (1965)
Massacre at Fort Perdition (1966)
Blackeagle of Santa Fe (1966)
Apache's Last Battle (1966)
Frontier Hellcat (1966)
Kid Rodelo (1966)
Massacre at Marble City (1966)
Last of the Renegades (1966)
Rampage at Apache Wells (1966)
White Comanche (1967)
The Hellbenders (1967)
Navajo Joe (1967)
The Tall Women (1967)
Shalako (1968)
Sabata (1970)

INDIAN BOY LOVES INDIAN GIRL AND/OR VICE VERSA AND/OR YOUNG MARRIEDS

Red Cloud (1908)
The Red Girl (1908)
The Bride of Tabaiva (1909)
Comata, the Sioux (1909)
Dove Eye's Gratitude (1909)
The Falling Arrow (1909)
An Indian Wife's Devotion (1909)
The Mended Lute (1909)
The Trail of the White Man
(1909)
A Cheyenne Brave (1910)
The Navajo's Bride (1910)
The Seminole Halfbreeds (1910)
Song of the Wildwood Flute
(1910)
The Legend of Scar Face (1910)
The Way of the Red Man (1910)
The Black Chasm (1911)
Black Cloud's Debt (1911)
The Cheyenne's Bride (1911)

309

The Empty Tepee (1911)
Grey Wolf's Squaw (1911)
The Indian Flute (1911)
An Indian Legend (1911)
Lone Star's Return (1911)
The Medicine Woman (1911)
A Noble Red Man (1911)
Owanee's Great Love (1911)
The Passing of Dapple Fawn
  (1911)
A Red Girl's Heart (1911)
Silver Tail and His Squaw (1911)
A Sioux Lover's Strategy (1911)
The Spirit of the Gorge (1911)
Starlight's Necklace (1911)
The Story of the Indian Ledge
  (1911)
The Winning of Wonega (1911)
The Warrior's Squaw (1911)
A Warrior's Treachery (1911)
Wenona's Broken Promise (1911)
A Young Squaw's Bravery (1911)
The Arrowmaker's Daughter
  (1912)
Before the White Man Came
  (1912)
The Deer Slayer's Retribution
  (1912)
Red Man's Honor (1912)
A Pueblo Legend (1912)
The Heart of the Red Man (1912)
An Indian Idyl (1912)
The Tribal Law (1912)
The Unwilling Bride (1912)
White Fawn (1912)
The Wooing of White Fawn
  (1912)
The Bear Hunter (1913)
The Big Horn Massacre (1913)
Children of the Forest (1913)
An Indian Maid's Strategy (1913)
The Romance of the Utah Pioneers
  (1913)
The Charmed Arrow (1914)
The Coming of Lone Wolf (1914)
The Death Mask (1914)
Defying the Chief (1914)
Lame Dog's Treachery (1914)
The Legend of the Amulet (1914)
The Navajo Blanket (1914)
A Romance of the Pueblo (1914)

The Sea-Gull (1914)
Star of the North (1914)
The Vanishing Tribe (1914)
The Village 'Neath the Sea (1914)
The Arrow Maiden (1915)
The Boundary Line (1915)
The Legend of the Lone Tree
  (1915)
The Race Love (1915)
The Western Border (1915)
The Great Alone (1922)
Red Love (1925)
Deerslayer (1943)
Apache (1954)
Taza, Son of Cochise (1954)
Chief Crazy Horse (1955)
Apache Warrior (1957)

INDIAN WOMAN LOVES
WHITE MAN

The Trail of the White Man
  (1909)
The Heart of a Sioux (1910)
The Indian Girl's Romance (1910)
Red Fern and the Kid (1910)
A Romance of the Western Hills
  (1910)
Wenonah (1910)
Red Wing's Loyalty (1910)
The Way of the Red Man (1910)
Bear Hunt Romance (1911)
The Broken Trap (1911)
A Daughter of the Navajos (1911)
The Indian Flute (1911)
Little Dove's Romance (1911)
Love in a Tepee (1911)
The Trail of the Pomos Charm
  (1911)
Kit Carson's Wooing (1911)
The Flower of the Tribe (1911)
At Old Fort Dearborn (1912)
The Curse of the Lake (1912)
The Outcast (1912)
The Redemption of White Hawk
  (1912)
Winona (1912)
Yellow Bird (1912)
The Flower of the Forest (1912)
His Little Indian Model (1912)

310

An Indian Idyl (1912)
The Vanishing Race (1912)
White Treachery (1912)
The Apache Kind (1913)
Broncho Billy and the Navajo
  Maid (1913)
Darkfeather's Sacrifice (1913)
Maya-Just an Indian (1913)
Mona (1913)
The Pride of Angry Bear (1913)
The Song of the Telegraph (1913)
Trooper Billy (1913)
Broncho Billy's Indian Romance
  (1914)
The Cave of Death (1914)
The Death Sign at High Noon
  (1914)
The Fate of a Squaw (1914)
Fatty and Minnie He-Haw (1914)
The Ghost of the Mine (1914)
Kidnapped by Indians (1914)
Grey Eagle's Revenge (1914)
A Message for Help (1915)
The Heritage of the Desert (1924)
Oklahoma Jim (1932)
Unconquered (1947)
The Prairie (1947)
Duel in the Sun (1947)
Flaming Feather (1951)
Cattle Queen of Montana (1954)
Ghost Town (1955)
Foxfire (1955)
The Far Horizons (1955)
Fort Yuma (1955)
The Oklahoman (1957)
Fort Bowie (1958)
Gunman's Walk (1958)
The Oregon Trail (1959)
Oklahoma Territory (1960)
The Unforgiven (1960)
Heaven with a Gun (1969)
Wild Women (1970)

INDIAN MAN LOVES
WHITE WOMAN

The Call of the Wild (1908)
The Paleface Princess (1910)
Red Eagle's Love Affair (1910)
The Return of Ta-Wa-Wa (1910)

Back to the Prairie (1911)
For the Tribe (1911)
The Redskin's Secret (1911)
Three Men (1911)
The Tribe's Penalty (1911)
Return of Company D (1911)
Her Indian Hero (1912)
Indian Jealousy (1912)
The Swastika (1912)
The Wooing of Wathena (1912)
Chief White Eagle (1912)
The Barrier of Blood (1913)
Bred in the Bone (1913)
The Call of the Blood (1913)
The Half Breed Sheriff (1913)
The Pale-Face Squaw (1913)
The Call of the Tribe (1914)
Grey Eagle's Revenge (1914)
The Greater Barrier (1915)
The Dawnmaker (1916)
A Daughter of War (1917)
The Half Breed (1922)
One Eighth Apache (1922)
The Scarlet West (1925)
The Vanishing American (1925)
Braveheart (1926)
Red Clay (1927)
Conquest of Cochise (1953)
Foxfire (1955)
Run, Simon, Run (1970)

WHITE MAN LUSTS AFTER
INDIAN MAIDEN

The Trail of the White Man (1909)
The Way of the Red Man (1910)
The Half-Breed's Daughter (1911)
How Tony Became a Hero (1911)
The Twin Squaws (1911)
The Ancient Bow (1912)
Justice of Manitou (1912)
His Punishment (1912)
White Treachery (1912)
Her Indian Brother (1913)
The Trail of the Silver Fox (1913)
Brought to Justice (1914)
The Gambler's Reformation (1914)
The Squaw's Revenge (1914)
The Indian Changeling (1915)
The Rainbow Trail (1931)

Canyon Passage (1946)
The Last Hunt (1956)
Heaven With a Gun (1969)
The McMasters (1970)

INDIAN MAN LUSTS AFTER WHITE WOMAN

In the Days of the Pilgrims (1908)
Iron Arm's Remorse (1910)
A Chance Shot (1911)
The Flower of the Tribe (1911)
The Disputed Claim (1912)
The Flower of the Forest (1912)
Early Oklahoma (1913)
The Last Blockhouse (1913)
The Gambler's Reformation (1914)
The Law of the North (1918)
The Last of the Mohicans (1920)
Fort Courageous (1965)

WHITE WOMAN LOVES INDIAN MAN

A Football Warrior (1908)
Her Indian Hero (1912)
Where the Trail Divides (1914)
Foxfire (1955)
Halliday Brand (1957)
Run, Simon, Run (1970)

WHITE MAN LOVES INDIAN MAIDEN

The White Chief (1908)
Red Fern and the Kid (1910)
How Tony Became a Hero (1911)
The Indian Flute (1911)
The Vanishing Race (1912)
The Pride of Angry Bear (1913)
The Paleface Brave (1914)
The Cactus Blossom (1915)
The Race Love (1915)
The Mohican's Daughter (1922)
Ghost Town (1955)
Gunman's Walk (1958)
The Unforgiven (1960)

INTERMARRIAGE — WHITE MAN AND INDIAN MAIDEN — SQUAW MAN

A Squaw Man (1912)
The Squawman's Sweetheart (1912)
The Squaw Man (1913, 1918, 1931)
The Squawman's Awakening (1913)
The Squaw Man's Reward (1913)
Reggie, the Squaw Man (1914)
The Squaw Man's Son (1917)
The Kentuckian (1908)
'Twixt Love and Duty (1908)
Comata, the Sioux (1909)
The Heart of a Sioux (1910)
Apache Gold (1910)
Indian Blood (1910)
Red Wing's Constancy (1910)
The Blackfoot Halfbreed (1911)
The Call of the Wilderness (1911)
Romance of the Desert (1911)
Kit Carson's Wooing (1911)
The White Chief (1911)
For the Papoose (1912)
The Loneliness of the Hills (1912)
White Dove's Sacrifice (1912)
The Oath of Conchita (1913)
Pecos Pete in Search of a Wife (1913)
The Brand of His Tribe (1914)
Indian Blood (1914)
Indian Fate (1914)
The Desert's Sting (1914)
Red Hawk's Sacrifice (1914)
The Hell Cat (1916)
The Ancient Blood (1916)
The Passing of Pete (1916)
Man Above the Law (1917)
The Snowshoe Trail (1920)
Behold My Wife (1921, 1935)
Colorado Territoy (1949)
Broken Arrow (1950)
Across the Wide Missouri (1951)
The Last Outpost (1951)
The Big Sky (1952)
The Wild North (1952)
Broken Lance (1954)
White Feather (1955)
The Indian Fighter (1955)

Distant Drums (1957)
Run of the Arrow (1957)
Bullwhip (1958)
Mohawk (1956)
Last Train from Gun Hill (1959)
Flaming Star (1960)
The Way West (1967)
The McMasters (1970)
A Man Called Horse (1970)
Little Big Man (1971)

SIOUX

Sioux Ghost Dance (1894)
Comata, The Sioux (1909)
The Mended Lute (1909)
A Cheyenne Brave (1910)
A Daughter of the Sioux (1910)
The Heart of a Sioux (1910)
The White Captive of the Sioux
   (1910)
The Cheyenne's Bride (1911)
Grey Wolf's Squaw (1911)
Owanee's Great Love (1911)
A Sioux Lover's Strategy (1911)
A Sioux Spy (1911)
The Winning of Wonega (1911)
A Young Squaw's Bravery (1911)
An Indian Martyr (1911)
Ogallalah (1911)
The Buffalo Hunt (1912)
An Indian Idyl (1912)
The Invaders (1912)
The Loneliness of the Hills (1912)
Battle of the Red Men (1912)
The Post Telegrapher (1912)
Campaigning with Custer (1913)
The Indian's Secret (1913)
The Land of Dead Things (1913)
When the Blood Calls (1913)
The Fight on Deadwood Trail
   (1914)
Sitting Bull, the Hostile Sioux
   Indian Chief (1914)
The Word of His People (1914)
Red Love (1925)
Warrior Gap (1925)
A Daughter of the Sioux (1925)
The Scarlet West (1925)

The Flaming Frontier (1926)
The Frontier Trail (1926)
General Custer at Little Big Horn
   (1926)
The Last Frontier (1926)
The Overland Stage (1927)
Red Raiders (1927)
Sitting Bull at the "Spirit Lake
   Massacre" (1927)
Sioux Blood (1929)
Massacre (1934)
The Plainsman (1936, 1966)
They Died With Their Boots On
   (1941)
Badlands of Dakota (1941)
Buffalo Bill (1944)
Winchester '73 (1950, 1967)
Oh! Susanna (1951)
Warpath (1951)
Tomahawk (1951)
The Savage (1952)
The Big Sky (1952)
Bugles in the Afternoon (1952)
The Great Sioux Uprising (1953)
The Nebraskan (1953)
Fort Vengeance (1953)
The Pony Express (1953)
The Black Dakotas (1954)
Saskatchewan (1954)
Sitting Bull (1954)
Chief Crazy Horse (1955)
The Indian Fighter (1955)
The Tall Men (1955)
The Gun That Won the West (1955)
7th Cavalry (1956)
The Last Frontier (1956)
Revolt at Fort Laramie (1957)
Run of the Arrow (1957)
Flaming Frontier (1958)
Gunman's Walk (1958)
Tonka (1958)
Yellowstone Kelly (1959)
The Canadians (1961)
The Wild Westerners (1962)
Buffalo Bill (1963)
The Hallelujah Trail (1965)
The Great Sioux Massacre (1965)
Red Tomahawk (1966)
The Way West (1967)
A Man Called Horse (1970)
Little Big Man (1971)

SITTING BULL

*Sitting Bull, the Hostile Sioux
    Indian Chief* (1914)
Flaming Frontier (1926)
Hands Up! (1926)
*Sitting Bull at the "Spirit Lake"
    Massacre* (1927)
Annie Oakley (1935)
Annie Get Your Gun (1950)
Fort Vengeance (1953)
Sitting Bull (1954)
Tonka (1958)
The Great Sioux Massacre (1965)

CRAZY HORSE

They Died With Their Boots On
    (1941)
Sitting Bull (1954)
Chief Crazy Horse (1955)
The Great Sioux Massacre (1965)

RED CLOUD

Warrior Gap (1925)
Tomahawk (1951)
The Indian Fighter (1955)
The Gun That Won the West (1955)
Revolt at Fort Laramie (1957)

GALL

Yellowstone Kelly (1959)

RAIN IN THE FACE

The Flaming Frontier (1926)

LITTLE CROW

Flaming Frontier (1958)

APACHE

Apache (1954)
Apache Ambush (1955)
Apache Chief (1949)
Apache Country (1953)
Apache Drums (1951)
An Apache Father's Vengeance
    (1912)
An Apache's Gratitude (1913)
Apache Gold (1910)
Apache Gold (1965)
The Apache Kind (1913)
The Apache Renegade (1912)
Apache Rifles (1965)
Apache Territoy (1958)
Apache Trail (1942)
Apache Uprising (1965)
Apache War Smoke (1952)
Apache Warrior (1957)
Apache Woman (1955)
An Apache's Gratitude (1913)
Apache's Last Battle (1966)
A Prisoner of the Apaches (1913)
One Eighth Apache (1922)
The Battle at Apache Pass (1952)
Stand at Apache River (1953)
40 Guns to Apache Pass (1966)
Fury of the Apaches (1965)
Fort Apache (1948)
*Young Wild West Cornered by
    Apaches* (1912)
The Sacred Turquoise of the Zuni
    (1910)
The Curse of the Red Man (1911)
*The Massacre of the Fourth
    Cavalry* (1912)
On the Warpath (1912)
The Trade Gun Bullet (1912)
The Tribal Law (1912)
A Wasted Sacrifice (1912)
The Indian's Secret (1913)
A Romance of the Pueblo (1914)
The Fight on Deadwood Trial
    (1914)
Riders of Vengeance (1919)
The Golden Strain (1925)
Tonio, Son of the Sierras (1925)
Bad Lands (1939)
Stagecoach (1939, 1966)
The Roundup (1941)

Valley of the Sun (1942)
Yellow Sky (1948)
Fury at Furnance Creek (1948)
Silver River (1948)
Ambush (1950)
Rio Grande (1950)
Only the Valiant (1951)
The Last Outpost (1951)
Indian Uprising (1952)
Lone Star (1952)
Arrowhead (1953)
Shotgun (1953)
Ambush at Tomahawk Gap (1953)
Hondo (1953)
Four Guns to the Border (1954)
Arrow in the Dust (1954)
Massacre Canyon (1954)
Foxfire (1955)
Fort Yuma (1955)
The Man From Laramie (1955)
Strange Lady in Town (1955)
Backlash (1956)
The Last Wagon (1956)
Walk the Proud Land (1956)
Quantez (1957)
War Drums (1957)
The Ride Back (1957)
Trooper Hook (1957)
Dragoon Wells Massacre (1957)
Escape from Red Rock (1958)
Fort Massacre (1958)
Fort Bowie (1958)
Ride Lonesome (1959)
Sergeant Rutledge (1960)
A Thunder of Drums (1961)
Six Black Horses (1962)
Stagecoach to Dancer's Rock (1962)
Young Guns of Texas (1962)
The Deadly Companions (1962)
Savage Sam (1963)
Buffalo Bill (1963)
A Distant Trumpet (1964)
Blood on the Arrow (1964)
Shatterhand (1964)
Bullet for a Badman (1964)
The Treasure of Silver Lake (1965)
Major Dundee (1965)
Duel at Diablo (1966)
Frontier Hellcat (1966)
Rampage at Apache Wells (1966)
Last of the Renegades (1966)

Massacre at Fort Perdition (1966)
The Tall Women (1967)
Hombre (1967)
Day of the Evil Gun (1968)
Shalako (1968)
The Stalking Moon (1969)
Mackenna's Gold (1969)
Land Raiders (1970)
Wild Women (1970)

COCHISE

Valley of the Sun (1942)
Fort Apache (1948)
Broken Arrow (1950)
The Battle at Apache Pass (1952)
Conquest of Cochise (1953)
Taza, Son of Cochise (1954)
40 Guns to Apache Pass (1964)

GERONIMO

Geronimo's Last Raid (1912)
Geronimo (1939, 1962)
Valley of the Sun (1942)
Fort Apache (1948)
Broken Arrow (1950)
I Killed Geronimo (1950)
The Last Outpost (1951)
Battle at Apache Pass (1952)
Indian Uprising (1952)
Lone Star (1952)
Son of Geronimo Apache Avenger
    (1952, serial)
Apache (1954)
Walk the Proud Land (1956)

MANGAS COLORADAS

Fort Yuma (1955)
War Drums (1957)

VICTORIO

Hondo (1953)
Fort Bowie (1958)

315

SEMINOLE

Seminole (1953)
The Seminole Halfbreeds (1910)
Seminole Uprising (1955)
The Seminole's Revenge (1909)
The Seminole's Sacrifice (1911)
The Seminole's Trust (1910)
The Seminole's Vengeance (1909)
The Indian's Revenge or Osceola,
    the Last of the Seminoles (1906)
The Exiled Chief (1910)
Silver Tail and His Squaw (1911)
Ramshackle House (1924)
Distant Drums (1951)
War Arrow (1954)
Yellowneck (1957)
Johnny Tiger (1966)

OSCEOLA

The Indian's Revenge or Osceolo,
    the Last of the Seminoles (1906)
Seminole (1953)

COMANCHE

Comanche (1956)
Comanche Station (1960)
Comanche Territory (1950)
Last of the Comanches (1952)
White Comanche (1967)
North of '36 (1924)
West of the Pecos (1934)
Young Buffalo Bill (1940)
Lone Star (1952)
Rose of Cimmarron (1952)
Conquest of Cochise (1953)
Overland Pacific (1954)
Kiss of Fire (1955)
The Searchers (1956)
Fort Dobbs (1958)
The Law and Jake Wade (1958)
Cowboy (1958)
Rawhide Trail (1958)
The Comancheros (1961)
Two Rode Together (1961)
War Party (1965)
Incident at Phantom Hill (1966)

Texas Across the River (1966)
Blackeagle of Santa Fe (1966)
White Comanche (1967)

QUANAH PARKER

Comanche (1956)
Two Rode Together (1961)

IROQUOIS AND THEIR NEIGHBORS

The Priest of the Wilderness (1909)
Fighting the Iroquois (1910)
A Mohawk's Way (1910)
The Last of the Mohicans (1911,
    1914, 1920, 1932 [serial], 1936)
Prisoner of the Mohicans (1911)
The Pathfinder (1911)
An Indian Legend (1911)
Gathering of the Council of the Six
    Nations (1911)
In the Days of the Six Nations
    (1911)
Deerslayer (1911, 1913, 1943, 1957)
The Battle of the Long Sault (1912)
When Broadway Was a Trail
    (1914)
Cardigan (1922)
The Mohican's Daughter (1922)
America (1924)
Drums Along the Mohawk (1939)
Northwest Passage (1940)
Unconquered (1947)
The Return of the Mohicans (1948)
The Iroquois Trail (1950)
The Pathfinder (1952)
Fort Ti (1953)
Mohawk (1956)
The Pathfinder and the Mohicans
    (1956)
Along the Mohawk Trail (1956)
The Long Rifle and the Tomahawk
    (1964)

CHEYENNE

Cheyenne Autumn (1964)
A Cheyenne Brave (1910)
The Cheyenne's Bride (1911)

The Cheyenne Massacre (1913)
The Cheyenne Medicine Man (1911)
The Cheyenne Raiders (1910)
The Missionary's Gratitude (1911)
A Sioux Spy (1911)
A Young Squaw's Bravery (1911)
Battle of the Red Men (1912)
The Battle at Fort Laramie (1913)
Satan McAllister's Heir (1915)
Wagons West (1952)
The Command (1954)
The Charge at Feather River (1953)
White Feather (1955)
Dakota Incident (1956)
Massacre at Sand Creek (1956)
Soldier Blue (1970)
Little Big Man (1971)

BLACK KETTLE

Wagons West (1952)

BLACKFOOT

Chief Blackfoot's Vindication (1910)
The Blackfoot Halfbreed (1911)
Owanee's Great Love (1911)
Camping with the Blackfeet (1913)
Kit Carson (1928)
Susannah of the Mounties (1939)
The Cariboo Trail (1950)
Across the Wide Missouri (1951)
Cattle Queen of Montana (1954)
Blood Arrow (1958)

HOPI

The Rights of a Savage (1912)
The Tribal Law (1912)
The Vanishing Race (1912)
The Fuse of Death (1914)
Hopi Raiders (1914)
The Coming of Lone Wolf (1914)
The Davil's Saddle (1927)
Heaven with a Gun (1969)

NAVAJO

The Navajo's Bride (1910)
A Daughter of the Navajos (1911)
The Navajo Blanket (1914)
The Desert's Sting (1914)
The Man Above the Law (1917)
The Heritage of the Desert (1924)
Drums of the Desert (1927)
Redskin (1929)
Daughter of the West (1949)
Navajo (1951)
Fort Defiance (1951)
Slaughter Trail (1951)
Ambush at Tomahawk Gap (1953)
Column South (1953)
Battle Cry (1955)
All the Young Men (1960)

CROW

The Winning of Wonega (1911)
The Buffalo Hunt (1912)
An Indian Idyl (1912)
Little Big Man (1971)

PAWNEE

Arrow in the Dust (1954)
Pawnee (1957)
Fort Massacre (1958)
Little Big Man (1971)

PUEBLO

Eagle Dance, Pueblo Indians (1898)
Wand Dance, Pueblo Indians (1898)
The Sacred Turquoise of the Zuni (1910)
Pueblo Indians, Albuquerque, N. M. (1912)
A Pueblo Legend (1912)
A Romance of the Pueblo (1914)
The Secret of the Pueblo (1923)
The Left Hand Brand (1924)

KIOWA

They Rode West (1954)
War Arrow (1954)
Santa Fe Passage (1955)
The Unforgiven (1960)
The War Wagon (1967)
The Scalphunters (1968)

SATANTA

War Arrow (1954)

SHOSHONI

Kit Carson (1940)
Devil's Doorway (1950)
Bend of the River (1952)
The Far Horizons (1955)
A Man Called Horse (1970)

SACAJAWEA

The Far Horizons (1955)

UTE

The Uprising of the Utes (1910)
A Perilous Ride (1911)
Finger on the Trigger (1965)

ARAPAHOE

Attack by Arapahoes (1910)
War Paint (1926)
The Oregon Trail (1959)
Yellowstone Kelly (1959)
Chuka (1967)

SHAWNEE

An Indian's Love (1911)
Rachel and the Stranger (1948)
Brave Warrior (1952)
Many Rivers to Cross (1955)

TECUMSEH AND THE PROPHET

Brave Warrior (1952)

CREE

The Trail of the Silver Fox (1913)
Pony Soldier (1952)

PAIUTE

The Dude oGes West (1948)
Kiss of Fire (1955)
Fort Massacre (1958)
Massacre at Fort Perdition (1966)

DELAWARE

The Light in the Forest (1958)

PEQUOT

Priscilla and the Pequot (1911)

MODOC

Drum Beat (1954)
Escort West (1959)

CAPT. JACK, SCARFACE CHARLIE, MODOC JIM, BOGUS CHARLIE (MODOCS)

Drum Beat (1954)

CHOCTAW

An Indian's Love (1911)

CREEK

The Loneliness of the Hills (1912)
The Frontiersman (1927)

ZUNI

The Sacred Turquoise of the Zuni
(1910)

HURON

The Huron Converts (1915)
Deerslayer (1943)

YUMA

On the Warpath (1912)

OTTAWA

An Indian Legend (1911)

PONTIAC (OTTOWA)

Winners of the Wilderness (1927)
Battles of Chief Pontiac (1952)

WINNEBAGO

Life and Customs of the Winnebago
Indians (1912)

PIEGAN

Piegan Indians (1913)

OJIBWAY

The Totem Mark (1911)
The Prairie on Fire (1912)

CALIFORNIA MISSION

Ramona (1910, 1914 [reissue],
1916, 1928, 1936)
The Little Indian Martyr (1912)

CALIFORNIA

Seven Cities of Gold (1955)
Island of the Blue Dolphins (1964)

LOUIS RIEL (METIS)

North Mounted Police (1940)

POCAHONTAS & POWHATAN

Pocahontas (1908)
Jamestown (1923)
Captain Smith and Pocahontas
(1953)

INDIAN HATER—MILITARY
A/O CIVILIAN

Fort Apache (1948)
Two Flags West (1950)
Devil's Doorway (1950)
Broken Arrow (1950)
Only the Valiant (1951)
Tomahawk (1951)
Warpath (1951)
The Savage (1952)
Pony Soldier (1952)
Stand at Apache River (1953)
Arrowhead (1953)
War Arrow (1954)
Yellow Tomahawk (1954)
Drum Beat (1954)
They Rode West (1954)
Fort Yuma (1955)
White Feather (1955)
Massacre at Sand Creek (1956)
The Last Frontier (1956)
The Last Hunt (1956)
The Last Wagon (1956)
Comanche (1956)
Apache Warrior (1957)
Run of the Arrow (1957)
Trooper Hook (1957)
Fort Bowie (1958)
Fort Massacre (1958)
Gunman's Walk (1958)
The Lone Ranger and the Lost City

of Gold (1958)
The Unforgiven (1950)
Rio Conchos (1964)

BLUE AND GREY
VS. INDIANS

Colorado (1940)
Renegade Girl (1947)
The Outriders (1950)
Rocky Mountain (1950)
Two Flags West (1950)
The Last Outpost (1951)
Red Mountain (1951)
Column South (1953)
Jack McCall, Desperado (1953)
The Great Sioux Uprising (1953)
Escape from Fort Bravo (1954)
Siege at Red River (1954)
Apache Ambush (1955)
Revolt at Fort Laramie (1957)
Yellowneck (1957)
Major Dundee (1965)

MOUNTIES

Breed of the North (1913)
A Tale of the Northwest Mounted
  (1914)
O'Garry of the Royal Mounted
  (1915)
A Fight for Love (1919)
Bring Him In (1921)
The Raiders (1921)
The Hate Trail (1922)
The Bloodhound (1925)
Moran of the Mounted (1926)
The Flaming Forest (1926)
Rose Marie (198, 1936, 1954)
Susannah of the Mounties (1939)
North West Mounted Police (1940)
Mrs. Mike (1950)
Pony Soldier (1952)
The Wild North (1952)
Fort Vengeance (1953)
Saskatchewan (1954)
The Canadians (1961)

INDIANS AND THE
TEXAS RANGERS

Galloping Vengeance (1925)
The Texas Rangers (1936, 1956)
The Comancheros (1961)

INDIANS AND THE LAW

The Arm of Vengeance (1914)
The Bottled Spider (1914)
The Ceremonial Turquoise (1915)
The Taking of Luke McVane (1015)
The Riding Renegade (1928)
Bad Lands (1939)
Badman's Territory (1946)
The Nebraskan (1953)
The Ride Back (1957)
Dragoon Wells Massacre (1957)
Escape from Red Rock (1958)
From Hell to Texas (1958)
Ride Lonesome (1959)
Posse from Hell (1961)
The Wild Westerners (1962)
Bullet for a Badman (1964)
Tell Them Willie Boy Is Here
  (1969)

INDIANS AND OUTLAWS

The Falling Arrow (1909)
Galloping Vengeance (1925)
Men of Daring (1927)
The Riding Renegade (1928)
Spurs (1930)
Prairie Schooners (1940)
Silver Stallion (1941)
Frontier Fury (1943)
Buffalo Bill Rides Again (1947)
The Plunderers (1948)
Blood on the Moon (1948)
Slaughter Trail (1951)
Four Guns to the Border (1954)
Quantez (1957)
Escape from Red Rock (1958)
Gun Fever (1958)
The Law and Jake Wade (1958)
The Bravados (1958)
Day of the Outlaw (1959)

Walk Tall (1960)
The Purple Hills (1961)

DEPRADATIONS AGAINST INDIANS—ATTACK ON VILLAGE

The Indian Massacre (1912)
The Blindness of Courage (1913)
Northwest Passage (1940)
Rio Grande (1950)
Devil's Doorway (1950)
Ambush (1950)
Broken Arrow (1950)
Conquest of Cochise (1953)
The Far Horizons (1955)
Massacre at Sand Creek (1956)
The Searchers (1956)
Flaming Frontier (1958)
Cheyenne Autumn (1964)
Soldier Blue (1970)
Little Big Man (1971)

CUSTER

On the Little Big Horn or
    Custer's Last Stand (1909)
Custer's Last Fight (1912)
The Masacre (1912)
Campaigning with Custer (1913)
Camping with Custer (1913)
Bob Hampton of Placer (1921)
The Scarlet West (1925)
The Flaming Frontier (1926)
The Last Frontier (1926)
General Custer at Little Big Horn
    (1926)
Last Frontier (1932, serial)
Custer's Last Stand (1936, serial)
They Died With Their Boots On
    (1941)
Little Big Horn (1951)
Warpath (1951)
Bugles in the Afternoon (1952)
Sitting Bull (1954)
Chief Crazy Horse (1955)
Tonka (1958)
The Great Sioux Massacre (1965)
Custer of the West (1968)
Little Big Man (1971)

INDIAN POLICE, INDIAN ARMY, SCOUTS AND INDIANS IN ARMY

The Call of the Blood (1913)
The Indian (1914)
Tonio, Son of the Sierras (1925)
Red Love (1925)
Spoilers of the West (1927)
Pony Soldier (1952)
War Arrow (1953)
Taza, Son of Cochise (1954)
Fort Yuma (1955)
Pillars of the Sky (1956)
Apache Warrior (1957)
Flaming Frontier (1958)
Tonka (1958)

INDIAN VS. ARMY

For Love of Country (1908)
Boots and Saddles (1909)
In Old Arizona (1909)
In the Bad Lands (1909)
On the Warpath (1909)
Across the Plains (1910)
Saved from the Redmen (1910)
Company D to the Rescue (1910)
The Flag of Company H (1910)
Attack by Arapahoes (1910)
The Colonel's Errand (1910)
Perils of the Plains (1910)
The Uprising of the Utes (1910)
The Battle of Redwood (1911)
Fighting Blood (1911)
Sergeant Dillon's Bravery (1911)
In Frontier Days (1911)
In the Days of the Six Nations
    (1911)
Return of Company D (1911)
Lieut. Scott's Narrow Escape
    (1911)
The Blackfoot Halfbreed (1911)
For the Sake of the Tribe (1911)
The Last Drop of Water (1911)
The Mascot of Troop "C" (1911)
The Rebuked Indian (1911)
The Red Devils (1911)
The Silent Signal (1911)
What the Indians Did (1911)

His Punishment (1912)
The Lieutenant's Last Fight (1912)
The Massacre of the Fourth Cavalry (1912)
The Arrow of Defiance (1912)
A Frontier Child (1912)
On the Warpath (1912)
The Post Telegrapher (1912)
A Soldier's Honor (1912)
The Crisis (1912)
For the Honor of the 7th (1912)
Geronimo's Last Raid (1912)
An Apache Father's Vengeance (1912)
The Colonel's Peril (1912)
The Colonel's Ward (1912)
The Army Surgeon (1912)
Captain King's Rescue (1912)
A Message to Kearney (1912)
A Soldier's Furlough (1912)
The Attack at Rocky Pass (1913)
Bred in the Bone (1913)
The Fight at Grizzly Gulch (1913)
For the Peace of Bear Valley (1913)
General Scott's Protege (1913)
The Green Shadow (1913)
The Land of Dead Things (1913)
The Snake (1913)
The Battle at Elderbush Gulch (1913)
The Big Horn Massacre (1913)
Trooper Billy (1913)
Hopi Raiders (1914)
The Hour of Reckoning (1914)
The Indian (1914)
Grey Eagle's Last Stand (1914)
The Brand of His Tribe (1914)
The Colonel's Orderly (1914)
Last of the Line (1914)
The Medicine Bag (1914)
The Tigers of the Hills (1914)
The Toll of the Warpath (1914)
Wolfe, or the Conquest of Quebec (1914)
The Corporal's Daughter (1915)
The Girl I Left Behind Me (1915)
The Renegade (1915)
The Deserter (1916)
Boots and Saddles (1919)
Winning of the West (1922)

America (1924)
The Iron Horse (1924)
The Golden Strain (1925)
The Scarlet West (1925)
Tonio, Son of the Sierras (1925)
Warrior Gap (1925)
Fort Frayne (1926)
The Frontier Trail (1926)
The Last Frontier (1926)
Under Fire (1926)
War Paint (1926)
The Bugle Call (1927)
The Frontiersman (1927)
Men of Daring (1927)
Red Raiders (1927)
Winners of the Wildnerness (1927)
Orphan of the Sage (1928)
Wyoming (1928)
The Invaders (1929)
The Overland Telegraph (1929)
Thoroughbreds (1931)
The Conquering Horde (1931)
White Eagle (1932)
For the Service (1936)
The Plainsman (1936, 1966)
Prairie Thunder (1937)
The Glory Trail (1937)
Ride, Ranger, Ride (1937)
Geronimo (1939, 1962)
Drums Along the Mohawk (1939)
Kit Carson (1940)
Wyoming (1940)
Northwest Passage (1940)
Badlands of Dakota (1941)
Ten Gentlemen from West Point (1942)
The Law Rides Again (1943)
Unconquered (1967)
Silver River (1948)
The Plunderers (1948)
Fort Apache (1948)
Laramie (1949)
Massacre River (1949)
Davy Crockett-Indian Scout (1949)
She Wore a Yellow Ribbon (1949)
Winchester '73 (1950, 1967)
Ambush (1950)
Rio Grande (1950)
Distant Drums (1951)
Flaming Feather (1951)
Tomahawk (1951)

Only the Valiant (1951)
Fort Defiance (1951)
Apache Drums (1951)
Cavalry Scout (1951)
New Mexico (1951)
Oh! Susanna (1951)
Red Mountain (1951)
Slaughter Trail (1951)
Warpath (1951)
Indian Uprising (1952)
Bugles in the Afternoon (1952)
The Battle at Apache Pass (1952)
The Half-Breed (1952)
Brave Warrior (1952)
The Savage (1952)
War Paint (1953)
Escape from Fort Bravo (1953)
Fort Ti (1953)
Arrowhead (1953)
The Charge at Feather River (1953)
The Stand at Apache River (1953)
Last of the Comanches (1953)
Conquest of Cochise (1953)
Fort Vengeance (1953)
Seminole (1953)
Arrow in the Dust (1954)
Apache (1954)
Massacre Canyon (1954)
The Battle of Rogue River (1954)
The Black Dakotas (1954)
Drum Beat (1954)
War Arrow (1954)
They Rode West (1954)
Taza, Son of Cochise (1954)
Thunder Pass (1954)
Yellow Tomahawk (1954)
The Command (1954)
Seminole Uprising (1955)
The Indian Fighter (1955)
The Gun That Won the West (1955)
Fort Yuma (1955)

White Feather (1955)
Santa Fe Passage (1955)
Run of the Arrow (1956)
The Last Frontier (1956)
Massacre at Sand Creek (1956)
Pillars of the Sky (1956)
The Last Wagon (1956)
7th Cavalry (1956)
Walk the Proud Land (1956)
Oregon Passage (1957)
War Drums (1957)
Trooper Nook (1957)
Apache Warrior (1957)
Shoot-Out at Medicine Bend (1957)
Yellowneck (1957)
Flaming Frontier (1958)
Ambush at Cimarron Pass (1958)
Fort Massacre (1958)
Fort Bowie (1958)
Ride out for Revenge (1958)
Yellowstone Kelly (1959)
Sergeant Rutledge (1960)
Frontier Uprising (1961)
A Thunder of Drums (1961)
Buffalo Bill (1963)
Taggart (1964)
Blood on the Arrow (1964)
Rio Conchos (1964)
Cheyenne Autumn (1964)
A Distant Trumpet (1964)
Apache Rifles (1965)
The Last Tomahawk (1965)
The Glory Guys (1965)
War Party (1965)
Fort Courageous (1965)
Finger on the Trigger (1965)
40 Guns to Apache Pass (1966)
Duel at Diablo (1966)
Red Tomahawk (1966)
Fort Utah (1967)
Chuka (1967)
Soldier Blue (1970)

Index

326